MIDDLE
AMERICA

BOOKS BY CHARLES MORROW WILSON

MIDDLE AMERICA

BACKWOODS AMERICA

ROOTS OF AMERICA

AMBASSADORS IN WHITE

CENTRAL AMERICA: CHALLENGE AND OPPORTUNITY

TREES AND TEST TUBES: THE STORY OF RUBBER

COUNTRY LIVING

AROOSTOOK

CORNBREAD AND CREEKWATER

MERIWETHER LEWIS; OF LEWIS AND CLARK

MIDDLE AMERICA

By

CHARLES MORROW WILSON

W · W · NORTON & COMPANY · INC · New York

11171

Copyright, 1944, by
W. W. NORTON & COMPANY, INC.
70 Fifth Avenue, New York

First Edition

A WARTIME BOOK

THIS COMPLETE EDITION IS PRODUCED
IN FULL COMPLIANCE WITH THE GOVERN-
MENT'S REGULATIONS FOR CONSERVING
PAPER AND OTHER ESSENTIAL MATERIALS

PRINTED IN THE UNITED STATES OF AMERICA
FOR THE PUBLISHERS BY THE VAIL-BALLOU PRESS

ACKNOWLEDGMENTS

GRATEFUL acknowledgment is made to *Harper's*, the *Reader's Digest*, the *Nation's Business*, the *Rotarian*, and the *Inter-American* for permission to publish here certain material which originally appeared in those magazines.

Also I wish to thank my associates, Drs. V. C. Dunlap and Wilson Popenoe, both of the scientific staff of the United Fruit Company; also Atherton Lee, former director of the Puerto Rico Experiment Station of the United States Department of Agriculture; and H. S. Wardlaw, until recently of the staff of the Imperial College of Tropical Agriculture of Trinidad, for generous and scholarly advice.

Thanks are likewise due various agricultural authorities serving the respective governments of Mexico, Cuba, Honduras, and Guatemala, who have provided welcome and helpful advice; also to the research facilities of the Middle America Information Bureau (conducted by the United Fruit Company), New York.

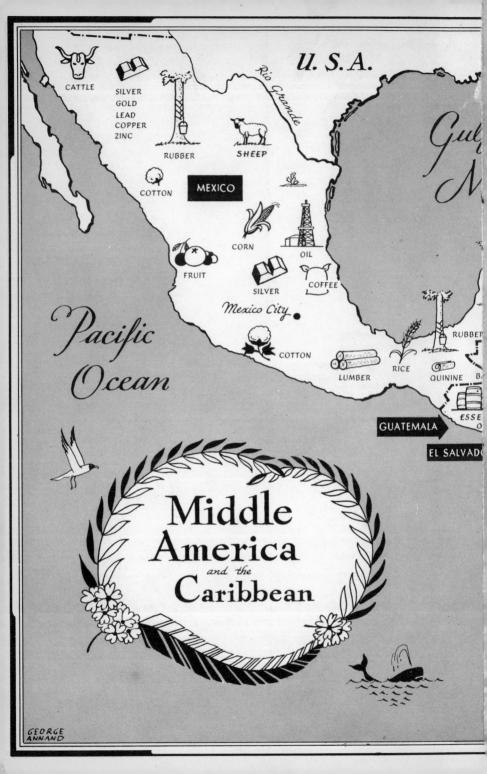

CONTENTS

ILLUSTRATIONS

11

CHAPTER ONE

~~~~~~~~

INTRODUCTION

THE nations of Middle America include Mexico; the six countries of Central America—Guatemala, El Salvador, Honduras, Nicaragua, Costa Rica and Panama; and the three Caribbean island republics, Cuba, Haiti and the Dominican Republic. To every one of us these nearest American neighbors are significant. They are cradle lands for many of the great farm crops upon which the economic structure of the United States is based. The ten nations of Middle America are also world laboratories for social and economic experiment. They are havens for the old and for the new. They constitute the geographic control board of our hemisphere. They comprise the littorals of the Caribbean, a sea of history and destiny.

In all, the nations of Middle America are the home of about 37,000,000 Americans. Their total land areas are nearly a third that of the United States. The strength of these Americas is confined to no one race or language. It is engendered of Indians, Negroes, Mestizos, Ladinos, and immigrant whites from Spain, South America, Europe, the United States, Canada and many other countries. Commercially the nations and peoples of Middle America are by odds our best customers. They buy from us more than three-fourths of all their imports. They sell us more than four-fifths of all their exports. They are our allies in war; our confederates in peace. Their good is our good and our good is theirs. To know and understand Middle America is to know and understand a great deal about the larger and more remote nations of South America. The nations of Middle America are close to us and destined to become closer. They are part of our past and our future; as well as our present.

The Japanese invasion of Malaya, the Netherlands Indies and other ancient strongholds of tropical fertility has brought the American tropics into the lives of each of us. As never before it has made Middle America—reservoir of manpower, food and other essential needs—indispensable to our present and future well-being. Basically Middle America and the United States are not competitive; each produces and exports what the other requires. Middle America wants our manufactured goods. We need the essential tropical crops, produced now or capable of being produced in the fertile soils and varied climates of Middle America; crops which we require and cannot grow ourselves.

We are already dependent on Middle America for a great part of our supplies of the following essential materials:

1. Our better quality coffees.

2. Our entire supply of bananas.

3. Natural rubber, which is a critical and desperately scarce war material; and a first essential in peace.

4. Abacá, a fiber needed for the making of Manila-type rope, a staple requirement for the operation of naval craft and merchant shipping; a fiber for which there is no effective substitute or synthetic.

5. Cacao (cocoa and chocolate), an important food beverage and the most cherished of flavors.

6. Sugar—Cuba is sugar bowl to the world, and despite our severe tariff walls, Cuba is our foremost supplier of sugars and nonfood sugar-cane molasses.

In addition, Middle America provides a potential larder of many other tropical crops needed by the United States and is already producing some of them in quantity. Among them are:

1. Quinine, an essential drug made from the bark of the cinchona tree, used in the treatment of malaria, the foremost communicable disease of this decade.

2. Rotenone, a superior insecticide, which is highly destructive of insect pests but relatively harmless to mammals, and therefore of immense value to United States fields, gardens, orchards, barnyards, and medicine.

3. Palm oil, required in vast bulk for chemical and industrial uses, critically needed in peace and war.

4. Tung oil, for quick-drying paints and varnishes, essential for military and civilian purposes.

5. Castor oil, an important pharmaceutical; also an indispensable lubricant for certain types of machinery.

6. Essential oils, such as citronella, lemon-grass oil, and vetivert, made from tropical grasses and basic to the manufacture of menthol, perfumes, insect sprays, toilet soaps, etc.

7. Mahogany, balsa, dyewoods, and other strategic timbers which can be grown only in the tropics.

8. Important tropical drugs, such as ipecac and senna, and many others.

9. Kapok or "tree cotton," a light fiber for filling material.

10. Vanilla, originally native to Mexico but more recently obtained principally from Madagascar, and various other important spices.

11. Sisal, jute and jute substitutes, and henequen, the staple fibers used for manufacturing cordage, bagging, binder twine, and other indispensable products.

12. Great treasuries of strategic and essential metals and minerals, which at present are not available in sufficient quantities within United States boundaries.

13. Tannin woods which are essential to United States leather industries.

14. Less known tropical fruits, such as avocado, papaya, pineapple, and many others which are indigenous to Middle America and may be destined to be of outstanding importance to our national diets.

This book will discuss the above mentioned and various other resources of the ever verdant Caribbean lands.[1]

Heretofore we have not adequately recognized the importance to us of the agricultural riches of the American tropics. Before the war, the United States depended almost entirely on the Pacific and South Pacific lands for tropical supplies. In 1938, for example, we imported about 94 percent of all essential crops from those regions; less than 6 percent from all Latin America.

War has proved the dangers and infamy of this policy. The capture of the Eastern tropics by our enemy and the disruption of the lengthy shipping routes via the Far Pacific, Indian Ocean, Red Sea and Mediterranean caused immediate serious shortages of vital materials. The United States turned to the nearby tropics in Middle America. Thus the importance of that area to the United States has been demonstrated again, along with the invincible truth that the well-being of Middle America *is* the well-being of the United States.

What course will be followed in the future, when and if the Far Pacific tropics are again open to Western trade? The most commonly mentioned advantage in a return to the Pacific tropics is the dubious advantage of an abundance of cheap, coolie labor. But the development, expansion and establishment of tropical crops in Middle America have several advantages: a safe, accessible supply of essential materials will lie within easy transport distance by protected shipping lanes, by already established air routes and by overland highways now in the building. Middle America will have a more

[1] See in particular Chapter Five.

solvent agriculture, and will be able to expand its trade with the United States, to the benefit of all the Americas. The cheap labor of the Eastern tropics can be offset—at least in substantial part—by efficient workers and scientific methods; the encouragement of low standards of living is grimly contrary to American principles.

In all events the vital interdependence of the nations of Middle America and the United States can be viewed as a great common asset and a platform for durable economic and cultural relationships among all the American nations.

For the assurance of hemispheric security and strength it is now supremely desirable that a reasonable proportion of these essential crops (which the United States cannot raise within domestic boundaries) be securely and promptly established within the boundaries of our nearest southern neighbors.

Better purchasing power is essential to the continuing progress and solvency of Middle America. Increased purchasing power is developed inevitably from higher wages and, more basically, from the capable production of valuable goods. Competition between Middle America and the tropics of the Eastern Hemisphere is inescapable. The seriousness of this problem must not be underestimated. It seems inevitable that still more effective reciprocal trade agreements will be indispensable if the wage levels, living standards, and solvency of Middle America as a whole are to be protected, at least until such time as the necessary experimental propagations can be made, and the desirable deficit crops can be established and brought into bearing. The time required for practical propagation varies greatly with the individual crops; from a year, or less, in the instance of certain valuable tropical grasses to a third of a century in the case of certain strategic tropical timbers. As an over-all average ten years would probably be a just and reasonable experimental period. And we have abundant reason to place complete confidence in the solvency of Middle American soil, the competency of Middle American workers, and the ever-strategic geographies of these lands of the Caribbean.

Satisfactory cultural relations with Middle America are inevitably allied with satisfactory business relations. The need and responsibilities for maintaining and assisting in the medical and sanitary welfare of Middle America are equally apparent.

The United States can never realize a truly worthwhile Middle American market or a dependable amity with these nearest American neighbors if it permits Middle America to become a tropical slum. You cannot live a good life in a pesthouse. You cannot realize an abundant life in a hell of poverty. You cannot trade with people or nations who have neither the money nor the credit with which to buy the goods you have to sell nor with which to produce the goods you wish to buy. In Middle America, or anywhere else, greater buying power builds for better lives, better health and more efficient government. These, in turn, spell greater security and prosperity for the United States. Middle America is part of our trading sphere, and Middle America is eager to buy what the United States has to sell, when, if and so long as that is possible.

The resources of Middle America are basically agricultural. The social and economic structures of Middle America are foundationed by land, some of the most fertile soils on earth. Millions of acres of Middle American lands are rich, deep and tropical—capable of producing goods, not four months of the twelve, but every day of the entire year. The principal export crops of Middle America are not competitive with the great domestic crops of the United States; they have never been, and almost certainly they will not be so. In war or peace, the United States must have many tropical products that cannot be grown within the boundaries of the United States. Yet the United States Department of Commerce table of imports for 1938, last of the relatively "typical" prewar years, given below tells much about the fantastic commercial favoritism which United States business at large has shown to the imperialistic low-wage colonies of the Eastern tropics, and the flagrantly antisocial and collusive cartels or international trusts with which United States business has so long crooked elbows and walked apace:

Commodity	Total U.S. Imports (*in thousands of dollars*)	Share of Latin America (*in thousands of dollars*)
Cinchona bark (source of quinine)	$ 588	$ 1
Cocoa (chocolate)	353	1
Cocoa beans	20,139	12,108
Coconut oil	11,401	—
Palm oil	9,125	—
Crude rubber	130,171	1,669
Sisal and henequen	9,571	4,734
Other vegetable fibers except cotton	10,657	524
Tanning and dyeing material	5,040	3,294

These entries become even more fantastic when one realizes that many of the great crops of Middle America have been lifted bodily from this hemisphere, established in the Far East, and sold back to the Western Hemisphere. Rubber trees, quinine trees, cacao or chocolate trees and many other great tropical crops are native to Middle America or South America. Yet the United States, as principal consumer of these products, has been buying them by the billions of dollars' worth, not from Middle America or South America or any other areas of the American tropics, but from remote and alien corners of creation which tolerate standards of life and wage scales that no American nation can endure.

World War II saw the strategic products of the South Pacific effectively cut off from us. Their harbors were blocked, their shipping lanes overwhelmed, their merchant shipping sunk or dissipated over sea lanes which no navy or combination of navies could protect.

Shipping distances from United States ports to Middle America are one-quarter to one-tenth those of the Pacific tropics. The major shipping centers of Middle America are actually closer to important and competent United States seaports than are the industrial and population centers of New England and the far Northwest—within our home boundaries. In transport value, one ship on a Middle American run can therefore do from four to twenty times as much productive work as it can now do in the Far East service, and Middle American shipping lanes can be protected with less naval tonnage than any other comparable shipping route.

The greater portion of Middle America is part of the North American mainland. Middle American products which fulfill both permanent and emergency demands can be transported to United States factories by railway and highway—as well as by ship and plane, for a new age of commercial aviation is sweeping over this hemisphere. In all events, Middle American crops can now be projected and planted and other resources developed with assurance that goods can be delivered to markets. But on the other side of the world, there is no assurance that the once great tropical crops of the Pacific East will be immediately or consistently available to the United States. Japanese conquests have dealt great and ominous injury to the established agrarian structures of the Pacific and South Pacific tropics.

To repeat, most, or perhaps all, valuable tropical crops can be grown in Middle America, beginning with natural rubber (the United States imported 866,000 long tons during 1941), ranging through the great and staple tropical fibers which the United States requires by the billions of pounds, through the several tropical plants with roots that yield rotenone, which has now become a principal and indispensable insecticide material with a more than casually significant bearing on the present and future of United States agriculture (United States needs for rotenone already exceed 6,500,-000 pounds per year), through the great drug crops and various other classifications and groups of other urgently needed products—all likely to become greater.

But the establishment of essential crops in Middle America or anywhere else is far from easy. Modern tropical agriculture is technical, exacting and scientific. It requires specialized education and numerous specialized skills. And in Middle America, aggressive sanitation and public-health efforts are imperative to the successful introduction and expansion of strategic crops and all other resources. These are big, hard orders. They can be filled only by a clear, insistent understanding of Middle America's human and social geography, present and past.

CHAPTER TWO

❧ ~~~~~~~

IN THE BEGINNING THERE WERE INDIANS

THE ever fascinating world that fronts the Caribbean was an Indian world. To a rather decisive extent it still is. The greatest of all the Middle American Indian nations was that of the Mayas, whose descendants, at least two million strong, continue to live and work in Guatemala, south Mexico, frontier British Honduras and many parts of Honduras.

The amazing empire of the Mayas appears to have been born somewhere on the lower Mexican plateau and in upper Central America at least 4,000 years before Christ, and perhaps as many as 5,000 years B. C. The life and the strength of the Mayas stemmed from their development of corn or maize —their classic and continuing staple food.

The Mayas were the master farmers of the New World. Their nation grew great as their people developed and expanded subsistence crops. Even today Mayas are notable farmers and the Mayan life was and is decisively a life of agriculture.

As far back as 1560 de Landa wrote of the Mayan community: "Before the Spaniards subdued the country the Indians lived together in well ordered communities; they kept the land in excellent condition, free from noxious vegetation and planted fine trees." [1] Contemporary Mayas keep well to this tradition.

[1] Friar Diego de Landa, *Yucatán, before and after the Conquest* (Maya Society Publication), Vol. XX.

In his study of contemporary Mayan Indians in Yucatán, Maurice Steggerda describes the village of Pista near Chichen Itzá, a Mexican pueblo of about 400 people. The dwellings are approximately rectangular with rounded ends. The walls are made of poles tied together with lianas or wooded vines. Sometimes the spaces between the poles are dabbed with mud. Four large poles support the palm-thatched roof. There are two doors, one at each end and directly opposite each other. The floors are bare earth. The beds are hand-woven hammocks slung from cross poles. In the yard beyond the house are fruit trees, and tiny vegetable gardens, frequently raised on poles as a protection against roving livestock or voracious ants. About the homes are clay pots bright with flowers.

In such villages the Mayas live today, much as their forefathers did. The Mayan women manage their homes, cook the food and weave their magnificent fabrics, while the men continue to put land to hoe and plow. Medicine men practice their age-old sleights. At nighttime the women make ready their husbands' baths. About the cottages the same naranja trees continue to bear and ripen small sweet oranges. The same wild animals continue to rove and breed, and the same birds sing. Mayan men still work hard in their cornfields. Mayan women and Mayan homes remain thrifty. The pottery and weaving have stayed much the same through many centuries.

On the whole the Mayas have never taken to the English language, and a great many of them do not speak Spanish. Hence Spanish- or English-speaking travelers and neighbors are very nearly obliged to learn Mayathan. In the cities and in easily accessible communities the living ways of the Mayas are changed, of course. Their people are beginning to wear ready-made clothes. They are being exposed to the radio and to the mechanical corn mill. But numerous endearing traits of the Mayas live on. They remain a courteous and a gracious people, as de Landa pointed out almost four centuries ago: "The Yucatecans are very generous and hospitable; no one enters their houses without being offered food and drink, what drink they may have during the day or food in the evenings. If they have none, they seek it from a neighbor. If they unite together on their oath, all join in sharing even if they have little for their own need."

Mayan children are still beloved and treated with dignity and courtesy. The Maya stays at peace. He is not particularly healthy. Among contemporary Mayas the birth and death rates are comparatively high. Malaria, dysentery, pellagra, pneumonia, and tuberculosis are still the principal enemies of these oldest of Americans. The child death rates are shockingly high, sometimes reaching 60 percent of the birth rate. In one rather typical village Steggerda estimates the average life span as 38.5 years, only a little more than half that in the United States today. As a rule contemporary Mayas do not live to a ripe old age. But their great race continues to live, and the Mayas remain men of the land.

Ancient picture writings of the Mayas tell a great deal about these premier farmers of the Americas. At least a thousand years before Columbus' time the Mayas had developed methods for recording on stone the appearance of a given plant, its seasonal character, its time of maturity, its food or medicinal value, its general appearance, taste, smell and feel, its practical use, its local and comparative importance.

The great mathematical attainments and the distinguished religions of the Mayas were concerned primarily with the nation's stake in agriculture. The Mayas worshiped the gods of planting, growth, fruition and harvest. They decorated their altars with flowers and fruits and grain. Their medicine men based their application of the healing arts on the use of medicinal plants that were indigenous to their empires.

Agriculture likewise foundationed the civic and political structure. Theirs was a communal agriculture; Mayan dependence on food crops was so commanding and direct that the land belonged to the social group, never to the individual.

De Landa [2] tells that the common tribal practice was to assign to each married man a plot of ground 400 feet square (roughly 3½ acres) which yielded an estimated average of 40 man-loads of maize or corn. This amounted to about 80 bushels, not a particularly good yield in our reckonings today, but an excellent yield at the time of de Landa's report. Ancient stone walls, many of them long lost in sunless jungles, continue to mark the boundaries of land parcels which the governments of the ancient agricultural cities assigned for the use of their citizens.

The testimony of archaeology indicates that Mayan ways of agriculture have not changed drastically during the past 2,000 years, that the productive routine remains in the ancient pattern: felling a tract of virgin bush or woodland, burning off the vegetation and planting the land to corn. When the first crop is made and repeated perhaps two or three times the land is permitted to lie fallow for the next two to six years, after which time it is again returned to cultivation. The Mayas had and in fact still have the custom of banding together in groups of sixteen to twenty citizens, foresworn to aid one another in preparing and planting the land. Their principle of land selection remains but little changed.

For century on century the Mayas have been a populous nation. And luckily for the Mayas, as for others, trees and vegetation grow rapidly in the tropics. The abandoned fields of one generation become the new clearings of the next. Even so, by the sixth or at latest the seventh century some of the Mayan city-states had completely exhausted their reserves of adjacent lands and so were forced to abandon their

[2] *Relacion de las Casas de Yucatán.*

proud stone cities and set forth to locate more and better farm sites.

So, through the centuries the Maya lived from the earth. His gods were of earth and sky and water. In his eagerness to understand the most desirable times for planting corn and squash and beans the Maya became a student of the rotation of the planets and the periodic movements of the heavenly bodies. As his knowledge of astronomy and meteorology increased, his agriculture became more and more efficient. The cities fed by neighboring checkerboards of fields and gardens grew stronger, and the arts gained momentum as the people became better and more securely planted to productive lands.

Mayan dependence on agriculture was all decisive. It is still so. Today when a Maya makes ready to clear new land for new planting he recites a sequence of prayers to the gods of the good earth. The Mayan harvest remains an occasion for true thanksgiving, and the living Mayas, like their ancient forebears, continue to bring the first fruits of their fields as offerings to the gods of the fruitful soil. The ritual of the harvest is still possessed of sincere intensity. A common expression consists of digging a deep hole in the earth, lining it with stone, and building a fire within. Then when the stones are thoroughly heated the worshipers remove the fire and place newly plucked ears of the first young corn in the pit which they cover with earth. When the all-provident ears are being cooked they are offered, not to cousins and uncles and visiting office mates, but to the invisible gods who have given harvests so that man may endure throughout another year.

Corn remains the staff of Mayan life, a principal entree of each meal. The preparation of corn has changed considerably with the passing centuries, but the age-old procedure is substantially the same: the grain is husked and softened overnight in a solution of lime and water. In the morning it is rinsed in clean water and then ground on a rubbing stone. In many Mayan homes grinding mills are replacing rubbing stones, but in some the ancient rubbing stones are still in use. When the stone "hand" has squashed and ground the softened grains to a fine paste, the woman (to the Mayas cooking has always been women's work) takes up the dough and with her fingers she kneads it into small thin pancakes. These cakes are baked over slow-burning fires, sometimes in earth pits; sometimes the fires are placed in pottery kettles, sometimes in primitive charcoal stoves built of stone or junk-yard metal. Tortillas are eaten as we eat bread, though more frequently and in greater proportion to the total fare. Frequently they are wrapped around meat and pepper sauces or chopped meat or eggs or other more or less attractive fillers, and they are still dipped in homemade chili pepper sauce. The corn dough is also used in making ever nutritious tamales of meat, beans, yams, potatoes or calabash.

Through the centuries, too, corn has supplied the Mayas with several staple drinks, among them *posole*, an immensely popular and a nonintoxicating thin gruel made of boiling corn meal in water and adding sweetening such as honey.

We of the United States have taken the classic Mayan maize as our greatest field crop. But neither from the standpoint of propagation technique nor the culinary arts have we added any item of consequence to what the Mayas have so long known about corn. Dr. Lyman Carrier, of the United States Department of Agriculture, points out:

A study of all available accounts fails to show that there has been any decisive improvement. . . . The description of the plants, the number of ears to the stalk, the number of rows of grains on the ear and the number of grains in a row, as given in the earlier accounts of Indian corn, correspond very closely with the average commercial varieties of corn now being planted and grown in fields of the United States.

As for corn dishes for human fare, we know little that the Mayas have not used in one form or another for hundreds or thousands of years, and they have dozens of edible and nutritious corn recipes which few of us have ever known.

Among other great Mayan crops is manioc, or tapioca, made from the starchy root Yuca. Centuries ago, the Mayas learned how to grate the root and squeeze the pulp in a basketry press and thus remove the toxic juice; how to press the pulp into cakes and heat them until all the remaining volatile poison is driven out. The end product was, and still is, cassava bread. Excellent beer and several stronger liquors can be made of cassava—all of which the ancient Mayas knew and made the most of.

The white potato was raised by the ancient Mayas and still is. The same is true of those two distinguished vegetable resources, the sweet potato and the tomato. For centuries while most white men considered the tomato deadly poisonous the Mayas were eating it; and they have cultivated and consumed sweet potatoes for thousands of years.

The Mayas also grew cacao, or chocolate, the oldest and still one of the most valuable of all Pan-American orchard crops. They developed and propagated the graceful, dapple-bodied cacao trees. They clipped off the small hard stems of the green-yellow squashlike pods, split open the pods first with flint knives and took out the slimy chocolate-bearing "beans" which they roasted and ground and boiled with corn meal and chili peppers. They ate the cured beans, but their principal chocolate food was corn gruel richly flavored with cacao.

Long before Columbus' time the roster of Mayan crops had also come to include various types of edible plums, the fruit of the breadnut tree, yams, canoches, squashes, okras and papayas, and through the centuries the Mayas have benefited from wild game of the Caribbean frontiers—native deer, wild hogs and wild turkeys; also tapirs and armadillos.

Great history lives in Mayan fields and forests. Agricultural practices have remained almost unbelievably consistent. Today in the many little known Mayan communities the land is still plowed with homemade plows drawn by gaunt tropical oxen. Today, as for centuries past, the majority of Mayan fields are small and frequently situated on roof-steep countrysides or other locations wherein the owner must till the land with his broad, heavy hand hoe. In thousands of Mayan homes the threshing is done the old way. Cereal grains, particularly barley, are planted in tiny patches, which on the steep hillsides must be kept in place by terraces built of stone.

Now, as of old, the Mayan farmer is likely to harvest his barley by means of a tiny reaping hook or sickle. In the autumn shortly before the corn is ripe the farmer continues to walk among the grain rows and to bend or break each stalk about a foot below the ear—causing the ear to hang down so that the rain will not soak into it and so spoil the grain. The corn harvest remains a hand harvest. Barley and other cereals are usually threshed by means of the age-old expedients of laying the grain ears on a hard earthen floor and driving horses or burros around and around the enclosures until the grain is separated from the chaff and straw. Then the Mayan countryman brushes away most of the straw with a triple-pronged tree branch or a cane broom, and separates the chaff by tossing the grain in the air with a homemade shovel and letting the wind lift away the lighter refuse.

The Mayas also had several nonedible crops of importance. The first rubber used by man is said to have come from Chichen Itzá in Yucatán. The Mayas used rubber for incense, also to tip drumsticks, and for waterproofing shoes, moccasins and clothing. They grew cotton and they were among the first nations of men to wear cotton clothing. According to the Spanish historian, Gomarro, the white-skinned discoverers of America were astonished "to perceive that the Indians [Mayas] were so richly and tastefully clothed. They wore shirts and cloaks of white and colored cotton." No one can be certain how long the Mayas have grown cotton; but now, as for many centuries, cotton remains their staple textile. Thousands of Mayas continue to garb themselves tastefully and ingeniously.

To Mayan people, past and present, we are also indebted for our supply of chewing gum, the basis of which is taken from the sap or "milk" of the chico-sapote tree. It is probable that the Mayas chewed gum for uncounted pre-Columbian centuries. (There is poetic justice in the fact that much of what we have learned about the Mayas has resulted from the jungle explorations made by the chicle hunters; the ancient trails of the *chicleros* continue to lead contemporary archaeologists into the ever fascinating ruins of earlier Mayan nations.)

The great epic of Mayan agriculture included numerous and valuable herb and medicinal crops—among them the coca leaf from which cocaine is derived, also quinine and cascara sagrada. Another great native crop developed in Mayan country is henequen, which the pre-Columbian Mayas used for making rope, twine, cloth and other strong textiles. Henequen is a member of the agave family, a dull-green thorny-leafed dryland shrub which has long been the most valuable export of Yucatán. And the same plant that provides farmers in Minnesota, Kansas and the Dakotas with twine with which to bind their grains for threshing also furnished the cordage for wrapping the crops which fed the ancient Mayan city-states, as well as the ropes that were used for towing and hauling the great stone blocks used in building the ancient and illustrious Mayan temples.

Some historians contend that the Mayas were emigrees from the lost continent—Atlantis; that ethnologically they are non-Asiatic. In no other part of the world do the Mayan hieroglyphs appear and there probably is no relevant similarity to their language anywhere outside the Mayan area. The same is generally true of their art and their architecture. Their origin is still further baffling to students in that they are among the few Indians practicing baptism, confession and atonement; that while they had a pantheon of gods, they believed in one supreme being for whom they made no image.

By the sixteenth century, when conquistadors came a-looting, Mayas peopled the greater parts of Yucatán, Vera Cruz, Tabasco, Campeche, Chiapas, in what is now Mexico, and most of Guatemala, Salvador, Honduras—an area of more than 150,000 square miles.

A tragic loss to the world was the burning by the Bishop of Yucatán of twenty-seven hieroglyphic rolls, recounting Mayan history and including works on astronomy, medicine and religion. The same bishop also brought about the destruction of some 5,000 idols, branding them as works of the devil and therefore to be annihilated by those who had come to convert the idolaters. Subsequently, however, Bishop Diego de Landa wrote a book on Mayan customs, their calendar and their organization, taking the material and testimony from living Mayas. De Landa's report has become the great source book on the Mayas—this together with the record on ruins which archaeologists are slowly deciphering. Through de Landa's book we learn of a people so highly civilized that in one given period of 200 years of their history there is no record of war; a people whose calendar was exactly right at that historical land-sighting moment when Columbus' calendar was allegedly eight to ten days in error; a people who apparently had no other culture to draw from, yet had the innate ability and social consciousness to develop an integrated and prosperous society in which flowered the arts and sciences.

From de Landa and the reports of various though generally reliable archaeologists, one learns that trade between the many scattered cities of Mayas was extensive. Merchants traveled by the North Star, a thousand years before the Vikings steered their high-prowed ships across the sea to Vineland. Trade moved across foot trails, sometimes along rock-paved highways, crossed great swamps, traveled over bridged rivers and over mountain passes. Slaves bore their masters' merchandise on their backs. As a symbol of their occupation Mayan merchants carried palm-leaf fans. Hanging from their belts were bags of cacao beans, the coin of the Mayas. Along the trails were sacred images, wayside altars, where merchants stopped to burn incense to the god Shaman-Ek, their protector. Trade followed the many religious festivals of the towns. Mayan cities built large central market places to which merchants brought their goods and provisions. A judge presided over the market to see that prices were fair, that cheating was not practiced.

Over land trails and waterways were carried copper, wax, rings, hatchets, ornaments, jewelry, feathers, raw or carved jade, vases, gourds, carvings, shells, stone implements, figurines, peppers, black beans, clay whistles, pottery, maize, honey, cotton cloth, embroidery, gums, charms and herbs. From El Salvador merchants carried the much-sought-for vases of a peculiar metallic luster. Salt was a most important article of commerce. The salt marshes were common property, the salt obtained from the sea by sun evaporation.

A system of business ethics was rigidly adhered to. There were no contracts or agreements except the word of the trad-

Photo by C. M. Wilson

The Open Market, Standard Resource of Middle American
Living, Is a Foremost Social Institution

Photo by Iris Woolcock

Assembling the Family Cart in Costa Rica

Indians Entering Primitive Dugout on Lake Atitlán in Guatemala

Middle America Information Bureau

Middle America Information Bureau

View from Morro Castle of Havana's Famous Melecon

View of Lake Atitlán in Guatemala

Middle America Information Bureau

ers. Loaning and borrowing were practiced, but without interest.

As already noted, cacao seeds were the most commonly used monetary unit of the Mayas. Their value fluctuated according to their supply and demand. At one period a slave cost 100 cacao seeds; a prostitute, ten. Small disks of stone were also used as coin, properly incised. So, too, were feathers. The owner of many great plumes was a man of wealth.

Gold was not used as money nor was it esteemed as precious as jade. Green was a sacred color as the good earth favors green: the growing crops, the forests, the plumage of birds, reeds on the river banks and medicinal herbs and leaves; so green was the Mayan symbol of value.

There was much barter trade—salt for chili pods; maize for black beans, etc. The counting system was in units and multiples of twenty. They used the cipher in their calculations, a symbol not in use in Europe until between the sixth and seventh centuries.

The Mayan cities, like the Greek cities, were independent of one another, each governed by a "king" who was probably also high priest; or by a body of nobles and priests, in some instances elective and in others, hereditary. (Among the Mayas today are perhaps the longest reigning royalty in all the world.) Later some of the cities united under a single ruler or chief.

The long years of peace indicate that this centering of many interests proved outstandingly successful. Otherwise there would surely have been wars over water, hunting and mining rights; quarrels over land and wealth.

The chiefs governed the towns, settled disputes and ordered and adjusted intercity affairs. A chief appointed a major-domo whom villagers having business in the central city consulted. The chiefs also appointed the governors who were charged with treating the common people justly and keeping the peace in the community.

Within this social system, stable for centuries, classes developed: ranks, castes, commoners, slaves. Cities were laid out in zones in which at the center were the temples, the houses of the priests and the nobles. Immediately surrounding them lived the wealthy, the merchants, the most esteemed, followed by the artisans. At the city limits lived the common people, the poor. Such a city was Uaxactun in Guatemala, thriving centuries before the Christian era. Scattered over Honduras and Guatemala were many such metropolises.

The national game, universally popular with all classes, was *pok-ta-pok*. The playing courts were from 100 to 200 feet long; the walls from 10 to 12 feet high and richly ornamented. Flowers and plants were planted outside the walls. The floor was smooth. In the center of the court, affixed to the walls, were two stones with holes in the center, encircled by the figure of the god of the game. A black and green line divided the court. A ball of solid rubber up to a foot in diameter was tossed into the court. The players, using only their buttocks and hips and heads, sought to land the ball in the center of their stone.

The game opened with religious ceremonies. Nobles bet their slaves, jewelry, rich stones, feather cloaks, adornments on their favorite players who were greatly admired by the populace. The rich gave them gifts, wined and dined them. The game required great skill, and so professional players played to great towns—and professional gamblers followed the players.

The Mayas were also fond of dancing, preferably from morning to night. But dancing was a manly art and recreation in which women were not permitted to indulge. The same was true of music, also beloved by the Mayas, who possessed small drums beaten by hand; hollow wood drums beaten with rubber-tipped gongs; also wind instruments shaped from turtle shells, flutes, whistles of bone or reed, conch shells and rattles. The rich banqueted and dined frequently, and each guest was obliged to repay in kind. If a guest died before he had met this obligation, his heirs inherited it. Mayan wines, made from honey and tree bark, were potent, and banquets traditionally ended in drunkenness.

The practice of medicine was in the hands of wizards or sorceresses and priests. Incantations, libations and exorcisms were incidental rituals, but the Mayas also had a superb pharmacopoeia consisting of herbs, barks, roots, oils and plants, which were used in connection with magic. Medicinal herbs which were gathered from highland forests and swamps were in continuing demand. Nightshade and ceterach were used medicinally; a sort of fennel, eaten raw or boiled, was a cure for sores. Sarsaparilla was known and its root was highly prized. They used cacao peel to cure cuts and chewed chicle as medicine, and an aromatic resin in holy water appeased the evil spirit responsible for disease. Burned, the same resin produced autohypnosis, dulling the senses and producing sleep.

The Mayas were a dark-skinned, round-headed, sturdy people. Both men and women loved adornment but the men were the more adorned. Both sexes tattooed their bodies. The men were particularly fond of mirrors, feathers and plumes. Men and women alike were frequent bathers and devotees of perfumes, and both wore nose ornaments, rings and necklaces. Figurines and decorated pottery have given us, in their traceries and reliefs, pictures of the daily life of the people, both commoners and aristocrats. They depict Mayan children as jolly, lively and mischievous, playing with whistles and bows and arrows. The conquering Spaniards, who may have smelled almost as badly as they behaved, were shocked at the frequent bathing of children; also by the fact that among the Mayas the women had charge of the child's education.

Life for the Mayas began propitiously. A sorceress was called in childbirth. Under the bed of the mother was put an image of an evil spirit to draw evil away from mother and child. Shortly after birth the child was taken to the priest that he might cast the child's fate and bestow a childhood name which he would keep till baptism, after which he was called by the father's name. A few days after birth the process of flattening the head began; boards were tied to the back and front of the head, then bound together tightly. A sugar-loaf head resulted. Because squinty eyes were regarded as a mark of beauty, dangling objects were tied on the forehead before the infant's eyes. That boys might not later grow beards, mothers scalded their faces with hot applications. Beards were considered most undesirable.

The ancient Mayas practiced baptism. The priest chose a lucky day for group baptism of boys and girls. On one side of the courtyard, swept clean and freshly strewn with leaves, ranged the girls with their godmothers; opposite, the boys with their godfathers. In the center of the courtyard sat the priest. To each child was handed a few grains of maize and incense, which he threw into the bowl beside the priest. After the last child had deposited the maize and incense a man was given the bowl and also wine. With these he ran from the town without looking back. Thus was evil cast out of the children. The priest donned a gorgeously plumed robe. White cloths were draped over the children's heads and they were directed to confess their important sins. With sins duly confessed the priest blessed each child and sprinkled water on him. The presiding noble then gave each child nine sharp taps with a sacred bone and rubbed perfumed water on his face. Finally came orations, offerings to the gods, gifts, feasting and a drinking orgy.

After the christening the youths were assigned to live alone in a large whitewashed community building which was surrounded by playgrounds. Here they played ball and other games. They painted their bodies black and lived apart until marriage time, which occurred when they were twenty, the parents making the choice of mates—with the aid of a professional matchmaker. A feast at the bride's home constituted marriage. Polygamy was not practiced but desertion and divorce were common with no penalty attached. Adultery was punished by the offended husband. It was his privilege to forgive or to deal violent death to the offending man. The women did not eat or drink with the men. At feasts and banquets they waited apart to take home their inebriated mates.

The Mayan manual arts and carvings on stone and wood, their work in gold and precious stones, the ruins of their impressive buildings have long been the astonishment and delight of archaeologists. Without the knowledge of the keystone principle in building the arch, with primitive tools, they erected great temples—necessarily narrow compared to their height—whose ruins still testify to the amazing skill of the Mayan builder. Great masonry steps, the risers high, the treads narrow and overlapping, rose course above course to vast heights, covered at the top by capstones. The walls of the temple, as well as great masonry courts, were covered with stucco and painted.

Mayan cities were vast complexes of rising pyramids, plazas, terraces, causeways, soaring altars. Retaining walls of solid masonry made of blocks of limestone terraced the hillsides, the terraces planted to corn. The beams in the temples and the houses of the nobles were richly carved in relief or incised. In the homes the common utensils, the vases, the urns were elaborately decorated. With the division of labor came weavers, feather workers, embroiderers, potters, metal-workers, carvers, sculptors. The Mayan artist used a roller to repeat a border design. He developed with movable, carved type blocks a stamp for designs on cloth.

From Mayan pottery and figurines are reconstructed the activities of a richly varied life, of a people artistically endowed. Here are incised, or in bas-relief, workers and their tools, clowns, pets, girls, slaves carrying loads on their heads, rich men traveling with their retainers, nobles in plumed headgear, grand processions.

Mayan weapons were bows and arrows, lances, shields, stones and slings, darts, spears, knives and hatchets. Two war chiefs commanded the military organizations, one of whom was hereditary and had little to do other than "to open the breasts of those sacrificed." The other chief, called the *nacon*, was elected for three years of field marshalry. The high priest went with the army, carrying the four war-gods of battle. A quota of men were chosen from each village as soldiers and paid only when at war by the lord under whom they fought. Women carried the supplies in the rear: food, drink and weapons. If the war was important and extensive then the whole manpower was conscripted. Noble captives were sacrificed to the gods and common prisoners were made slaves.

With faces painted, wearing wooden helmets and carrying shields down to the knees, the battle opened with terrific howling, shouting, blowing of whistles, beating of drums, wild yelling. The army divided into two wings with the priest and war-gods and war-captain in between. The dart throwers were first in battle, hurling their darts, then running to the rear where the women were ready with fresh supplies. The dart throwers were followed by the lance and sword fighters. During the month of Pax soldiers took the captain from his home to the temple where he was treated as an idol. Incense was burned; gifts given. The soldiers danced before him the solemn dance of the warriors.

Such were the Mayas at war; but most of the time the Mayas were at peace, and in peace as in war their ever amazing history shaped enduring mosaics of inter-American affairs.

Unquestionably the Mayas were the most distinguished and powerful confederation of Middle America, first shapers of Caribbean destinies and the provers of Middle America as a world-significant agrarian laboratory. After the Mayas, and to some measure despite the Mayas, were other distinguished Indian races. Among the competing Indian empires were the Mexican Aztec, with whom we associate the almost fabulous Montezuma who reigned long as emperor absolute at the height of Aztec power.

But the Aztecs, or Mexitl (tribal war-god), were of comparatively humble origin. Unlike the Mayas they were a nomadic people from the north of Mexico. When finally they settled in old Tezcuco Lake, one of the five lakes in the Valley of Mexico, they lived a hard and ungracious life—naked, ill fed and housed only in mud hovels or caves. There is no reason to believe that the ancient Aztecs had any noteworthy agriculture. Apparently they ate insects, fish and roots plucked from the lake bottom.

Then by slow evolution they began to devise means for using the rich soil which bedded the drying lakes. This was accomplished by way of their talents for weaving with reeds which grew in swamps or among the beds of the drying lakes. With swamp reeds the Aztecs built the *chinampas*, huge woven baskets which were sometimes as much as 300 feet long, 300 feet wide and 10 to 50 feet high. Laboriously the landless Aztecs filled these giant baskets with rich soil carried from the lake bottoms. Thus they created their "basket fields," and in them planted corn, beans, sweet potatoes, squashes and sometimes cotton and other crops. The number of the *chinampas* increased and presently towns appeared among the unique garden fields, and the greatest town became the city of Tenochtitlan, on the site of present-day Mexico City. This great city was not built on a solid mass of earth or stone. It grew up on a group of islands which were developed via the earth baskets—crisscrossed with wide avenues and canals, a sort of New World Venice which ultimately was builded into the New World metropolis, Mexico City.

Like the Mayas, the Aztecs eventually developed distinguished talents in agriculture, and their military prowess far exceeded that of the Mayas. The Aztecs became great and decisive conquerors, the Romans among Middle American Indians, even as the Mayas remained the Greeks. And like the Mayas, the blood of the Aztecs still carries through important population groups in Mexico, Guatemala, El Salvador and other Middle American lands, despite the centuries of conquest, pillage and murderous oppression by white men.

To the south, other grand nations of Indians were tumbled into slavery by the seemingly eternal villainies of white destroyers. The incalculable tragedy began with the magnificent Incas, those ancient masters of the Andes who built great highways to join their empires with the Pacific and dug tunnels through vast stone mountains; who worked and planned and built until the lands of the Incas ran north to include what are now Ecuador and Colombia, and south to what we now call Chile and Argentina. (Incas created and maintained the highland cultures of South America, much as the Mayas did in Mexico and Central America.)

There were other notable Indian nations in the Caribbean lands. The bitter tragedy of conquests by Spaniards and other pale-skinned pillagers saw the Mayas carried as slaves to many of the Caribbean islands. After the "War of Castes" in Mexico thousands on thousands of surviving Mayas were sold as slaves to the sugar planters in Cuba (standard price sixteen pesos a head).

Before Columbus time several remnants or colonies of South American Indians found their way into Central America; such peoples as the Chibchas of Colombia, talented goldsmiths and silversmiths and weavers who colonized in what is now Panama. On the islands of the Caribbean lived still other tribes and nations of Indians such as the mild-mannered Arawaks, who lived in huts built of mud and bamboo, wove cloth from the kapok of Ceiba trees, and slept in hammocks (which they originated). The Arawaks were a gracious and kindly people, but with the Spanish conquest, their race, perhaps numbering into millions, was quickly annihilated by massacre, privation and disease. In the Bahamas lived the Lucayos who apparently intermingled with the Arawaks and so produced the more populous of Cuban Indians—the Ciboneys and Tainos. Also there were the great and brave Caribs for whom the Caribbean was named. They were a dark-skinned and warlike people, with lineage clearly established in South America. By 1492 the Caribs had gone far into the West Indies. They had invaded areas of Cuba and were strongly ensconced in the Lesser Antilles and on mainland areas which we now call Honduras.

In his sociological summary entitled *Rio Grande to Cape Horn,* Carleton Beals presents some brilliant etymological testimony of continuing lingual influences of pre-Columbian Indians of Middle America. He points out, for example, that "tobacco" is the ancient Ciboney word for the weed which has now foaled the all-time fantasia of advertising buncombe; that *huracanes* (a Carib word) still tumble Cubans out of their *hamacas* (Sarawak); that the Aztec *cacique* remains the unscrupulous political boss of Spanish-born politics in four continents.

Still other Indian peoples lived in what we now call Central America, many of them imaginative and inventive peoples who lived at peace and strove for a higher civilization, using their lands sufficiently, receiving from the soil all the necessary elements to make them healthy and content, and, if we believe the records, to live to comparatively ripe old ages. Such men and women of peace were easy prey to the Aztecs and easier prey to the white Spanish invaders whose peculiar military genius far excelled even the most formidable might of the Aztecs.

As the conquering armies of Spain continued to push into the lands of the Caribbean, the smaller nations of Indians collapsed in oblivion and slavery. For, as Diego de Landa (who destroyed the Mayan books and manuscripts when the Mayas declined to abandon their gods for his) wrote so casually: "The Indians took to the yoke of servitude grievously and in great suffering." But during four centuries in which white men have smeared most lands with tyranny, war, and corruption, the Indians of Middle America have survived.

Today the Indian peoples of the Caribbean are majority publics. Spiritually and socially they can be a decisive public. Today and almost certainly tomorrow Mexico, Guatemala, El Salvador, Honduras, Nicaragua and Panama are preponderantly nations of Indians, some "mestized" or mixed with Europeans, but millions of them pure-blooded Indians. Guatemala and Nicaragua are distinguished and preponderantly Indian lands. Panama is the home of primitive Indians, such as the island-bound San Blas—some of whom wear rings in their noses—and the comparatively well "assimilated" Chiriqui peoples, and others. Honduras is Indian, Spanish and Negro, but principally Indian. El Salvador, like Mexico, is preponderantly Indian with considerable admixture of bloods. Costa Rica, the so-called white Spanish democracy, is considerably and perhaps beneficially tinged with Indian blood; it has a considerable Negro population on the Caribbean side.

"Mestization," a nineteen-carat word effectively mounted by Mr. Carleton Beals and others, has long been an important resource of these Americas. For the mestizos, admixtures of the bloods of conquering Spaniards and native Indians, are a principal American population of the highlands of Mexico and Central America, while among the continental lowlands and islands of the Caribbean the Negro endures as a majority race.

Negroes came to Caribbean lands soon after the Spaniards, and (possibly) in some instances before. As early as 1517 Charles V of Spain had extended concessions for the export of slaves to the West Indies. A mere twenty years later Spain and Portugal were diligently engaged in the capture and export of African peoples into slavery. By the early eighteenth century all major European powers, including Britain, France and Holland, were devotedly grabbing the Negro from all inhabited Africa and reselling him in slavery to the American tropics or anywhere else.

The Negro victims numbering high in the millions (the French alone are said to have enslaved 3,000,000; Spain and Portugal together, three or four times that number) were shanghaied from all parts of Africa and from among most types of Africans—from lowliest bushmen to Moslem aristocrats; from the Eboe whom other Negroes had previously enslaved in Africa; from the Congos, the Mandingas, the Luemies and others; from the Fanti, Ashantis and other warlike Negroes.

Spaniards, Negroes and Indians intermarried at their own volition. French and British pirates, most of them licensed by the royal gangsterdoms of those times, added to the intermixing. Would-be and abortive invaders increased the fervency of the melting pot. The clashes between Cromwell Puritanism and deeply imbedded Catholicism were another force behind the intermingling of island peoples. Britain, France, the Netherlands, Portugal, Sweden and even Denmark scrambled for holds on Caribbean islands, winning and losing their stakes as the fortunes of war directed; trading, exploiting and matching race against race and slave against slave.

The destruction by native revolutionaries of feebly established imperial governments, as in Haiti, the seizures by British fifth-columnists as effected in the coastal slice of Guatemala now called British Honduras, and more noticeably the extensive importation of Asiatic laborers, East Indians, Chinese, Tengils and others—these further added to the racial conglomeration of the Caribbean countries.

The racial laboratory of the Caribbean islands and continental frontiers continues to show tremendous activity. Thousands of refugees from Nazi terrorism and European debility have emigrated to Caribbean lands during the past decade. Orientals, particularly Chinese, have continued to filter in, frequently without passports. Negroes from the overpopulated islands have persisted in moving to the mainlands. Unverified numbers of acutely crowded island peoples, such as Haitians, have spilled into less crowded islands, such as Cuba; this despite the frequent or usual protest of the unwilling national host.

Within the islands and along the jungle-strewn Central American shores, the Caribbean complexion continues to grow darker. The transplanted sons and daughters of Africa are the prolific children of the lush tropics and the verdant subtropics. They are potent replenishers of most of this palm-scattered oval of sea frontier. As Carleton Beals puts it: "For these [the Negroes] are the breeders in this vast circle of ocean, island and sky. Spaniard, Frenchman, Englishman, Dutchman —they came, they conquered, they faded away in the poisonous sweet arms of the Cariba and Chibcha girl."

Caribbean island populations continue to multiply—populations have increased tenfold as in Hispaniola, or even twentyfold as in some of the Lesser Antilles during the past century. In Barbados the density of population touches peaks of more than 1,000 people per square mile—well over twenty times United States averages. Carleton Beals again speaks pertinently when he says: "The Caribbean is an enormous black incubator." And the preponderant occupation and economy of these black men, like that of the Indians, remains agricultural. They crowd the soil. They strain the soil. And as in Puerto Rico, with ten times the current per square mile population of the United States, or in Haiti, where the average private farm holding is less than one acre per family, without good leadership they may scratch their way to anarchy and starvation.

Closely south of us lie the most densely peopled nations of this hemisphere. Closely south live, increase and amalgamate some of the most impressive Indian populations in the world today and some of the most highly unified and rapidly increasing of Negro populations.

Middle America is a foremost working laboratory for crops, for plant life and for the races of man; in particular the colored races. There is no widespread likelihood of racial suicide or white supremacy. The Caribbean is not and will not be a "white man's world."

CHAPTER THREE

THESE ARE THE LANDS TODAY

A COLLEGE professor, with a desolating aptitude for generalities, used to speak of the Caribbean countries as "those low swampy jungle lands," sometimes adding the epithet—"hell-holes of the hemisphere."

The latter is readily dismissable as crass ignorance. But the misconception that Middle America is a succession of jungle-strewn swamps is about as unfortunate. It is therefore well to know at least something of the geography of this Caribbean world; of its almost immeasurable resources in variety and contrasts.

This reporter is beyond the age of believing in typical countries or average citizens. Nevertheless if there is one Caribbean nation that can be listed as *generally* typical of the rest, it seems to me that that nation is Honduras.

Honduras is about the size of Pennsylvania. As in Pennsylvania, the principal area is mountainous—mountains which stated geologically comprise the basic "core" of Central America.

Honduras is preponderantly a land of farms, forests and wilderness, and as such it is divisible in three parts. The better known of these is the Caribbean coastal plain, stretching from the Guatemalan border to Cape Gracias a Dios. By no means continuous, the plain is broken by random mountains (Pico Bonito, near La Ceiba, is 8,000 feet high). To the northwest frontier is the rich, lush plain of Sula, where rainfall is as great as 150 inches per year. Southward the country becomes less level and less rainy. The banana land capital of San Pedro Sula has a mere forty to sixty inches of rain per year, with a usual dry season between January and May.

Bananas are the principal crop of this Caribbean coastal plain; cattle, sugar cane, corn and rice are of considerable importance, but bananas are the key crop—the most productive and valuable banana acreages anywhere in the world.

Inland and westward are the "Sierra" lands, made up of minor mountain ranges, some of them separated by steep, canyonlike valleys. Here forest and livestock ranges are the principal resources and here the soils are comparatively shallow—no more than two feet deep on the average. In some areas the bedrock, principally light-colored volcanic rock and mica schists, is clearly exposed. The rainfall corresponds to United States averages, i. e., thirty to sixty inches a year, with severe dry seasons. It is a milpas country; cultivations are principally limited to small or garden-sized fields of corn, beans and other subsistence crops. For centuries past the lack of roads and trails has been a principal barrier to the settlement and development of these sparsely peopled Sierras. Now that more roads are being opened, and with plane transportation showing distinguished progress, the interior mountain country of Honduras can at least be listed as a habitable, and for that reason a significant, frontier country.

The Pacific coastal plain of Honduras is another still too little known frontier of this New World. Here most of the farming lands are located in the valleys of three rivers, the Choluteca, the Nacaome and the Goascoran, all emptying into the Gulf of Fonseca. Sharply contoured volcanic peaks rise rather unexpectedly from the farspread coastal plains which front the Gulf. But these particular volcanoes are long dead; they are sedate and old, not the furious mountain hell pits which continue to erupt, belch and smoke in the mountain fastnesses of nearby Guatemala, Nicaragua and Costa Rica.

Only recently has Honduras' potentially great role as an agricultural nation become effectively recognized. In the fifteenth century, Spanish colonizers brought with them the seed and planting stocks of sugar cane, wheat, barley, plantains (cooking bananas), citrus fruits, peaches, grapes, and other staple crops. But the silver and gold deposits of the land served to divert the newcomers' attention from agriculture. Also, in the highlands where the climate is particularly attractive, the fertile lands are scattered and the intervening mountains and rivers were formidable barriers to travel and development.

But at any rate in its modest way colonial Honduras has helped prove the tremendous agricultural possibilities of the Caribbean frontiers. In its plains and highlands and valleys were planted and grown practically all the great crops, including cereal grains, fruits, sugar cane, tobacco, coffee, plantains, potatoes and corn—an astonishing roster of most of the principal crop stand-bys both of the tropics and the temperate zones.

The agricultural implication is truly outstanding, for the country provides the three decisive altitudes which shape the final destinies of tropical agriculture: mountain lands 5,000 to 6,000 feet above sea level (such as the lands of the Intibucá Department, which can and do produce superb highland coffee and limited quantities of temperate-zone fruits, i. e., apples, peaches and plums); the medium lands, mountain valleys and fringing plateaus with elevations ranging from 2,500 to 3,500 feet, lands well suited to tobacco and cereal grains and corn, also oranges, mangoes and avocados; and the great banana lowlands of the north coast, lands which have made Honduras the foremost banana-producing country of the world, with exports as great as 25,000,000 bunches per year. Citrus fruits, abacá—the Manila fiber plant, rice, oil palms, hevea rubber trees and dozens of other great crops grow lushly in the rich lowlands of the north coast. In the Lancetilla Valley, the United Fruit Company has established one of the most effective tropical experimental stations of the New World. The past importance of this station is considerable. Its future importance may be tremendous. For Honduras is a distinguished agricultural laboratory, and one of the least developed of the great farming nations.

North and west of Honduras is Guatemala, one of the most densely peopled nations of Central America and the most impressive stronghold of comparatively unspoiled Indian life that remains anywhere in the New World. It is the northernmost of the Central American republics and the ancient capital for Central American administration. The country, in all about the size of New York State, is geographically divisible into four principal regions: the jungle-strewn and generally fertile lowlands of the Atlantic and Pacific coastal plains, the low level and heavily forested plateaus that make up the sparsely settled province of Petén, the ragged, volcanic mountains called Sierra Madre, and the rolling, cool and sunshiny highlands.

The westward lowlands take the form of a plain, a *tierra caliente*, lands of crowded jungles and of grassy mesas. Here is an ancient stronghold of animal life—wild animals such as tapir, wild swine and jaguar; of domestic animals particularly beef cattle, sheep and swine. The *tierra caliente* is also a cotton country and produces some of the best cotton of the hemisphere. Though not invariably well watered throughout the year, the soil is outstandingly rich; it is a potential and to some measure a developed stronghold for the production of tropical fruits, including pineapples, bananas, plantains and avocados, and of sugar cane.

The coastal plains give way to powerful and ragged-top mountains, volcanic mountains with some of the volcanoes still violently active. Guatemala has a bona fide census of twenty-seven volcanoes which have produced the highest mountain peaks in all Central America; Tacaná, Tajumulco to the north, Santa María, Agua, Fuego and Acatenango in the area of Antigua, the ancient, proud and almost incredibly beautiful capital of earlier centuries. This chain of volcanic mountains is most valuable as coffee lands. Most of Guatemala's population lives and survives among the highlands, particularly in the high and relatively dry valleys which are protected by surrounding peaks. Corn, beans and cereal grains, principally wheat, and thousands of sheep, principally black sheep, are grown in these lofty valleys, and the great towns are likewise built among them at altitudes ranging from 5,000 to 8,000 feet. To the east and north the Sierra Madre slope downward by a succession of plateaus, some of them virtual deserts, to the lush, low strip of coastal plains, which, second only to Honduras, now support the highest yielding and most valuable banana lands in the American tropics. North of this wet, hot Caribbean littoral are the limestone plains of Petén, in all about a third of the area of Guatemala, with a population from sparse to nonexistent (averaging only two to the square mile), the great stronghold of chicle and of valuable tropical forest trees such as ebony, logwood, Spanish cedars and Castilla rubber trees.

Inland waterways are important to Guatemala. The Motagua River, which empties into the Gulf of Honduras and is more or less navigable to within 100 miles of Guatemala City, provides one of the richest alluvial valleys in the world. Rio Polochic, which also empties into the Gulf of Honduras via the Golfo Dulce, is another notable carrier of rich alluvial soils. So in some measure is the Usumacinta and its three tributaries, Rio Chixoy, Lacantun and de la

Pasión, which follow the general course of the Guatemala-Mexico border to the Gulf of Mexico. In the highlands are a number of renowned and fancifully beautiful mountain lakes—Izabal, Flores, Atitlán, Amatitlán and others.

Like Honduras and indeed like practically all of Middle America, Guatemala is primarily an agricultural nation. Its greatest crop is corn. Its principal export crops are coffee and bananas. Despite rugged terrain and comparatively dense population, Guatemala is very nearly self-sufficient in terms of food production. However, the supplies of beef and dairy products are still inadequate. The dependence on coffee is unfortunately heavy in view of the present gravely complex coffee market. Strangely enough, Guatemala as a whole is not yet really well known. We know comparatively little about the value of its forests. Millions of acres of its low-lands and level plateaus have never been opened to cultivation. Practically nothing is known of its mineral resources. Gold and silver have been "found" in various areas. The ancient salt mines in Santa Rosa and Alta Verapaz are still active. Various but inadequate surveys suggest that there are resources of lead, tin, copper, zinc, manganese and perhaps coal and iron, but the hope and promise of mineral resources have never yet been properly proved or disproved. It is trite though convincingly realistic to repeat that the foremost resource of Guatemala is Guatemalans, more than half of whom are full-blooded Indians and most of the rest of mixed bloods.

El Salvador, south of Guatemala, is the smallest and most densely peopled of Central American countries, and in terms of United States acquaintance it is probably the least known of all the Middle American nations. That is because its geographic situation permits no Atlantic coast line, and although there are five established ports on its 125 miles of Pacific frontage, that is, La Libertad, La Union, Concordia, El

Triunfo and Acajutla, comparatively few traders call at these ports.

El Salvador is a comparatively modern country. Its road systems and towns are among the best of Middle America. Its lands are thickly populated, principally with farming peoples. Its great crop is coffee, and in terms of agricultural establishments it is one of the most beautiful of New World nations.

Like Guatemala, El Salvador is preponderantly Indian country. Even during the Spanish conquest more than 1,000,000 farming Indians are said to have lived in the little country, diligent farming Indians, descended of Toltecs and Aztecs, farming peoples who raised corn, cacao, tobacco and other staple crops upon which their economies and caste systems were foundationed. The classic centers of this agricultural nation were originally in the interior, with the coastal peoples the poorest and least advanced. But during recent centuries the Salvadoran Indians have lost for the most part their tribal tradition, their eye for color and for costume, and much of their racial distinction.

It might be well to point out here that the technique of the fifth column is intimately related to the beginning of El Salvador's history. For example, in 1486, Ahuitzol, the Aztec king in Mexico, is said to have made preparation for invading this territory. He sent in emissaries disguised as merchants, with instructions to settle in the land, become spies and otherwise make way for an invasion by Aztec armed might. The infiltration was not effected entirely as planned, for only six years later the distinguished admiral named Columbus made way for the first Spanish settlements in Middle America, and a mere generation later, in 1519, Hernando Cortes swept into mainland Mexico to launch the conquest of the Aztecs who were pre-eminently the warrior Romans of pre-Columbian Middle America.

Below El Salvador and south of Honduras is Nicaragua, about the size of England, the biggest in area of the Central American countries and, except for Mexico, the biggest in Middle America. In contrast to mountainous Honduras on the north and mountainous Costa Rica on the south, most of Nicaragua is a warm, wet and comparatively low country. Elsewhere in Central America, except in Panama, the principal cities and population centers are in the highlands. But Nicaragua's highlands are sparsely settled, as one deduces while traveling through the comparatively densely peopled lowlands, which begin at the Gulf of Fonseca and sweep diagonally toward the Caribbean along the broad plains of the San Juan basin. Most Nicaraguans live in these lush, hot lowlands. The hill people have always been in a minority.

One also notices that the human geography of Nicaragua is rather vitally concerned with lakes. Lake Nicaragua, about four times the size of the Great Salt Lake of Utah, and the smaller Lake Managua, which are connected by a river, are the principal denominators of settlement and commerce in the fertile and somewhat steamy interior. These are the largest inland waters between our own Great Lakes and Lake Titicaca of Peru and Bolivia. All of Nicaragua's larger cities and most of the decisive agricultural centers are situated along the lakes, particularly the west and north shores of Lake Nicaragua. Here the rich wet soils are the principal loadstones for a nation of farmers whose principal crops include coffee, cacao, sugar, tobacco, cotton and bananas.

The Nicaraguan highlands are principally volcanic. Their tallest peak is Volcan Viejo, some 6,000 feet above sea level; and the west shores of the two inland lakes are studded with volcanic cones, a few of them destructively active, as was evidenced in 1931 by the volcanic razing of Managua, the capital.

The three principal cities of Nicaragua are inland.

Managua, the capital, has about 70,000 people. It is both a national metropolis and the newest of Western Hemisphere capitals. Next is León, within easy reach of the port of Corinto, an old city of some 50,000 people and the first capital of independent Nicaragua. The still older agricultural stronghold is Granada, with about 25,000 people, some of whom are descendants of the first Spanish colonists.

Nicaragua lies casually along the Caribbean—a low, hot coastal front of about three hundred miles. This is the Mosquito Coast, of sparsely settled, densely green jungle country, peopled largely with West Indian Negroes; a lumbering country, and recently a part of Nicaragua's fast expanding gold frontier. Gold is the fast-gaining wealth of Nicaragua; in 1940 over 60 percent of the nation's total exports consisted of bar gold and bullion. But farming remains the principal occupation and enduring life of Nicaragua, as of every other Middle American country.

South of Nicaragua is Costa Rica, which is Middle America's premier stronghold of proprietary agriculture. It is a small and mountainous country about the size of West Virginia and not greatly different from West Virginia's topography. About two-thirds of the country's population of about 600,000 live in the 3,500-square-mile arena of farm lands in the central plateau. The plateau stronghold of agriculture includes the provinces of San José, Cartago, Heredia and Alajuela. Here the climate is perhaps as near to ideal as any temperature range of the world, and here are many of the oldest of white man's cultivations in the New World. Four centuries ago Coronado saw this great central plateau as ideal farming sites for the real farming peoples of Spain. Accordingly, he directed the importation of cattle, horses and swine, and Costa Rica came into being as a beautiful and remote agricultural province. It has remained so, and now reaches a more comprehensive realization of its truly great agricultural resources.

Its Pacific coast province of Puntarenas is being opened to valuable banana and cacao productions. Guanacaste, also facing the Pacific, rapidly gains importance as cattle lands and as timber resources. Earlier banana centers in the area of Puerto Limon on the Caribbean are playing important roles in the development of abacá, hevea rubber and many other valuable experimental crops. Steady improvement is apparent in the agronomy of subsistence crops, including rice, corn, beans, sugar cane and vegetable crops.

Steadily and surely Costa Rica grows closer to the United States in trade and general developments; for contrary to certain journalistic romanticisms, Costa Rica is really and vitally a New World nation, not a miniature transplanted Spain. Its Indian blood and its Negro blood, though in a minority, are nevertheless important, and its present and future, like its past, are bound immutably to the common strength of the Americas.

Below Costa Rica is Panama, of the ten Middle American nations the farthest away from the United States and situated far south of the high arched hump of north-coast South America.

Panama is also the newest of American republics, and except for the canal strip and the two well-known entrance ports of Colón and Panama, it is one of the least-known American nations and, relatively, one of the least developed. Of its area of somewhat more than 32,000 square miles (roughly the size of Maine or Indiana) less than 5 percent of the lands believed to be tillable are at present in cultivation. On the whole, Panama—the name is a forthright pre-Columbian Indian phrase which means plenty of fish—is the most impressively tropical of all the Americas. Much of the ocean fronts are crowded with impish mangrove forests, and inland one meets mile after mile of jungle lands, all infinitely colorful and interesting. The greatest variety of palm plants known anywhere in the world grow in these ever-crowded jungle areas where herbaceous life seems too joyously prolific to permit of time or space for death. Accordingly, Panama's jungles are the perennial paradise for botanists and botanical revelations.

Actually Panama has many other resources, including the most strategic geography of this hemisphere. Centuries before white men spilled over into the New World, Panama's place as control board of a hemisphere was clearly proved and duly respected. During most of four centuries Spain exploited this premier resource of location and was able to hold its New World empire at least partly because it was able to dominate the land route of the isthmus.

But centuries before Columbus, Panama was a shaper of American destinies. Through the same narrow, hot, wet isthmus walked the New World's pre-Columbian men of destiny: Andean Indians from the countries that we now call Ecuador, Peru and Bolivia: the great dark Caribs who pushed northward into Panama from their ancient homes in the Amazon Basin and from the shores of Panama set forth to conquer and colonize the West Indian islands. Descendants of all these decisive Indian people still live in Panama: the primitive, fascinating San Blas Indians, who are believed to be of the original Carib blood; the western or Chiriqui Indians, who are descendants of the great Andean Indians; and the surviving remnants of what may have been outmost colonies of the Mayas.

In Panama, Columbus sought confusedly for the great Khan of Tartary, but discovered that his Arab interpreters were of no use. In Panama, Columbus discovered and named the land-locked harbor of Porto Bello, saw gold ornaments dug from Indian graves and made his futile and tragic effort to establish the colony called Saint Mary of Bethlehem. In Panama, too, Columbus heard of the vast repositories of gold which were to be found farther to the south and west; also in Panama, Columbus dared to match wits with the Indian leaders, such as the powerful cacique Quibian, and came out second best.

Beginning in 1508 Spain's king-emperor, Ferdinand, centered his audacious colonization plans for the New World on the decisive if too little known geography of Panama. The great Balboa, thirsting for the gold which shrewd Indians suggested as being the only cure for the fever which burnt the Spaniards, fought his way across 60 miles of isthmus, leading 190 men and an estimated 1,000 Indian burden bearers and slaves, and a pack of blood hounds which were conspicuously out of place. As every schoolchild knows, that particular twenty-five-day journey proved a major epic of the New World, and having completed it the youthful Balboa looked upon the vast ocean which he called the Great South Sea, claiming the land, the newly discovered sea and all lands touched by its waters for the king-emperor of Spain.

By 1532 the land of the isthmus was world famous as the pathway of the incessant streams of Peruvian gold. Thereafter a surprisingly large percentage of New World history is built about the struggle for the isthmus, a struggle which dealt various renown to such names as Sir Francis Drake; Henry Morgan, the freebooter; and Spain's Governor Juan Perez de Guzman and his ill-fated defenders. In November, 1821, the still stouthearted province of Panama declared its independence from Spain, joined the newly born republic of Colombia and noted in its understanding Indian way that Spain was too much preoccupied with fighting Simon Bolivar's army of liberation and seeking to subdue the rebels of Chile and Argentina to actively defend the jungle wonderland which had written so much of New Spain's history.

In 1849 Panama again leaped to world prominence, this time as the trade route and land passage for the California gold rush. With the completion of the Panama Railroad in 1855 and the opening of steamship lines from west-coast United States, the desirability of a canal once more gained ascendancy. Spain had projected the building of such a canal as early as 1520. In 1826 Simon Bolivar had projected a Panama canal to be built and controlled by a congress of the American nations, and the Colombian republic proffered the necessary rights free of charge for the common good of the Americas.

The tragic story of Ferdinand de Lesseps and his ill-fated, badly managed French canal company served as unintentional overture to United States purchases of the rotting French properties and the acquisition of United States rights to the canal strip following the overnight incubation of the so-named republic of Panama, which was followed by the successful building of the world's most decisive canal.

Yet besides being a supremely important geographic location, Panama in its own name and rights is a highly significant American nation, an important proving ground for tropical agriculture: the country with two of the truly memorable agrarian centers of our hemisphere, the first centered about Almirante on the Caribbean coast, the other at Boquete and Puerto Armuelles in the Chiriqui frontiers.

Panama is our farthest Middle American neighbor; Mexico is our nearest. Mexico is the magnificent giant of Middle America; one of the great Indian nations of the new world; the second power of North America; a distinguished reservoir of the American past and the American future. Its area is approximately that of Texas plus the three Pacific coast states of the United States, with Montana for good measure. Its capital, Mexico City, is the metropolis of all Middle America, and one of the world's most beautiful cities.

Its Pacific coast line is about 4,500 miles, featuring the 760-mile-long peninsula of Lower California, and its Caribbean frontage about 1,700 miles. Mexican terrain is dominated by two mountain ranges between which is a huge tableland or plateau 5,000 to 8,000 feet high; also hot, fertile valleys, alluvial flood plains and other rich pockets of lowland. The decisive agricultures are therefore immensely varied and include bananas, cacao, cotton and rice of the hot lowlands; corn, sugar, wheat, coffee, beans, sisals, tomatoes and peppers of the midlands and tablelands; the world's principal supply of the hard fiber, henequen, from the spreading plains of Yucatán; the huge highland reservoirs of grass, the tens of millions of acres of forests which include vast treasuries of spruce, cedar, rosewood and other logwoods.

Mexico is one of the world's most versatile nations; astonishingly old and astonishingly new. Its national university was founded in 1553—some half a century before John Harvard was born. Its ancient cathedrals and medieval palaces point back into a magnificent if mysterious past whence comes the Mexico of today and tomorrow; with burros plodding beneath the sweeping shadows of fast flying planes; with forked stick plows at work within sight of gleaning diesel tractors; with vast snow-capped mountains overlooking dense and flowery jungles.

There is no one Mexico. It is a million distinguished locales and a thousand centuries scattered pell-mell to form a nation. It is colored with an American civilization which was grown great while Europe, even as today, was afflicted with roving savages. Mexitl, tribal war-god of the Aztecs, for whom the country was named, was even himself an immigrant creation. Toltecs and Mayas preceded the Aztecs, and many more nations of Indians may have come before them, for temple pyramids such as Cuicuilco are believed to have been ancient even before the Pharaohs planned their own imperishable tombs along the Nile.

Spain's conquest of Mexico was one of the more infamous stories of man's history. By the end of the sixteenth century most of Mexico had become a viceroyalty of Spain, a great colony of mining, cattle ranching and sugar planting. Steadily the Church gained strength, and throughout all Mexico, not excepting the sites of the ancient temples, new churches rose, and new saint days were created, until every day became a saint's day in one or more places in Mexico.

Then Napoleon invaded Spain and overturned the dynasty of Charles IV, and in Mexico began the New World era of liberation from Spain. By 1810 Miguel Hidalgo y Costilla and his followers led the revolution of New Spain, claiming land and independence for Mexico's peoples. The first revolutionist paid with his life. But others followed in invincible succession, climaxed by the full-blooded Zapotec Indian, Juarez, one of the greatest of all New World statesmen, who fought and served to save Mexico from the wrath of the three-part conspiracy of France, Britain and Spain.

Through the intervening years the Mexican struggle for liberty and an era of the common man has carried on. It is strong and clear today. It will be so tomorrow. It is a heritage of all 20,000,000 of the Mexicans, some 90 percent of whom are even now of Indian blood. The mood, the folklore, the artistic genius of the Indian remain the continuing life of Mexico.

Without possibility of doubt, Mexico is the hemisphere's number-one reservoir of valuable metals and minerals. Following the brutal execution of Cuauhtemoc, the last of the

Aztec emperors, the Spanish conquerors opened a ruthless and widespread exploitation of Mexico's mineral wealth. With little cessation of extravagance, this exploitation has continued for 400 years. Yet Mexico's storehouses of precious and useful metals seem little depleted; in fact the surface is but barely touched. For more than 400 years Mexican silver has flown forth in an almost uninterrupted stream. Alberto Terones Benitez, the distinguished mining attorney of Mexico City, estimates that the total production of Mexican silver since 1521 is at least 210,000 metric tons, and adds, "yet apparently silver mining may continue indefinitely at its present rate." [1]

There is no doubt that mining is more variedly developed in Mexico than in any other nation of the present-day world. In silver, copper, lead, zinc and petroleum, Mexico holds a foremost place. In iron, coal, gold, mercury, antimony, manganese, tungsten and tin, Mexico holds an important place. In the course of World War II, Mexican mineral and metal resources have touched their all-time high of strategic importance. The world-renowned silver mines, such as Real del Monte, La Reforma, Santa Eulalia, and Fresnillo Pachuca, are once more world-leading producers of silver. But numerous old mines and heretofore undiscovered mines are likewise awakened to impressive activity.

Though new producing areas are well known and in some instances capably surveyed, most of the actual mining is being done in the well-established areas. Mexico's copper, for example, continues to come forth from the age-old strongholds of copper, such as Greene-Cananea and Moctezuma in Sonora and Compagnie du Boleo in Lower California. The great iron mountain, the Cerro de Mercado in Durango, holds its place as a principal iron-producing center. Blast

[1] *Engineering and Mining Journal,* Latin-American number, August 1942, pp. 98, 99.

furnaces and steel mills of Monterrey roar on to greater activity. That Mexican zinc and lead mining has continued full blast is due substantially to the heavy purchases of the Metal Reserve Company, a procurement arm of the United States Government, which recently purchased 250,000 tons of lead and 200,000 tons of zinc from Mexico alone. Antimony and mercury mining show apparently incessant increase. New deposits are being opened with each passing month. Here again the number-one mine, the Huitzuco in Guerrero, long the foremost producer of antimony and mercury concentrates, remains the number-one producer. Recently new antimony mines in Oaxaca and San Luis Potosí have begun export of the concentrates to the United States. "Showings" of the immensely valuable steel-hardening metal, tungsten, are reported in many areas, though for the time being most of the tungsten is being lifted from the Santo Domingo mine near Nacozari. Manganese, still in modest quantities, is forthcoming from mining areas in Lower California and from several established mines in San Luis Potosí, Durango and Michoacán. Stream tin has been certainly located in Durango. That Mexico has cadmium, arsenic and bismuth is now beyond question.

The year 1940 marked the all-time high in Mexican metal production. According to the *Engineering and Mining Journal* that year's totals were as shown in table on page 63.

The majority of Mexican mines are comparatively small. Of approximately 300 in operation during 1942, 225 reported a monthly output of less than 100 tons; 60, of between 100 and 1,000 tons; and only 16 of more than 10,000 metric tons. The latter are owned by United States interests, but today practically all small and medium-sized mines are owned by Mexicans. During the past five years co-operative mining societies have been established among workers in many mining communities. Here the miners themselves are the owners, and

Metal	Output in Metric Tons [*]
Gold	27.5
Silver	2,570.4
Copper	37,602.5
Lead	196,253.4
Zinc	114,955.1
Antimony	12,267.5
Mercury	401.7
Tin	350.7
Iron	93,179.0
Manganese	1,696.4
Molybdenum	515.5
Tungsten	103.1
Arsenic	9,267.6
Bismuth	185.4
Cadmium	815.7
Graphite	12,327.1

[*] Metric ton = 2204.6 pounds.

profits are divided among the members of the co-operative society in accordance with each miner's efforts on behalf of the group. This experiment, while challenging, has not yet proved uniformly successful. A few are succeeding, two outstanding examples being the El Rosario Mine Co-operative and the Dos Carlos Mining Company. In answer to urgent war needs, the government of Mexico has encouraged the production of various strategic minerals by helping to organize and in some instances by subsidizing small mining enterprises: by effecting temporary labor contracts, by permitting the immigration of mine and mineral technicians and by expanding the nation's resources in roads and railroads. During 1942, President Camacho issued a decree which exempts from taxation all new investments in the mining of strategic minerals.

The future of Mexican mining is enormously promising. But it calls for more and better organization, for sanitation efforts, higher wages and better living standards for the workers, and for ever more rigid control of foreign investments; and it calls for more and better survey and appraisal.

The need for more and better survey and appraisal applies more or less uniformly to all Middle America. We know in a general way that Honduras, for example, has important copper deposits, but to date, so far as this reporter knows, the necessary analyses have not been made. Recently ore samples from Panama have been assayed in reliable United States laboratories as containing 99 percent pure metallic antimony. Here again, so far as this reporter knows, nothing has been done about it. World War II has helped reinstitute the mining of Cuban iron, manganese and chromium. It has motivated passing notice of such certainties as Nicaragua's great resources in copper—perhaps the most important between Mexico and South America—aluminum and manganese. The United States Bureau of Mines wrote with eloquent brevity that: "Nicaragua is regarded as rich in minerals with extraction to date having barely tapped the country's deposits."

The same may be true of much of Middle America. There is no question, for example, that the volcanic areas northwest of San José, Costa Rica, hold important sulphur deposits, as does the Guanacaste area.

It is at least possible that still remote areas of south-coast Panama hold notable deposits of copper. It is certain that the diverse, scarcely known mineral wealth of Guatemala includes limestone, iron, chromium, antimony and copper, none of them adequately developed. Much of Middle America may be destined to become world important in mineral and metals. That much is for the significant possibility file. The enduring life of Middle America remains agricultural, and nowhere is this more fascinatingly evident than in the three Caribbean island republics.

Indian Women on Way to Market, Chichicastenango, Guatemala

Presidential Palace at Havana, Cuba

Bud-grafting High-yielding (Hevea)
Rubber Trees in Costa Rica

Budded Clone of Hevea Rubber,
Honduras

Portaging Ball Para Rubber around the January River Rapids on Its
Way to the Amazon on Down to Belem

Most of Middle America is tropical. Cuba, largest of the Caribbean islands and largest of the island republics, is essentially subtropical—a propitious merging of the temperate climates with the deep tropics; of tropical crops and temperate crops, with particular emphasis on sugar cane, Cuba's master crop which happens to be one of the more decisive grasses born of many climates, from hottest tropics to subarctic.

Cuba is best divisible as Havana and the rest of the island. Havana endures as the magnificent capital of the Antilles— one of the oldest of the New World capitals, one of the most incessantly varied and one of the most perennially inviting. Havana was founded in 1514, almost a century before Jamestown Colony. In 1551 it replaced Santiago de Cuba as capital of the colony, and by 1634 it had become Spain's most powerful New World naval base. Accordingly, Britain lusted for the city and in 1762 the fighting forces of Britain's Lord Albemarle captured it and established Havana as a capital for the fantastically profitable British slave trade.

Spain eventually rewon its proud fortress city, and Havana, like all Cuba, eventually won comparative independence. Through the parade of history-shaping events, Havana has grown and flowered until today when the theoretically average citizen of the United States thinks of Cuba he usually thinks of Havana, which is understandable, though not necessarily fortunate either to Cuba or to the ever fictitious average United States citizen.

For Cuba is a truly memorable country. West and south of Havana one becomes acquainted with the province of Pinar del Río, some 5,000 square miles of immensely attractive countryside traversed by three great mountain ranges and marked by a rolling fertile plain which is crowded with sugar plantations, citrus groves and other fields—all beautiful and readily accessible countryside. Off the south coast of the island, about ninety miles from Havana, is the fascinating Isle of Pines, which Columbus discovered in 1492, and about which Robert Louis Stevenson wrote a book called *Treasure Island.* The Isle of Pines is about thirty miles north and south, and forty miles east and west; a kind of lost world, with wild mountainous country descending to jungle swamps and with magnificent forests of tropical cedars. High cliffs of tinted marble face the rising sun, and inland one finds a sheltered oasis for citrus orchards and year-round garden farms.

East of Havana one meets the province of Matanzas, a green, lush countryside bright with flowers, dotted occasionally with palm-made shacks, a rather gay and decidedly hospitable countryside of which Matanzas, the sugar town, is capital—an old city with narrow, crooked streets, iron-grilled windows and bright rainbows of tiles. Continuing eastward one meets the province of Santa Clara, another sugar province, which occupies the approximate center of the island. East of Santa Clara is Camagüey Province, the second largest state of Cuba and one of the great farming states, a lowland area which is also the cattle and livestock center of the island, as well as one of the decisive political centers. The green, rich, eastmost end of the island is the province of Oriente, of which Santiago de Cuba is the aging capital. This is the largest province of Cuba, the most mountainous and the richest in minerals and forests. Santiago de Cuba, with about 100,000 people, is the second city. From Santiago, Cortes set out for Mexico in 1519; and here, too, in 1868, Carlos Manuel de Céspedes first proclaimed the independence of Cuba. Santiago was Cuba's strategic city of the Spanish-American War. Here the Spanish fleet under Admiral Pascual Cervera was blockaded and taken by the fighting United States Navy, and nearby was fought the battle of San Juan Hill. Many times Santiago de Cuba has been the city of Cuban destinies and it may be so again.

But the final denominator of the Cuba of present and future is not one of cities. It is a denominator of growing fields and of productive earth and a preponderantly agricultural people, a gracious people who continue to love the lands on which they live. And the same can be said of the other Caribbean republics.

Haiti is a country of uniqueness and of superlatives: it is the most densely populated independent nation in the world; it is the world's first Negro republic and the scene of the first Spanish settlement in the Americas; it is the smallest in area of all American nations; it is the only French-speaking American republic; it was the first New World colony to gain independence from an Old World power.

The Negro republic occupies the western third of Hispaniola, the second largest island of the West Indies. Most of its land surface consists of two approximately parallel peninsulas, and Port-au-Prince, the capital and principal seaport, lies at the strategic crux of these peninsulas. Haiti's area is approximately that of the State of Vermont, but the population, numbering at least 3,000,000 and perhaps more, is more than six times that of Vermont.

The country as a whole is decidedly mountainous; "Haiti" is an aboriginal Indian word meaning "mountainous country." For the most part the Haitian mountains are a bright, exuberant green, and to the voyager they appear to leap gaily and irresistibly out of the bright blue Caribbean. The life-giving soil is principally in the fertile valleys that separate the mountain ranges, particularly the Artibonite and the Plaine-du-Nord, both of which are strongholds of farms, coffee fincas and sugar plantations, of small watered fields and unpredictable midget deserts, of cactus growth and jungle growth in strange and somewhat inexplicable proximity.

The valley of the Artibonite is the agricultural stronghold

of the Haitian nation and provides a substantial part of the country's timber resources which include cedar, rosewood, dyewoods and some types of mahogany. But there are other valleys to sustain this most densely populated of nations, smaller valleys such as Cul-de-Sac, close behind the capital, and Les Cayes, a sugar-cane country. Haiti is dominantly agricultural, and for a long time France was its principal outlet for timbers, bananas, sisal, cotton, sugar, pineapples and leathers. At present the United States is Haiti's trade associate.

At least nine-tenths of all Haitians are direct descendants of African slaves. French is the official language, though the popular spoken language is a sort of Creole which includes adaptations of African dialects and bizarre mergings of English, French and Spanish.

Much of Africa lives on in Haiti. So also does a great deal of the New World, past and present. Despite long continued overcrowding, and despite an almost incredibly high birth rate, Haiti's place as an agrarian proving ground is still of decided importance. The most formidable problem of Haiti is that of overpopulation, and of sea-bound land surfaces which cannot conceivably be expanded. The great resource remains the good lush tropical soils from which the unique nation survives.

Adjoining Haiti is the Dominican Republic which occupies all the remaining two-thirds of the island that Columbus called La Española and that later comers changed to Hispaniola. Santo Domingo was the name of its ancient Spanish colony—which has lived longer than any other Spanish settlement in the hemisphere—but Republica Dominicana—Dominican Republic—is now the approved designation of the country. Barely 1,400 miles away from New York City, the Dominican Republic is one of the more distinctive and impressive of American nations. Its land area is about 19,000 square miles, somewhat more than the states of New Hampshire and Vermont combined. It is crossed by four mountain ranges lying northwest to southeast and is bounded by Haiti and some 1,500 miles of seacoast.

The Dominican mountains are the highest in all the West Indies. The Cordillera Central has peaks, such as Pico Trujillo, which stand more than 10,000 feet. The Royal Plain, Vega Real, which lies north of the great central mountain range, is one of the richest valleys of all the West Indies. Somewhat similar is the rich soil of the coastal plains which also produce most of the staple crops of the warmer Americas, including bananas, rice, sugar cane, sisals, coffee and numerous subsistence crops. The three most strategic rivers are Rio Yaque del Sur, Rio Ozama, and Rio Yaque del Norte.

The nation is preponderantly agricultural. The population, principally Spanish speaking and obviously fast multiplying (the census estimate is 1,800,000 as of 1942, compared with 1,450,000 in 1935), lives principally in the rural communities which are clearly separated from the principal towns. The distribution of land is distinctly in favor of the small farms, many of them proprietor owned. The remoteness of country to town, in so small a nation, is perennially puzzling. The majority of the wealthier Dominicans live in the cities. But the majority population consists of yeomen who practice subsistence farming with corn, molasses and sugar cane, native tropical fruits, honey, and livestock, particularly goats, as principal stand-bys. There are several thousand sugar workers who are more or less regularly employed by the "centrals," but to this date at least the operation of large plantations is neither the mood nor the essential economy of the island. Modest, self-contained subsistence farming remains Dominica's preponderant way and means of life. Surprisingly, a considerable part of the island nation remains an undeveloped frontier, and thus provides both a refuge and working front for present and future generations of tropical pioneers.

These, briefly, are the nations of Middle America, agricultural nations which must be measured ultimately in terms of agriculture.

CHAPTER FOUR

GREAT CROPS MOVE

As THE races and nations of men migrate, so do the families and species of valuable plants. A distinguished social and racial laboratory, Middle America is also a world laboratory of crops and a world cradle of crops.

The over-all history of agriculture is sketchy and considerably clouded with uncertainties. But the fact that the lands of Middle America and the closely adjacent American tropics have given to the United States and the world several of the most valuable food crops is beyond question.

The first of these is corn or Indian maize, by odds the largest and most valuable field crop of the United States and all the Western Hemisphere as well as a rapidly increasing food source for China, India, Australia, Central Africa, southern Europe, lower Russia and many other food-producing centers from the equator to the subarctic. Surely and rapidly corn crowds ahead of rice as the foremost grain of mankind.

Corn, or maize, is an own child of the American tropics. At least three major empires of tropical American Indians were foundationed upon corn, bred and developed from basic strains of lush wild grasses. For when these great Indians learned how to feed themselves handsomely from hoe crops that were readily produced, they developed indigenous arts and otherwise lifted themselves to comparative greatness. The white or "Irish" potato, by all odds the most important vegetable crop of the United States, Central Europe, the British Isles, Scandinavia, Russia and many other nations, is like-wise an own child of the American tropics. Its particular homeland is the Andean highlands of what is now Peru, but its indigenous range includes many Caribbean lands. This range has increased until, like corn, the potato has become a pre-eminent world crop. In one year the potato crop of the United States alone is probably worth more in money than all the gold that all the conquistadors took out of all the Americas. Most of the edible beans which have long since earned second place among our edible vegetables are her-baceous offspring of the American tropics. The same is true of most of the great melon crops; of that tremendously im-portant legume called peanuts; of peppers, tomatoes, tobacco (first among the great crops of man which cannot be eaten or drunk); of the cacao or chocolate tree, which, second only to milk, is now become the foremost food beverage of man-kind and one of the most widely coveted of flavors.

This list can be extended. The plain, newsworthy truth is that the list is being extended at a rate heretofore unprece-dented. More emphatically than ever before, Middle America is today the number-one agrarian laboratory of the world. For many of its soils are almost fabulously rich; its topography and climates are so remarkably varied that virtually any crop grown anywhere, and perhaps every tropical crop, can be grown in the rich and variable lands of the Caribbean na-tions. Therefore it is no wonder that Middle America is be-come an action center for what is almost certainly the most significant crop migration in history.

One of the most exciting developments of the global war has been the sensational growth of "seed flying"—carrying seed by airplane from country to country and even from con-tinent to continent. The seed flyers have not only contributed to the winning of the war but also to making an exceptional contribution to world history by enabling the native crops of one land to move to other lands and take up residence there.

For example, various groups of military flyers have flown selected hevea or rubber-tree seed from Jap holdings in Sumatra to points in India and other tropical areas. To Madagascar, south China, Burma, and Egypt they have delivered high-yielding hybrid corn, the seed of long-staple cottons, and disease-resistant wheat and rye from the United States. In a few instances they have flown live ewes and rams into wool-short Africa to replenish the African wool and meat supplies. Many times they have carried live predators of various crop-destroying beetles from one hemisphere to the next.

The work of these flyers is merely one of hundreds of instances of the unprecedented and in many cases the almost instantly successful world-wide migration of great crops. In the fourth year of World War II this migration of crops touched an all-time high.

It is definitely a two-way traffic—not simply an export of crop seed and of planting stock from the United States, but a corresponding import of crops to the United States from all continents and from scores of islands. The acorns of cork oak have been flown from Spain to southern California; the seed of staple drug crops, from southern Europe to the Carolinas and Tennessee; of Cryptostegia, or vine rubber, from Madagascar to Florida, Arizona, Haiti, Mexico, and other areas south of the Rio Grande. The seed of kok-saghyz, the rubber-bearing "Russian dandelion," have been flown from various areas of the U.S.S.R., particularly the Republic of Kazakstan, for experimental planting throughout the United States.

Though Japan has seized the principal sources of many valuable crops that we sorely need, the seeds of these crops can be readily smuggled out—and now are traveling halfway round the world to go to work for us. The seed of cinchona, or quinine, trees are reaching us from the Philippines and the Dutch Pacific islands and proceeding via Washington to Puerto Rico and many republics of the American tropics. Teak seed (which will eventually produce that strategic shipbuilding timber) have recently been brought from Siam and Burma for planting in experimental farms in Central America. The seed of Derris and other plants which produce rotenone (one of the most important insecticides) are being brought in from the Dutch Indies and Malaya to the United States Department of Agriculture's brilliantly run Tropical Experiment Station at Mayagüez, Puerto Rico, whence they are being reshipped to select Latin-American areas at 50,000 cuttings per planeload. And the essential-oil grasses, such as lemon grass, citronella, and vetiver (source of soap, perfume, and spray ingredients), are being flown or otherwise carried out of the Dutch Indies and Malaya, where the Japanese would like to be able to monopolize them.

It is not by any means a new discovery that crops can migrate by plane. For the past seven years Pan American Airways, co-operating with our principal domestic airlines and more recently with the air-express division of the Railway Express Agency, has been making two-way airplane shipments of important seeds and planting stocks. These include outbound shipments of hybrid corn seed, rust-resistant wheat, high-yielding queen bees, long-staple cotton seed, and other planting stocks from the United States to most of Latin America, much of Africa, and some of the Far East. Air traffic in practically any kind of planting material promotes the successful migration of that material. Corn, for example, which is the greatest domestic crop of the United States, is also the number-one crop in most of Latin America. Successful plane shipments of seed of high-yielding hybrid corns developed in our Midwest are improving the ever-important

South American yields and making a sound contribution to inter-American agriculture and nutrition.

During the latter 1930's Pan American Airways began to carry live chicks from hatcheries in Florida and Texas to poultry growers in the Caribbean countries. The American tropics, like most other hot countries, are deplorably short of good poultry. Eggs do not incubate well in the tropics, and therefore imported chicks are in particular demand. The Pan American Airways chick traffic climbed promptly into the millions, and even before the war suitable hatch space in most southbound "Panam" liners was crowded to capacity with live chicks. Since newly hatched chicks do not require feed for at least seventy-two hours, Pan American urged its hatchery clients to crate and load their downy cargoes within twelve hours of hatching time, thus permitting delivery to any point that could be reached within sixty hours, counting not only flying time but time taken at the terminals. That meant that they could be sent distances that would have seemed incredible a decade before.

In any country good poultry is a major nutritional blessing. But many other kinds of livestock also migrate by plane. In northern South America the Pan American–Grace Airways have developed a remarkable traffic in live animals, particularly breeding animals, to and from otherwise isolated ranches. TACA Airlines has developed and exploited similar traffic in many remote areas of Middle America, and Canadian commercial flyers have hauled a lot of animals in western Canada. Where cargo space permits, air transport of breeding animals helps greatly to improve the quality of livestock and thus to make the soil more fertile and the farm establishments more prosperous.

During the past decade Soviet Russia has offered the most ambitious demonstration of this. Soviet planes have hauled

tens of thousands of tons of breeding animals, probably 25,-
000 tons or more yearly during 1937, 1938, and 1939, principally sheep and cattle, to remote Soviet republics—an accomplishment which no doubt has had a great deal to do with
the success of the Russians in feeding and supplying the magnificent Soviet Army.

The transport of breeding animals by air is supplemented
by the rapid development of the techniques of artificial insemination. Here again major credit is due the Russians.
Artificial or mechanical insemination began to be used during
the last czar's reign (about 1912) with stallions and mares
on the government stud farms where cavalry horses were
developed. The experiments were sufficiently promising to
cause Soviet veterinarians to reinstate the project in 1923 and
thereafter. During the past decade the use of artificial insemination has been standard and successful husbandry procedure in many areas of Russia, greatly increasing the values,
usefulness, and "service range" of superior stallions, bulls,
and rams. The semen of highly valuable sires can be packed,
insulated, flown thousands of miles by plane, and used to
impregnate dams in another country or even on another continent.

In the United States, too, artificial insemination is succeeding. Introduced by progressive horse ranches, principally
in the Far West, it is already of substantial importance to our
domestic dairy industries. Several hundred dairymen's associations or clubs in various sections are now taking advantage of this important technique whereby the breed value of
a given sire can be increased tenfold and its superior offspring can be established practically anywhere that better
livestock is needed—which is practically everywhere. During 1939 veterinarians of the American Jersey Cattle Club
used plane-transported semen taken from a champion bull

exhibited at the New York Fair to breed a prize cow on exhibit at the fair in San Francisco. In due course the cow delivered a healthy calf in Arizona.

It is now undeniable that strategic semen as well as strategic seed can be distributed effectively by plane to most of all habitable places on earth.

Another important phase of crop migration is the dispatch of "insect commandos," the natural enemies or predators of the insects and fungi which have been destroying important food sources. This strategy began half a century ago with the importation of the Vedalia beetle from Australia to combat the cushion scale in California. The venture proved successful, and to date similar feats in "biological control" have wiped out or helped to control at least twenty-five major insect pests and have proved to be the cheapest and most rational defense against at least some of the ever-increasing hordes of insect enemies.

Practically all plant diseases and insect enemies came into the Americas as stowaways on imported nursery stocks or other plant materials. Having once given their natural enemies the slip, the pests frequently thrive and multiply with great virulence. Since 1921 our Department of Agriculture has exported breeding stocks of fifty-three species of insect parasites and predators to Latin America for defense against major insect pests which prey upon important crops grown by our southern neighbors. These exportations have established effective natural predators to combat such crop ruiners as the citrus black fly, citrus mealy bug, cushion scale, Mediterranean fruit fly, apple aphid, San Jose scale, pink bollworm, horn fly, and sugar-cane borer.

Until the continents became linked by airlines the strategic use of insect commandos was severely limited by the fact that only a comparatively few insect predators can survive more than a week of travel. But by plane they can be flown practically anywhere in the world in less than a week, which indicates that the comparatively new strategy of protecting or saving crops by means of biological control also shows great promise for the immediate future. It is at least a partial safeguard against the migration of destructive pests which is likely to follow the increasing migration of crops. We shall say more about this.

Incidentally, a few of the important "new" crops are not immigrants at all, but neglected natives. A good example is allspice, harvested from a common and hardy tropical myrtle tree. Allspice, so named because it tastes like a mixture of its three principal rivals—nutmeg, cinnamon, and cloves—grows wild in most of the Caribbean countries. Now that Japan has seized most of our principal spice sources, some of our near southern neighbors, particularly Jamaica, are reinstating allspice simply by clearing brushlands and giving the myrtle seedlings a chance to develop. With such consideration the tree comes to bearing within seven to ten years and at maturity produces as much as 100 pounds of dried spice per year.

This item is mentioned because, owing to the now desperate scarcity of can metals and refrigeration equipment, spices may have a chance to resume their earlier roles as preservatives of meats. The more important spices are tropical crops, and because of Japan's seizure of the Far Eastern supply, many are again migrating to this hemisphere. For example, Mexico, Guatemala, Costa Rica, Haiti, and the Dominican Republic are again beginning to do well with pimento trees, which thrive in their shallow limestone soils. At last Mexico's famous vanilla plant is being brought back to Mexico. Black pepper and white pepper, harvested from the same perennial tropical vine (which yields as much as a ton or even two tons of dry spice per acre), are also coming back to Middle America. So is cinnamon, made from the inner bark of big and hardy cassia trees. Clove trees, heretofore a virtual monopoly of east-coast Africa, are growing splendidly in several Caribbean countries; and nutmeg trees, though natives of the Moluccas, now thrive after emigration to Brazil and the West Indies.

The plane that now speeds so casually, sometimes so ruinously, over nations, oceans, seas, and continents is the foremost activator of the current migration of crops, and in the instance of a great many highly perishable seed (which include hevea rubber trees and many other tropical crops) long-range plane transport is virtually essential to successful herbaceous migration, just as it is beneficial to migration of live semen and insect predators. As the war brings aeronautical progress to its all-time high, today in terms of proved and practical aeronautics there are no more really isolated people, plants, or animals anywhere on earth.

But important as aviation is to the contemporary migration of crops, the general proposition stands that many staple crops have been migrating approximately as long as men have (although, like men, they have not invariably migrated wisely or sufficiently). Here in the United States, except for tobacco and a limited list of fruits and berries, none of our great domestic crops is indigenous. Our livestock comes to us principally via Spain, Britain, Scandinavia, and the Channel Islands; corn, beans, peas, white potatoes, peanuts, and the common melon have come to us from the American tropics; citrus fruits from the Iberian Peninsula; our common cereals and root vegetables from the British Isles and Europe.

For generation after generation the migration of plants has created and perpetuated American wealth. Repeatedly it has helped to save domestic crops from annihilation by natural enemies. For example, rust-resistant types of wheat, without which much or all of our hugely important wheat industry might have perished, have been produced and perpetuated by assembling and interbreeding selected varieties of wheat from many countries—Russia, Poland, Germany, Switzerland, France, etc. More recently our sugar-cane crop was saved from destruction by mosaic disease by the importation —via the superb *proofstaatens* of Java—of various rust-resistant canes, which in turn had been developed by cross-breeding sugar grasses taken from the valleys of India, the mountains of Afghanistan, the dry plateaus of Turkey, the hillsides of East India, and other widely separated places. Crops such as long-staple cottons, raisin grapes, wine grapes, market pears, oranges and lemons, dates, figs, avocados, and a hundred other of our important food crops are here only because plants and plant materials can be and have been moved here from many parts of the earth.

The usual prerequisites for the selective breeding of plants are to assemble diverse species, strains, or clones of a given crop from the greatest possible variety of environments, and from these to develop new and virile strains that amplify the advantages and minimize the faults of the diverse parent strains. Obviously, this constructive feat can never be accomplished on a really adequate scale unless and until capably directed plant migration is attained. Our Department of Agriculture has known this for the past third of a century or longer.

B. Y. Morrison, head of the Department's Division of Plant Exploration and Introduction, describes his division's procedure in tracking down a desirable alien plant and bringing it back alive somewhat as follows:

While traveling abroad the Department's experienced plant hunters begin by collecting that portion or stage of a given plant that will bear transport with minimum risk, i. e., the dormant seed, bulb, or shoot. When the plant material is received in the United States qualified inspectors examine it for diseases and pests and assign the planting stock to specialists in the Plant Introduction Section, whose job it is to set out the herbaceous immigrant in an "introduction garden," which is usually equipped with quarantine greenhouses, propagation greenhouses, nursery greenhouses, refrigeration and cold storage, and whatever other facilities are needed for nursing it along. The current introduction of the cinchona or quinine tree into Middle America is a timely example of this procedure. Recently Plant Introduction received a shipment of the seed by air mail from a point in the Far Pacific. The envelope was opened at the Inspection House and examined by disease experts of the Bureau of Entomology and Plant Quarantine, who gave the seed a serial number and passed them on to the Plant Introduction men, who planted the seed in a Division greenhouse within taxi distance of the White House. In about three weeks the seed germinated, and for six months thereafter the puny seedlings were nursed along with exquisite care. Then the infant trees were taken out of the soil, fumigated, tagged, assigned certificates, and transported by plane to carefully selected experimental gardens in the tropics, within a few miles or a few hundred miles of the original home of quinine.

Practical gardeners were waiting at the tropical nurseries, men with "warm hands" or "green fingers"—the practical and intuitive talent for putting plant materials into soil and making them grow, come hell, high water, drought, or hurricane. Thanks to the Latin-American and *norteamericano* gardeners who received the feeble hothouse trees and nursed them along, as immediate local conditions of soil, rain, elevation, shelter, prevailing winds, subsoil drainage, and a hundred other more subtle factors require, the seed from the Pacific are prospering on Pan-American earth. Thus they reinforce the virtual certainty that eventually the Americas will again produce and process quinine to safeguard Americans from the types of malaria that quinine can best arrest or cure.

Like human migration, crop migration brings about many melting-pot problems—problems that result in many individual failures. But the present year appears to be establishing new records in successful introduction of crops, thanks to improved supervision and clearance of plant materials, to plane transport, and most of all to the urgent or crucial needs begot by the global war and the prospects of grim and hungry years ahead. But even as the tempo and range of plant migration increase, one wonders why the interchange of essential crops should not have been more actively encouraged or sponsored in the past. Throughout the centuries the great majority of all farm populations have stubbornly and futilely planted degenerate seed of a severely restricted range of crops in weary and impoverished soils. Then to escape starvation or intolerable poverty, men have moved themselves to other lands where too frequently, as in so much of our own country, they have reinstated similar routines of bad seed, poor livestock, and insufficient variety of crops.

The sower of seed is still a shaper and provider of nations, and it is now entirely evident that no nation can continue to perpetuate a really solvent agriculture or to feed its people adequately unless the quality and variety of its seed and the breed standards of its livestock approach a practical maximum. Otherwise intensive agriculture, however desirable in theory, is virtually impossible.

In the past people migrated by millions and hundreds of millions in the hope of profiting from richer and more abundant lands. In most cases ill-planned and even disastrous human migrations have been substituted for what might have been the inexpensive and well-studied migration of the staple crops by which people live.

Such fantastic defiance of economy and logic is no longer tolerable. In view of our crucial war needs and our even more crucial postwar needs for the valid foods and materials that soils must produce, our failure—or any other country's failure —to permit the free migration of crops or the effective circulation of seed supplies which other nations need so desperately is suicidal. For in tomorrow's world, plant populations—not human populations—must of sheer economic necessity do most of the migrating.

While surveying the huge task of administering relief to starving Europe, hungering Africa, and a disrupted and widely destitute Orient, Governor Lehman pointed out that it is infinitely better for the United States to supply desirable seeds and breeding animals than to try to supply millions of tons of harvested foods—particularly when there are not enough ships or facilities for food storage anywhere in the world to make such gigantic handouts even remotely possible.

We do not need to look into the future or to look ahead, however, to gauge the importance and the promise of this new stream of crop migration. The fact is that we urgently need new crops and more kinds of crops right here in the United States if we are ever to succeed in feeding our own people satisfactorily.

The principal subsistence of the United States is taken from about 30 crops. All told, our farmers grow about 300 different crops—more than most temperate-zone nations and far more than most tropical countries. But these are not enough. China produces and harvests about 6,000 different plants of nutritional value, which is an important reason why China has been able to survive the withering Japanese onslaught.

It is hardly likely that the United States needs as many as 6,000 different field and garden crops. But it seems definitely probable that the United States would fare better if we could establish, say, 600 valid crops instead of 300, and if we could employ still more advantageous foreign plants to "breed up" and otherwise improve the planting stocks of our ready-set bread-meat-milk-and-vegetable stand-bys. If food is the staff of life, the United States of America is still leaning upon a rather limber reed.

It is true that about 80 percent of mankind eat starches preponderantly and that we are among the fortunate fifth who are able to escape some of the loathsome diseases, the impaired livers, the rotting teeth and fouled muscles that usually result from the preponderant starch diet. Yet some of our wisest medical men keep right on insisting that better varied and better balanced protein-vegetable-fruit diets could eventually succeed in obliterating about half of the sickness that is still current in the United States. Unquestionably, the methodical and selective migration of crops can do a great deal to improve our United States standards of health and nutrition as well as our farm income.

But even if we elect to continue a let-well-enough-be attitude toward United States agriculture (and through no particular virtue of our own it is easily the best in the world today) we can be certain that the feat of improving and expanding the migration of useful crops can help in protecting other nations against degrading and war-breeding want.

The determined introduction of more and better crops can certainly help people in such desperately impoverished hells as parts of India, Borneo, North Africa, and (getting closer to home) Puerto Rico. It can help to erase such tragic paradoxes as the plight of one South American country, viz., Chile, which despite its immense treasures of fine soils has remained one of the worst fed and most unhealthy nations in the world, in substantial part because its crop range is ridiculously small. Almost certainly many of the rural slums of Europe, particularly of the Balkans, Spain, Italy, and Poland, could be lastingly benefited by the relatively inexpensive introduction of better seed and more varied crops.

Wherever the place or whatever the major agrarian prob-

terms, the continuing migration of crops tends broadly to restore and increase the active reservoirs of human nutrition. The real goal of reciprocal crop migrations is to make better use of a given soil by establishing those crops or species of crops which best fit the local conditions of soils, climate, and human needs; to improve the vitality of a given farm product and increase its value to both grower and consumer; and thus to improve the chances for the successful intensive cultivation of crops so that the maximum amounts of valuable foods and materials can be produced at minimum cost and in minimum time; and finally to avoid the excessive cost of moving peoples and of having to use millions of tons of fertilizers or soil concentrates instead of a comparatively few pounds or ounces of seeds, cuttings, or sperms.

The goal of wisely encouraged crop migration is certainly not to filch the indigenous agrarian resources of one nation or hemisphere and establish them in another to the lasting injury of the first. Nor is it to throw one particular farming area into bitter or demoralizing competition with another —as, for example, to enable the American tropics to smash the Eastern tropics, or vice versa. For it so happens that both the Eastern and Western tropics are permanent parts of our little world and both are far too important to their respective peoples, and to us, to be indiscriminately knocked down or pushed up.

As a matter of proved history, the most bitter and destructive competition between areas or nations producing the same crops usually occurs when the crop range of each is so rigidly limited that the competitive farmers are deprived of reasonable flexibility of marketable plantings. In general the greater the variety of crops that can be produced the smaller the chances of head-on crashes between producing areas.

The free migration of crops means the end of crop monopolies, and it can very well mean the end of the audacious cartels which would "freeze" a given crop to a given locale in order to augment the profits and prestige of any self-seeking group. From now on, if free men and free nations are to survive, crops, like air and water, must be for all men of good will who can use them well. The free migration of crops offers the one reliable assurance that this can happen.

The seeds of beneficial crops and livestock are also seeds of democracy. The valid and selective migration of crops can very well become one of the foremost benefits derived from this war, which, like the peace that follows it, is going to be won with food. There is, therefore, poetic justice as well as enlightened strategy in the fact that British, American, and Russian planes and ships are now being used to speed the seed and planting stocks of valid crops to suitable fields and gardens throughout the freedom-seeking world. It is inspiring to see at least some of our strategists, both military and civilian, shaping plans to use well-selected and well-distributed seed to help in remaking Europe into a productive community of gardens, instead of monopolizing our precious ships and further imperiling our overworked railroads to make Europe a perennial bread line or soup kitchen.

In terms of international and intercontinental migration of crops Middle America is both a giving center and a receiving center of distinguished and unprecedented importance.

CHAPTER FIVE

CROPS FOR MIDDLE AMERICA

EVEN during these dynamic times tropical life generally is strangely, perhaps fatalistically, repetitious. So, almost inevitably, is tropical reporting. In the instance of Middle America, as in most other tropical lands, agriculture remains the basic denominator. Agricultural news is, or at any moment can become, the decisive news. That is the case today in Middle America. It has been so through the centuries and will probably remain so. In terms of the pre-eminent migration of crops which is now in progress, Middle America is most strategically placed. But the true significance of this situation cannot be indicated in general or theoretic terms.

It seems to me that any intelligible appraisal calls for consideration of specific crops. This particular chapter seeks to set forth the contemporary stations and prospects of some of the more promising herbaceous migrants, with some predictions and suggestions regarding other crops ready borne or yet to be borne at our southern doorways.

1. QUININE

On the high slopes of a volcanic mountain in western and central Guatemala one can now observe a unique harvest. Indians are at work in a grove of tall, gray-barked trees. They fell the trees and, swinging their sharp, broad-headed axes, slash away the small limbs and twigs, then chop the trunk logs and larger limbs into "junks" four to six feet long. That done they take sharpened digging tools and dig up the stumps and roots and scrape away most of the earth or mud. Then they lay down hoes and axes, take up wooden mallets and begin pounding the wet logs and the cleaned roots.

That done, the Indian workmen begin peeling off the bark in thick layers, which they leave to dry in the sun. Not all the bark can be loosened by the mallet blows. Sometimes, particularly in knotty areas, knife work is required. In such cases the workmen employ stubby, thick-handled knives, the blades of which are made of bone. If you ask them why they don't use steel knives, they will nod solemnly and advise you in peculiar dialect Spanish that the "bite" of the bark (meaning the alkaloid content) will quickly eat away any metal, including, alas, the cutting edges of axes, which at best are short-lived. Or if they do not speak Spanish, they will merely nod in solemn politeness and go right ahead scraping.

They call the tree under annihilation "quina"—after the Dutch "kina." The tree's usual name is cinchona or "fever tree." Its bark provides people with quinine, man's surest and best proved defense against malaria.

Because of their work and the astonishing, if paradoxical, tree that occasions it, these Guatemaltecans have become particularly significant Americans. They are midwifing the rebirth of quinine as a valid Pan-American cultivated crop at this time when malaria remains mankind's most widespread communicable disease—in our hemisphere endemic to seventeen states of the United States South and Southwest, to all the American tropics and to all South American countries. No less urgent is the fact that malaria intermittently smolders throughout North Africa and much of South Africa, in all countries fronting the Mediterranean, in most of southern Asia and Asia Minor, Malaya and nearly all the Pacific tropics. India remains the number-one hell of "tropical fevers,"

QUININE

89

with a normal yearly toll of about 1,500,000 malarial deaths. Here, as in most other malarial lands, the toll increases alarmingly.

As World War II swings farther and deeper into the tropics, antimalarial drugs become crucial ammunition for our armed forces. Quinine still leads the list of antimalarial drugs. The synthetics called atabrine and plasmochin are able complements, but quinine stays far, far in the lead.

Today, as for centuries, the fever tree means life for people in the tropics. Now, as during most of the past century, quinine supplies are not sufficient to meet urgent human needs. While condoning the millions of underprivileged tropical peoples who quake and rot with malaria, it is notable that even in the United States, according to United States Public Health Service estimates, we have about a million cases more or less of chronic malaria, causing the loss in working time alone of at least three-quarters of a billion dollars per year. Every state of the United States, even southern Canada, has one or more types of anopheline mosquitoes capable of transmitting the blood-poisoning parasites of malaria from sick people to well people. Since the Japs grabbed the Netherlands Indies, Japan has more than nine-tenths of the world's established quinine supply. Our Far Pacific enemy is using this to his best possible advantage, particularly to bait and bribe the more apathetic tropical peoples of the Far East.

Accordingly the likelihood that for the first time in half a century the Americas can and will become at least partially independent of Far Eastern quinine sources is significant. For this, honors are due many Americans and several American nations, among them, Guatemala, which now reveals one of the most important supplies of harvestable quinine in the Western Hemisphere or the free world. Inside Guatemala there are now an estimated 1,600,000 cinchona trees, some of them planted as long ago as 1884 and most of them old enough to yield the bitter-tasting bark which has saved tens of millions of people from painful and lingering death from malaria and can save tens of millions more. On El Naranjo Finca, situated on the Pacific slope of the Santa Clara volcano —just west of the world-famed crater lake, Atitlán—Guatemala has established one of the world's most effective cinchona research stations.

Credit is also due earlier pioneers in Guatemala—men like Julio Rossignon, a Belgian coffee planter who first set out cinchona in the Coban area back in 1860; Franz Sarg, who planted more quinine trees in the same area in 1875; Guatemala's late president, General Justo Rufino Barrios, who worked valiantly to establish the fever tree in his country and to this end employed the world-renowned British Indian cinchona expert, Colonel W. J. Forsyth, to supervise experimental plantings. The resulting cinchonas, principally hardy succirubas (red saps), grew well even where local authorities set them out along highways or in schoolyards.

Credit is likewise due the present president, General Jorge Ubico, who probably more than any other American has facilitated the work of expert agronomists, botanists, geneticists and chemists in restoring cinchona horticulture to our hemisphere. Until recently Guatemalans had almost completely lost interest in quinine as a crop. In some instances they had felled the trees and left them to rot or burn. Repeatedly cinchona wood has been used to build bridges and houses.

The story began to change during the early 1930's. In 1932 Mariano Pacheco Herrarte, working with Dr. Francisco Cruz, then minister of agriculture, began collecting bark samples from all known cinchona trees in the Republic, wild trees included. By examining about 150 bark specimens Herrarte found that 29 were true cinchonas containing quinine sulphate, ranging in amounts from 1.52 percent to a maximum of 5.4 percent of dry-bark weight.

In 1934 under President General Jorge Ubico, Guatemala's Department of Agriculture began helping with the planting of selected quinine seed on several well-managed plantations—"El Naranjo," "Las Charcas," "Finca Panama," "Helvetia," "Moca," "Patzulen," "El Zapote," "Samac" and others. Long neglected cinchona plantings like those on "El Porvenir," a great plantation south of the Tezumulco volcano, began returning to usefulness. "El Porvenir," like several nearby plantations, is well suited to cinchona. Of the 800,000 to 1,000,000 quinine seed planted there in 1884, between 40,-000 and 50,000 of the original trees survive. Six of these, measuring more than four feet in diameter and standing some sixty-five feet high, are probably the world's largest cinchonas. Yet not too long ago a proprietor of "El Porvenir" had an estimated 700,000 of the fever trees felled in order to open lands for planting coffee bush. He burned most of the wood and bark and used a little for building timber.

But the now precious cinchonas simply stubbornly declined to be exterminated. The felled trees resprouted—usually from four to twenty or more shoots to the original trunk. Tens of thousands of wild shoots sprang up from wind-blown seed. Gradually a dense forest of fever trees replaced the original and orderly planting—as many as ten to the square yard. Presently Guatemalans began planting the trees in packed rows in order to form "living fences." (In many areas of the Guatemalan highlands the living fences of cinchona still flourish, the tree trunks standing only a few inches apart.)

With the outbreak of World War II, Guatemalans, like most other Americans, began to heed the long neglected cinchona resources. A Guatemalan woman, Señora Maria Raskin-Pinol, socially prominent proprietress of "Las Charcas" plantation, proved herself the most effective reawakener. Early in 1938 this señora began traveling throughout the republic, locating supplies of the "medicine bark" and seeking to interest farmers in harvesting the long-dormant crop. She succeeded in assembling a test shipment of two tons of bark samples. These proved to be low in contents of quinine sulphates. But Señora Pinol persisted, and because she did, about fifty tons of bark taken from the trees on "El Porvenir" plantation were shipped to the United States during 1941.

The finca "San Pablo," with about five thousand harvestable cinchona trees, began to export bark which brought an average of twenty-five cents per pound. The plantation "Los Desamparados" also opened commercial harvest of bark from old-stand trees. Between January 10, 1941 and March 15, 1942 Guatemala exports of cinchona bark climbed to 466,975 pounds—at least that many ounces of refined quinine —enough to supply a half million fighting men for a year. In 1943 Guatemalan cinchona trees were being harvested in sixteen different producing areas, in all more than 1,500,000 bearing cinchonas, which provide enough quinine for millions of Americans who now need the drug as they never needed it before.

Supplementing the old plantings that are widely scattered throughout Guatemala's almost fantastically beautiful highlands, particularly on the Pacific slopes of the volcanic mountains, are the new plantings of hardy roots bud-grafted to Javan strains of ledger cinchona which are particularly high in quinine content. Most of these new plantings are in the departments or states of Retalhuleú, Alta Verapaz, and Escuintla—at elevations ranging from 3,500 to 4,500 feet. Several thousand young trees planted in the middle 1930's are already big enough for harvest, or at least for bark analyses that indicate quinine sulphate recoveries as high as 12 or 13 percent of bark weight, i. e., at "maximum quinine areas"—about three feet above the ground. That is an excellent quinine recovery anywhere in anybody's language or country. Also significantly, Guatemalan planters are taking new lands for quinine. The altitude range of the earlier planting is under 5,000 feet. New plantings are being made at higher levels —up to 6,200 feet—in efforts to test the possibilities of the "zone" immediately above that in which coffee can be grown profitably.

But in terms of diligent and modern horticulture the little known hero of the revival of the inter-American horticulture of cinchona is the youthful scientist, Jorge M. Benitez, who directs Experimental Plantations, an all-Guatemala cinchona experimental center on finca "El Narayano" in the high mountainsides of Chicacao. Ecuadoran by birth, Dr. Benitez has studied and worked at the Lancetilla (Honduras) Tropical Experiment Station. From Lancetilla he went to Guatemala and took over what experts consider the most exacting cinchona-propagation venture yet undertaken. Here Dr. Benitez occasionally puts aside his mountainous records—he keeps a detailed "biography" of each one of tens of thousands of seedling cinchona—and speaks with mature skepticism (he is almost thirty) to the effect that he is only a minor paradox seeking to discover a major paradox—the latter being the fever tree.

Here, in part, is why he feels that way. Cinchonas must be propagated from seed—so tiny it takes twenty-five hundred to weigh a gram and about seventy-five thousand to weigh an ounce. During the germination period (three to four weeks) the seed require a little moisture and a great deal of shade. The seed beds must be well ventilated and are usually placed east-to-west so that light can be admitted with gradually increasing intensity from the north side. While the seed are germinating, the north ends of the seed beds must be blacked out with mats of cane or bamboo, so that the light can be gradually increased. Sheet iron roofing (lamina) protects the beds from the direct rays of the sun, and diligent spraying must defend the seedlings against insect and fungus enemies, since the seed beds must be surfaced with an inch or two of rich, bug-luring leaf mold.

After a nursery period of from six to ten months—or as soon as the midget trees are about two inches high and "hardened" by gradual exposure to light—they are ready for transplanting to shaded nursery beds to "harden up" for bud grafting. Thus an outstandingly hardy adult tree must grow from one of the puniest seedlings known.

The technique of quinine bud grafting is similar to standard United States nursery practices for bud-grafting apples, peaches, pears and other standard fruit trees. The leaves of the scion stem (of the more desirable tree) are carefully trimmed off with the grafting knife and a diagonal cut about two inches in length is made toward the lower end. This cut is placed against a long shallow cut on the side of the stock plant (grown from seed), so that the cambium layer of the scion comes into direct contact with that of the stock. The graft is then bound with waxed tape and painted over with warm, melted wax. Union of the two plants takes place in four to six weeks. After the scion has commenced to grow vigorously, the stock plant is cut back gradually so that the most highly productive tree will grow from the healthiest root. In about one year's time the grafted plant is ready for moving into its permanent location in the field. The required field culture is much the same as for coffee—hand weeding and occasional hoeing.

So far as we now know there are no formidable natural enemies of cinchona in the American tropics except careless, greedy man. Jorge Benitez is out to erase this exception. He nurses every seedling. On the story sheet of each he notes the rate of growth, the thickness of the bark, the quinine content, the branching habits, the age of first flowering, the leaf form, and so on. After the tree is two inches in diameter and three feet above the ground, he inaugurates bark sampling. The tree comes to flower during its fourth or fifth year, and as a rule the bark harvest begins at about the same time. The harvest is a matter of "selective logging." The first trees to be uprooted are those that have started badly—as an average about one-fourth of the total stand. First yields rarely exceed 125 pounds of dry bark per cultivated acre. Each year thereafter the trees are thinned until in fifteen to thirty years all of the original trees are removed.

As already noted, the harvest of quinine bark is a process of complete annihilation of the growing crops. A good average yield from healthy mature trees is eight tons of bark per acre; 16,000 pounds—good for some 16,000 ounces of effective malaria cure.

Cinchona varieties with the highest quinine content came originally from regions in the Andes where mountainsides are covered with a thick layer of humus (the accumulated leaf fall of centuries) and where clouds piling up from the lowlands keep the air and leaves more or less perpetually moist. Throughout the world most commercial quinine plantations are situated on the slopes of volcanoes—in Java on the slopes of the Preanger volcanoes and the plateaus between them; in Guatemala the tree is flourishing on the Pacific slopes of the volcanoes. Plenty of rain is another requirement—100 inches a year preferably; in Java's Preanger and Cheribon areas as many as 210 inches.

Ten years is the average time required for the cinchona to reach its maximum yield. The Javan plantations are ordinarily operated on a "rotation" schedule. A ten-year rotation, for instance, would direct that one-tenth of the total acreage be felled for harvest each year after the fourth or fifth, with a similar amount of land planted to new trees. Preparation of the bark for market is simple. It is dried and then ground to a coarse powder for shipment to the manufacturers, who use chemical formulae to extract the quinine and the minor alkaloids such as cinchonidine, quinidine, and cinchonine, which also have considerable medicinal value. (Five years ago the Philippine Bureau of Science began producing a drug called totaquine, which uses all the alkaloids of cinchona bark, is normally cheaper than quinine, and makes every pound of the now precious bark go further.) Thus far the ledger types of cinchona are the best quinine yielders. But the distinguished tropical botanist, Dr. Wilson Popenoe, points out: "There may be in Colombia, Ecuador, Peru, Bolivia, or elsewhere in Latin America wild forms which when brought into cultivation will prove even more productive and disease resistant."

The newest chapter of the paradoxical story of cinchona is rooted deep in New World history. It so happens that all trees which yield quinine are native to the American tropics —from south Bolivia north to Costa Rica. The Washington-and-cherry tree version of how white men learned of quinine dates back to 1629 when that magnificent Spaniard, Luis Geronimo de Cabrera y Bobadilla, Fourth Count of Chinchon, arrived in Peru as Spain's viceroy. The count was stricken with malaria. His physician, Dr. Juan de Vega, was unable to cure him. In due time the Countess of Chinchon learned of a bitter bark which local Indians described as a fever cure. Probably without the physician's knowledge she gave the ground bark to her husband, who eventually recovered. So the bitter bark was called "Countess's Powder" (Polvo de Condesa) and presently won an accredited place

Photo by Iris Woolcock

Harvesting Latex of a Hevea Rubber Tree in Costa Rica

Photo by Iris Woolcock

Walter N. Bangham, Goodyear's Distinguished Rubber Tree Botanist, Examines the Flower of Hevea Tree on Goodyear Plantation in Costa Rica

U.S.D.A. Photograph

Topping Castilla Elastica Rubber Tree, La Zacualpa, Mexico

Bud-grafting a High-yielding
Cinchona or Quinine Tree in
Guatemala

Roselle Plants Ready for Harvest, Sant.
Rosa, Honduras

Cluster African Palm Oil Nuts, Lancetilla Experiment Station, Honduras

in medicine, thanks largely to the Jesuits who did most to distribute it.

That is the staple history-book version, and highly improbable, even though it was once published in *Fortune*. The Peruvian version of how quinine was discovered tells of an Indian of Loja, a certain Pedro de Leyva, who suffered a great thirst resulting from fever, and drank from a spring at the edge of which several cinchona trees were growing. Pedro promptly recovered from the fever, pondered, and administered the same bitter water to his friends who suffered from malaria. When they recovered, too, Pedro trudged to Lima and told the Jesuits of the cure, whereupon the Compañia de Jesus became the foremost sponsors of quinine.

Last year both these stories were blasted by Dr. Juan A. Dominguez, a distinguished Buenos Aires botanist, who presented forceful evidence that the empire-building Incas of Peru and neighboring South American lands used cinchona powder medicinally late in the thirteenth century, thereby predating the Countess Chinchon's discovery by three and a half centuries—also predating by three centuries the apparent fable of Pedro.

Another cinchona paradox is one of spelling. Cinchona (usually pronounced *sinkona*) was named by the Swedish botanist Linnaeus (one of the world's worst spellers) for the Countess Chinchon. He dropped an *h*. Sir Clements Markham and many other renowned botanic scholars have tried in vain to make correction.

In any case, until about 1750 practically all the world's supply of quinine bark came from the forests of Loja near the Ecuador-Peru boundary. Thereafter demands continued to climb as men struggled to fight malaria, as more and more valuable alkaloids were recovered from the bark (at present about thirty are extracted, some of which are used nonmedically in vulcanizing rubber, mothproofing furniture, etc.), and as medical workers discovered quinine's efficacy in treating colds as well as malaria.

Starting about two centuries ago the harvest of quinine bark became a specialized trade among various South American Indians. The "cascarilleros" hunted out the cinchona trees, felled them, stripped off the bark, dried it in the sun or before fires and carried the dry bales via burro or mulepack to market ports—to Arica (from Bolivia and Peru), to Guayaquil (from Ecuador), to Barranquilla or Cartagena (from Colombia), and to Puerto Cabello or Maracaibo (from Venezuela). From these ports buyers shipped the barks to the dominant drug markets of New York, London, Hamburg and Paris.

Thus the more valuable fever trees were destroyed without replacement. The quality of the barks was irregular; the supplies were erratic and immigrant traders profiteered outrageously. Even before the American Revolution, demands had leaped ahead of the wilderness supplies. In due time British and Dutch speculators began collecting seed for planting in India, Ceylon and Java—a lush money crop, suited to the rainy slopes of volcanic mountains too high and steep to accommodate most other tropical crops.

In 1852 quinine seed collected in Bolivia by John Weddell were first dispatched to Java. Seven years later the British Government made plans for establishing cinchona cultivations in India, and handed the plans to the aristocratic botanist, Clements R. Markham, who went to South America to collect the seed. Markham succeeded via the efforts of Charles Ledger, a respectable Londoner who had lived for twenty years in Peru and Bolivia. In the latter country Ledger meticulously picked the seed of superior-yielding trees. The seed were sent to Java. There they provided the parentage for more than 50,000 acres of ledger cinchona orchard which, before Pearl Harbor, supplied most of the world's quinine via the Kina Bureau of Java and Amsterdam, the most audacious, antisocial and fabulously successful cartel the world has ever known.

Of the thirty to forty alleged species of South American cinchona (botanists do not agree as to the exact number), the ledger and succiruba, or red sap, have become the orchard stand-bys for the entire world. In time Dutch planters began grafting buds of the former to rootstocks of the latter to develop a healthy orchard tree with the highest possible quinine yields (known to be as high as ten tons per acre yearly from mature trees). But such "horticultural miracles" did not occur overnight. The Dutch Government began to subsidize the methodical introduction of South American quinine into Java during the late 1860's. By 1920 Java and its Dutch colonial neighbor, Sumatra, were producing around 97 percent of the world quinine supply. But that was after half a century of the peculiarly stubborn, perhaps inspired dividends of the practical botany of the colonial Dutchman.

The Dutch pioneer efforts to cultivate cinchona in Java failed utterly. The venture succeeded only with the introduction of the thick-barked Bolivian strains first identified by Ledger. Even so, the successful adaptation of quinine from South America to the rugged and otherwise low-value mountainsides of Java was one of the most illuminating feats in all the history of horticulture. Its example value to the Americas can hardly be exaggerated.

As late as 1880 Colombia was the world's leading source of quinine bark, exporting 6,000,000 pounds against 1,170,000 from India (the second runner-up), 950,000 from Bolivia, Peru and Ecuador combined, and a mere 70,000 from all of Java. But by 1911 Colombia's exports had fallen to a mere 35,000 pounds, India's to less than 500,000, while Java's had spurted to 20,000,000—proving once more that wild-growing

crops simply cannot compete in international trade with skillful cultivation of the same crops. In 1938 the United States
Tariff Commission records showed that the total Latin-
American production of cinchona bark was somewhat over
2,000,000 pounds or 7.4 percent of the world's supply—as
compared with 464,000 pound or 1.7 percent in 1929. Bolivia
now exports the major portion of wild bark—1,950,000 pounds
for 1938, as against 185,000 pounds from Peru; one lone ton
from Colombia, and another lone ton from British India,
while the Netherlands Indies produced the decisive 24,665,-
000 pounds.

In 1940, after World War II was burning strong, United
States imports of cinchona barks spurted to about 5,500,000
pounds—most of it directly from Java. Luckily, during 1941
the United States Government had succeeded in securing
large stocks of East Indies cinchona—enough to make at
least 6,000,000 ounces of refined quinine sulphate. Our allies
were not that lucky. Our armed forces now hold practically
all the refined quinine in the world—outside the Axis. Even
so, quinine sulphate is no longer on our civilian markets. If
you require quinine, you must now have a doctor's prescription; and even with that you will get only the ground-
bark solution called "totaquine," which contains in various
proportions a considerable list of quinine alkaloids. During
1942 our imports of Latin-American cinchona climbed sixfold
from 23,000 to 149,000 pounds—the latter total now increased
by the month and week.

Today Latin-American planters and governments, including Bolivia, Mexico, Peru, Colombia and Guatemala, are
definitely interested in cinchona as a durable Pan-American
crop. During 1939 the United States Department of Agriculture sent 1,000 seedlings of ledger cinchona to Brazil for
planting at the Agronomical Institute at Campinas, São Paulo.
As already pointed out, Guatemala has effected the most im-

pressive renaissance of quinine horticulture in the present-day world. (The Pan-American Union suggests: "It is quite possible that a revived Latin-American cinchona bark industry hinges on the experimental and commercial results . . . to be obtained in Guatemala. . . .")

On March 13, 1943 an official announcement from San José stated that the United States and Costa Rica had signed an agreement granting the former a twenty-five-year concession of ten thousand acres (about fifteen square miles) of land for planting of cinchona trees, with the understanding that all the properties will revert to Costa Rica at the end of the twenty-five years. In Colombia experimental growing of cinchona—in the modern manner—is being carried on at the Coffee Experiment Station in Chinchinas, Caldas. Here seeds and planting stock were recently brought from Guatemala by Dr. Gilberto Zapata. Our Department of Agriculture is detailing expert foresters to survey the quinine resources that can be developed in Colombia, to "scout" the stands of wild trees, and work out plans for getting the wild bark to seaport.

Recently, when Sergeant Barney Ross, Marine fighter on Guadalcanal, told how the shortage of quinine had cost the lives of many of our fighting men in the Solomons, scores of United States druggists, following the lead of Druggist Oscar Lasky of Los Angeles, began to donate millions of capsules of quinine in stock for the use of our fighting men in the faraway tropics. Officials of the Red Cross received the donations with the comment that the gifts of quinine were infinitely better than any comparable donation of money. No more pertinent testimony of professional esteem for the bitter powder from the fever tree could be offered.

For quite regardless of what the real or would-be science columns may say, there is no synthetic quinine. The molecular structure apparently cannot be duplicated. Of the two extremely important quinine substitutes or partial substitutes, plasmochin lacks the curative power of quinine, but helps greatly in stopping the spread of the disease; while atabrine is proving itself a valuable antimalarial for the defense of people. Neither atabrine nor plasmochin, nor both together, takes over completely the role of quinine, because quinine remains the best-known over-all defense against malaria—a group of infectious fevers caused when red blood cells are destroyed by malignant parasites which are spat into the human blood stream by anopheline mosquitoes. Quinine helps destroy within the blood the asexual forms of the parasite and thus "cures" the patient of fever attacks. It also destroys the gametocytes or sexual forms of the parasite which transmit the disease through the agency of the infected mosquitoes. Plasmochin and atabrine are proving of enormous worth as tide-overs in the most crucial of quinine shortages. We are getting them, particularly atabrine, by the hundreds of millions of tablets. But we still need quinine in unprecedented amounts, since quinine's ability to double-score against the ruinous cycle of malaria assures it a lasting place among the essential therapeutics.

At this time when all workable antimalarials are so essential to victory in our global war, the malariologist's standard dream of freeing the world of malaria without seeking the impossible, i. e., literal destruction of mosquitoes, seems more nearly possible than ever before.

And more imperative. For our all-decisive war sweeps ever deeper into tropical lands where malaria is rampant. Into such malarial traps we continue sending hundreds of thousands of temperate-zone fighting men whose resistance to the number-one scourge of the tropics is at a minimum.

Fortunately, our medical corps are aware of this dilemma. Both Surgeon General James Magee of the Army and Surgeon General Ross T. McIntire of the Navy state openly that malaria is one of the more serious menaces to American fighting forces throughout the world. Nor do they overlook the other mosquito-borne diseases which include dengue or "breakbone fever," an influenzalike ailment, particularly prevalent in Australia (and still lacking a proved cure), and filariasis, another mosquito-borne blood parasite disease current in Africa and equally lacking of treatment. But malaria remains the devastative bad hombre among communicable diseases, a force from which both military and civilian medicine continues to take frequent and humiliating defeats. When Bataan fell United Press correspondents reported that more than half of all United States troops were in hospitals or otherwise out of action with malaria.

But when one grants the importance of malaria control to United Nations victory, one all but inevitably finds oneself predicting that the malaria curve is likely to keep ascending after the war is done. Troops who come home from the tropics or subtropics are most likely to bring malaria to most if not all temperate-zone countries. That happened to us after the Mexican War, the Civil War and the Spanish-American War. (In 1899–1900 the return of our Cuban expeditionary forces resulted in serious malaria epidemics in such northerly points as Greenwich [Connecticut], Duluth, Buffalo, Syracuse and Cleveland, and the Cuban Expedition veterans numbered only a few thousands—not millions.)

More fervently than ever before American medicine prays for God's own plenty of antimalarial ammunition: billions of doses of atabrine, more billions of doses of quinine, all of which can and must be made available at low prices. In the past there has never been enough quinine to supply the crucial needs of the impoverished millions who suffer from malaria. During the past two decades League of Nations medical statisticians insisted that Kina Bureau prices, effective throughout the world, have kept quinine out of the buying range of nine-tenths of the malaria sufferers. (As a long-term proposition malaria is a poor man's disease, and usually it is worst where food supplies are most deficient.)

Malariologists, particularly those with long and distinguished experience in the tropics, are growing more unanimous in the belief that malaria can never be competently controlled without plenty of drugs—inexpensive therapeutics of standard strength and uniform quality which will not be adequately supplied by power-politics cartels or manufacturing chemists in business to make financial killings. The so-called quinine substitutes are already sewed up by patents and other invisible commercial ropes. But quinine, so long dominated by collusive cartels, now has a chance to be free again.

It would seem probable, if not inevitable, that climatically, botanically, and morally quinine can be and is being grown by free men in the relatively free Americas. In Guatemala and elsewhere in Latin America quinine is being grown with prospects sufficiently encouraging to offer the promise that in time malaria can be made comparatively obsolete. Middle American countries have begun to realize this. Nobody is fooling the malariologists with assertions that quinine is "obsolete." Any competent malariologist knows that quinine is not obsolete—and therefore that the new bud-grafted cinchonas which begin to grow on Guatemalan hillsides can very well be the most significant trees in the world today.

But at this moment quinine as a continuing and expanding cultivated crop is no absolute certainty in Guatemala, South America or anywhere else. We now know that certain hardier types of cinchona tree—though not necessarily the ledger strains which have served to provide both the Java "monopoly" and the refined quinine sulphate with which the Kina Bureau of Amsterdam has so long reigned—can be grown in various highlands of Central and South America. But the proved possibility and the established facts are by no means identical. For that matter the Dutch-Java, cartel-sponsored monopoly of ledger-type cinchona trees is by no means assured. While this book is being written it is reported that the Japs have dealt no extensive damage to the remote, mountainside cinchona orchards in Java. Indeed it appears as if the Japs have not succeeded in recovering enough of the quinine to meet the crucial antimalaria needs of the Japanese fighting forces. It seems probable that thousands of acres of the new plantings of cinchona have been let die because Javan planters have been unable to employ and pay the labor required to protect the younger trees from otherwise ruinous weed growths. Even if the harvestable trees are left standing, the probability is that in seven to ten years from today Javan quinine orchards will be out of production for four years or longer.

This adds to the quinine-malaria dilemma. It may also serve to better the possibilities of American-born cinchona as a valid and socially essential inter-American crop.

2. MISNAMED MANILA HEMP

Manila rope (for which there seems to be no substitute or synthetic) is made from the tough resilient fiber of a tropical, bananalike plant called abacá. Before Pearl Harbor, the Philippines, probably the native home of the plant, produced about 95 percent of the world supply of abacá fiber; the Netherlands Indies produced most of the rest. Directly after Pearl Harbor, Japan seized the established sources of the strategic fiber; that is, all but a little noticed seed plantation which an American company had developed in the hot lowlands near Almirante, Panama. With good reason the Nipponese rated the seizure of the established sources of Manila rope a major victory. In war or peace the product is high up on the list of maritime necessities. For many years United States marine authorities have requested that no American ship leave a port without an emergency supply of Manila rope—made of abacá fiber—for use in emergency towing or other mishaps at sea.

When twisted into rope abacá fiber has maximum resistance to water and salt, tremendous strength (tensile strength 15,000 or more pounds per inch) and exceptional resiliency—a "stretch capacity" as great as 20 percent of the original length of the fiber. Thus, when a ship must be towed, particularly in stormy waters or swells, abacá or Manila rope makes the only reliable towing rope. Such a rope or hawser will "pull steady" even when a steel cable of twice its diameter snaps like a toothpick. No metal and no other cordage have sufficient "give" to keep from breaking under the terrific jerks, stresses and strains of a rough sea. When Nazi submarines began harassing our shipping, the needs for Manila rope were intensified. When a crew or fighting component has to leave a ship in double-quick time for attack, or to save their own lives, they use multiple Manila-rope ladders or "embarkation nets"—quickly lowered and quickly and safely used regardless of rough seas or listing ships.

In peace or war abacá is a stand-by of the shipping front. Giant loading baskets, made of Manila rope, put invaluable war cargoes aboard the thousands of cargo ships and battle crafts which are the life lines of our far-scattered fighting fronts. Manila rope for pulleys, winches and hatch drives has long been the stevedore's indispensable. Tugs use Manila hawsers to dock and discharge the bigger ships. Other types and sizes of Manila rope secure ships to piers or other anchorage.

In this, an air age as well as a ship age, Manila rope has become all but indispensable to military and commercial aviation. It tethers hydroplanes, anchors barrage balloons, tows powerful bombers and cargo planes to their runways, and tows gliders to and from battle. We must have it, and during 1943 for the first time, we began getting abacá fiber from the American tropics—particularly the Central American republics of Panama, Costa Rica, Guatemala, and Honduras, a few tons a week at first, then 20 tons, 50 tons, and more. Each year now the Middle American production is tripling or quadrupling. These new plantings are already yielding the best Manila fiber ever put in use (currently rated as 6 percent above United States Navy specifications, the world's highest), and yielding from 1,000 to 1,500 pounds of fiber per acre yearly—compared with Far East tropics yields of 500 to 1,000 pounds.

The plant that yields the fiber is one of about thirty members of an immensely interesting family of bulbous tropical plants known as the *musae*. The three most important members of this Musa clan are the edible bananas of which the United States normally consumes well over 1,500,000 tons per year; the abacá plant, source of Manila hemp (of which our country now requires at least 250,000,000 pounds per year); and the plantain or cooking banana—not important in the United States but a basic starch food of millions of Middle American peoples.

Abacá can also be propagated from seed or suckers. But planting rootstocks is the preferred method. The heavy rhizomes, each big enough to cram a peck measure, are cut into pieces or "bits" weighing at least two pounds and having at least two good "eyes" or leaf buds. The planter simply buries these bits in shallow holes and covers them with two or three inches of soil. Within a week or two first sprouts appear and within a few months they are as tall as a man. Each good eye thus becomes a plant, and just as with bananas, each plant when it reaches a definite stage of growth propagates itself by producing side shoots or suckers.

The plant flourishes only in true tropics. It grows best under at least 100 inches per year of well-distributed rainfall. It is quickly damaged by drought or by standing water. For protection against the latter, good drainage is required—deep ditches that keep the water table low at all times. During the first few months of growth, weeds and jungle growths must be cleared away from the planting. After being "started," abacá is a hardy crop comparatively free from ruinous insects and other natural enemies. The crop is harvested throughout the entire year. There is no particular harvest season. Three varieties are now being grown in Middle America: Bungulanon—the most important—Libuton and Maguindanao. All originated in the Philippines and all three were first brought to the American tropics by Henry T. Edwards, a distinguished plant explorer for the United States Department of Agriculture. Mr. Edwards, incidentally, is still much alive and at work.

Eighteen to twenty-two months after planting, the healthy abacá plant (it isn't a tree) is somewhere between eighteen and thirty-five feet tall, with a central or main shoot five to ten inches in diameter. These are surrounded by several smaller shoots of "plantillas"—biding their time for future harvest. The best stems for fiber are those that have just "shot" their lush purple blossoms (about the size and shape of a big artichoke), or that have begun to bear their fruit—small bunches of finger-length and inedible bananas.

The fibrous stalks are harvested with a sharp machete—the famous all-purpose knife of the American tropics. The cutter selects the bigger plants that have newly blossomed and whacks down the sturdy stalks with his machete. If the stalk is eight or ten inches in diameter, several hard machete blows are required to fell it. Next, the harvester cuts the stalks into lengths suitable for milling. These pieces, called "junks," are from four to six feet long and usually weigh between twenty and thirty pounds each and yield about one pound of dried fiber. In low, wet country, which is ordinarily best suited to the crop, the junks are loaded on mule packs and borne by mules or burros (fifteen to twenty junks per load) to the loading point on the narrow-gauge steam railroad which serves the individual plantation. Flatcars, piled shoulder high with the heavy cargo, are then drawn to the mill where the junks are cleaned and "decordicated."

At the mill, workmen peel off the discolored outer layers from the stalks. This leaves a gleaming white stem which is made up of crescent-shaped, tightly overlapping sheaths. The powerful fibers, which average around 2 percent of the gross weight of the stalks, are located on the edges and in the cell walls of these sheaths. Otherwise, the stem contains air cells, pulp, pith and water. To avoid sun damage the fiber should be recovered within two days after the junk is cut.

After the junks are stripped, they are fed into initial rotary crushers which flatten them into "blankets" and squeeze out most of the juice. Conveyor belts then carry the crushed junks to the "decordicator" where automatic metal blades mounted on high-speed wheels scrape lengthwise along the fibers, loosening and removing the waste materials and leaving only the good fibers, which are automatically washed by high-pressure water sprays.

The wet, clean fiber is then placed on poles and carried outdoors into drying yards where intense tropical sun quickly removes most of the moisture. (New-style mills dry the fibers in carefully regulated drying ovens.) Then the "hanks" are placed in mechanical dryers (hot-air rotary drums) where the last of the sap is removed. From the discharge end of the dryer, a set of stiff-wire mechanical brushes separate and comb the fibers and leave the hanks orderly and free of snarls. Next the fibers are assembled in steam or hydraulic presses and squashed into compact 200-pound bales, which are shipped by rail and ship to United States factories, at the present time almost exclusively to Army and Navy rope-walks.

If you examine the "raw" fibers, you discover that your hands are barely strong enough to break a single filament. But the almost fabulous strength of abacá or Manila rope is better appreciated when one has watched its manufacture. One of the world's best rope factories is the United States Navy's ropewalk at the Boston Navy Yard. Here hanks of the fibers, four to six feet long, are made into giant rope, sometimes thousands of feet long, by a process of mixing the individual fibers so that they overlap and the ends do not come at the same place. Then the combed fibers are twisted together so that the friction of filament against filament holds them tightly together.

When the bales arrive at the rope plant, they are opened and the fiber is fed into the first carding machine. Here fast moving metal teeth pass through the fibers, combing them into parallel strands. Expert operators feed in new hanks of ready carded and mixed fibers, making certain that the in-dividual "filaments" are shuffled so that the ends do not come at one place. These strands, sized as desired, are fed out of the carding machine in the form of a ribbon or "sliver," prop-erly mixed and sized for ropemaking. The next step puts a twist into the parallel fibers. The yarns are next wound on spools, then wound together into strands by a process of feed-ing the yarns into the guides and twisting the strands by means of the revolving motion of the power-driven reels. Finally, three strands of the desired size are mechanically laid together to form the completed rope. The combination of left- and right-hand twists previously given the yarns and strands causes the fibers to lie lightly against one another, further increasing the strength of the rope.

The skilled American manufacture of indispensable rope from American-grown abacá is one of the newer chapters in the story of an indispensable commodity which until Pearl Harbor most Americans merely took for granted. In 1521, when he discovered the Philippines, Magellan reported having seen Filipino natives dressed in coarse garments made from the fiber of an indigenous plant which they called abacá. Apparently white men did not learn to appreciate the value of the fiber until centuries later. About 1800, first samples of abacá rope were brought to Salem, Massachusetts. Sailing men of that renowned seaport quickly recognized the unique value of the fiber and began importing it for use on Yankee clippers and other sailing ships. Presently the trail-blazing Yankee clippers began carrying cargoes of the fiber directly from the Philippines and distributing it throughout the world.

Since Manila was the principal export center, the name "Manila hemp" was coined. But abacá is not a hemp at all though its fiber fills many of the common uses for hemp. (For centuries abacá fiber has been used in the Philippines to make hats, cloth, fish nets, matting, shoes and slippers, rugs and baskets.)

By 1900 the United States had become the number-one consumer of the rope, and United States manufacturers had learned that in addition to ship and marine uses Manila rope fills thousands of other needs. Deep drilling, particularly for petroleum, depends abjectly on the strength of Manila rope. Harbor patrolmen, firemen, and coast guards have long used the rope for lifesaving missions. Usually the scaffolding that swings from cornices of tall skyscrapers in construction depends for its sure holds on abacá fiber.

Until Pearl Harbor the Philippines remained the predominant source of abacá. It is difficult to say why, because its agriculture is unusually simple. The plant is a perennial; it frequently remains in bearing for twenty years or longer and, as already noted, it has few natural enemies. Yet for one reason or another most of the world chose to let abacá remain a resource of the Philippines (where it is still one of the three leading crops).

During World War I, United States importation of abacá fiber shot to about 50,000,000 pounds yearly and our authorities listed it as an indispensable war material. About 1920, planters of the Netherlands Indies began to take the seed stock out of the Philippines and plant it as a Dutch colonial crop. Disliking this, the Philippine Government (in 1925) enacted a law to prohibit further export of the planting stock from its islands. By that time the more or less stealthy Jap entered the picture. For nearly fifty years Japan has been the third greatest importer of abacá (after the United States and Great Britain). Besides making rope and cordage, the Japanese used large quantities of the fiber for manufacturing "Lagal" hat braid which they exported widely; also for making cheap shoes to sell to the normally barefoot millions of south Asiatics.

Most Philippine abacá is grown in Mindanao Province, particularly in the Davao area. Around the turn of the century, Jap immigrants, or subsidized colonists, began moving into the area of Davao, to work as abacá laborers, and presently to become abacá producers. Gradually the Japanese owned or controlled the decisive acreages. By 1930 the Davao area, leading the world in total output of abacá, as well as in yields per acre, was commonly called the "New Japan," though this title was not necessarily indigenous to Davao.

The American cordage manufacturers, recognized as the world's best, were disturbed by the Japanese role in abacá. So were the distinguished and too little honored plant explorers of the United States Department of Agriculture. In

1925 one of the latter, Mr. Henry T. Edwards, after traveling in Davao and the Netherlands Indies, brought out a hand-
bagful of abacá "bits," carried them to Panama, and planted
them on United Fruit Company land near Almirante, on the
Caribbean coast. The venture was purely experimental. Part
of the first plantings flourished. From time to time other Department of Agriculture men brought more rhizomes and
planted them in the plots at Almirante. United Fruit Company botanists supported the experiment, but the company
made no attempt to exploit it. During 1932, the late H. C.
Clark, a veteran New England manufacturer and president
of the Plymouth Cordage Company, called on the president
of the United Fruit Company and urged that the company
use its facilities to introduce abacá as a crop for the American tropics. The banana company agreed to sponsor the
experiment. Accordingly, at its own expense the company
expanded the plantings from 50 acres to 1,000 acres; then
after 1937 it doubled the latter acreage as soon as sufficient
planting stock had become available. When Pearl Harbor
doomed the Philippines and millions of other square miles of
the tropical East, the "seed plantation" of 2,060 acres in Panama was the only source of abacá planting stock anywhere
in the Western Hemisphere, and all our established sources
of abacá were lost to our Pacific enemies.

Immediately after Pearl Harbor the United Fruit Company transferred its ownership of the seed supply to the
United States Government, through the agency of the Defense Supplies Corporation. Early in 1942 the company contracted with the Defense Supplies Corporation to plant 20,-
000 acres of abacá in Central America, to harvest and process
the fiber and sell it at cost to the United States for the ful-
fillment of urgent war needs. United Fruit has now planted
the first 30,000 acres in Central America: about 11,500 acres
in Costa Rica (a field of 9 square miles now comes to bearing

in the Puerto Limon area), 6,500 acres in Panama, 5,700 acres in Guatemala, and 5,000 acres in Honduras—in all about 44 square miles of a great crop which never before grew in this hemisphere.

The plantings may be further increased. The first decordication mill, now at work at Almirante, Panama, supplied its entire output to the armed services of the United States. Early in 1944 additional mills were being built in Costa Rica and Honduras, and the recovery of the strategic fiber was more than doubled. With the completion of five decordication plants—one in Panama, two in Costa Rica and one each in Honduras and Guatemala—the 1945 production is expected to reach a stride of perhaps 45,000,000 pounds per year.

Through the co-operative efforts of the Department of Agriculture, the Defense Supplies Corporation, and the United Fruit Company, planting stocks from the basic seed plantation are also being distributed among native farmers of Nicaragua, Costa Rica, Haiti and other American nations, with the hope that the abacá will also succeed as a home crop for citizen farmers of the American tropics. This hope is supported by a number of noteworthy facts. In terms of daily wage, Middle American farmers and farm workers cannot conceivably compete with the coolie wages of the Far East. But first yields of abacá in Panama and Costa Rica are almost twice the Philippine average. Far East abacá remains a hand-labor crop. There, practically all the fiber is stripped by hand and dried in the sun, whereas practically all Middle American fiber is machine stripped.

In the Philippines each plant is cut by hand and each leaf sheath is split the entire length of the plant. One end of the outer sections, containing all the best fiber plus a great deal of useless cellular material, is clamped under a serrated knife blade, then pulled back and forth to free the fiber from the cell pulp. The hand processing is tiresome and discouragingly slow. The fiber that is mechanically processed is a better product (according to United States Navy tests).

Here again richer soil, better planting and cultivation methods may yet succeed in overcoming the ever-doubtful "advantage" of a deplorably low wage scale, with the deplorable social results thereof.

3. ROTENONE

The unique principle called rotenone is also winning a conspicuous place among the many strategic tropical crops which the Americas need permanently and at present desperately because Japan seized and gravely upset the principal established supply. Rotenone is one of the most effective insecticides because it is highly destructive of insects and other "cold-bloods" and comparatively harmless to men, livestock and other "warm-bloods." In addition to its insecticidal value, rotenone is probably the most effective agent for ridding fighting men and others of lice, mites, and other skin tormenters. The substance has become a stand-by for veterinarians who use it regularly and in quantity for ridding cattle, hogs, sheep, poultry, dogs, cats and other livestock of injurious parasites. More recently rotenone has won a place in human dermatology.

Since 1930 United States requirements and uses for rotenone have increased almost unbelievably, and United States consumption has been limited only by the available supply, even though plantings of rotenone-bearing crops in Java, Sumatra, Malaya, and other Far Eastern tropics have been doubled and tripled time and time again. For home gardens, for improved-livestock programs, for maintaining human health and comfort and for other good causes we now need rotenone more urgently than ever before.

Several of the plants that supply the crystalline substance

are indigenous to the American tropics, where the material was discovered. In the American tropics it was originally called "fish poison" because many Indians dug the quasi-poisonous roots (of Cube, Lonchocarpus and other unique "weeds"), shaved the roots into their fishing pools, and waited in tranquil ease until the fish died. Then the Indians ate the fish without ill effect to themselves. Early plant explorers were fascinated and puzzled by this phenomenon—of a substance that kills fish without injuring the people who eat the fish. They brought back and laboriously analyzed the roots and recorded the toxic principles of rotenone, which actually smothers insects and fish by a process of paralyzing the breathing organs.

Particularly in Java, Dutch botanists and planters began exhaustive experimentation with possible rotenone crops and presently agreed on the Derris plant, a hardy tuberous-rooted tropical perennial (not indigenous to the Americas), as the most efficient source of rotenone concentrates.

Improved Derris now reaches bearing age within eighteen to twenty-four months after the root cuttings are planted, and under good conditions the harvests are as great as a ton or a ton and a half per acre. Net rotenone content of these roots averages around 5 percent of dry-root weight. The market price is quoted on a basis of a 5 percent net return of rotenone crystal. Bounties, now averaging five cents per pound extra for each percent of rotenone over five, are paid for the higher yielding harvests. Herein lies a white hope of rotenone as a valuable durable crop for Middle America. In Honduras, Haiti and other areas, test harvests are yielding 8 or 9 percent of root weight in refinable rotenone—with record recoveries of 10 and 11 percent, as against established Far Eastern averages of 4 or 5 percent, thus approximately doubling the value of the harvest.

The superior recoveries result from selective breeding of

the plants, rich soils, and expert cultivation and harvest, plus near ideal climate. Export records indicate that the Pacific tropics were producing at least 76 percent of the world's supply of rotenone at the time of Pearl Harbor, though in this particular instance almost half of the United States supply came out of the Americas. (During the three years ending January 1, 1940, United States imports of rotenone-bearing roots showed a progressive increase of from 2,412,000 pounds in 1937 to 5,138,000 pounds in 1939, to about 7,000,000 pounds in 1940, the latter sufficient to make about 35,000,000 pounds of commercial insecticides.) Our total current needs are estimated as between 15,000,000 and 20,000,000 pounds per year of the root powder, or around 100,000,000 pounds of the finished insecticides.

Though it has been identified for almost a century, rotenone remains one of the newest of the great commercial crops, and in terms of Middle America, one of the more important war crops. According to British records the first use of rotenone as an insecticide dates back to 1848 when an English planter in Jamaica, one William Oxley, used a decoction of Cube roots to spray his nutmeg trees. Since 1929 planters and plant hunters in the American tropics have been propagating various species of rotenone-bearing plants, which are variously identified as derris, barbasco, cube and timbo.

Further distinguished work is being accomplished by United States Department of Agriculture workers at the Tropical Experiment Station at Mayagüez, Puerto Rico, where the highest recorded yields—about 3,000 pounds per acre of Derris roots—have recently been recorded. From Mayagüez and with the blessings and frequently the transport planes of the United States Government, root cuttings of high-yielding Derris have been and are being flown to scores of plantations and experiment plots throughout the American tropics.

In Guatemala, Honduras and Costa Rica, the United Fruit Company is co-operating successfully with the Department of Agriculture's Derris project, the expressed purpose of which is to develop rotenone as a strategic hemispheric crop and in due course to establish its propagation on farms and plantations that are owned and operated by independent citizen farmers of Middle America.

Meanwhile constructive research in additional uses for rotenones keeps pace with the all-time high of urgent needs for practical propagation and prompt distribution of the product. There seems to be no other toxic agent so capable of destroying so large a variety of harmful insects—and with such remorseless speed. For example, the Chemical Dictionary [1] says that rotenone, as a crystalline insecticidal principle, is "harmless to birds and mammals but 30 times as toxic as lead arsenate to silkworms and 15 times as toxic as nicotine to aphids." Kingzetts Chemical Encyclopaedia (London) points out the distinguished values of rotenone when used in flea powders, in fly sprays and in mothproofing of wool. The Reinhold Condensed Chemical Dictionary (New York) describes the premier insect destroyer as a white odorless crystal, soluble in ether, alcohol, acetone, chloroform and other organic solvents. The Industrial and Engineering Chemistry Magazine (New York) points out that the development of rotenone in the immensely important field of commercial insecticide has been greatly facilitated by the persistent work of the Insecticide Division, Bureau of Soil Chemistry of the United States Department of Agriculture, by the Food and Drug Administration, and the Bureau of Entomology of the same federal department. More than any other scientific agency in the world, our Department of Agriculture has worked to change rotenone from an obscure name to an effective commodity, with a sound role in winning the war of food and of

[1] P. Blakiston Sons and Co., Philadelphia.

defending people from the perennial menace of insect pests.

The actual agronomy of rotenone-bearing Derris is comparatively simple. It is a matter of planting select seed and root cuttings, transplanting as desired and harvesting when the roots reach maturity, which is never less than eighteen months from planting time and usually not more than two years. Routines for harvest and processing vary considerably. As a rule the roots are dug and dried, preferably in gas or wood-fired kilns, and pressed into bales weighing between 100 and 200 pounds each. Such root is admitted into the United States duty free.

The final milling is comparatively difficult. The dried roots must be pulled from their container by hand and fed into a chopping machine which reduces the material to a mill-sized chip. In the mill the chopped root is ground into a basic powder, which is then converted to air-float dust. Each lot must be assayed separately for rotenone content, with the result that mill runs are usually limited to 1,000 pounds or, at most, a ton. The moisture content of the root should not exceed 6 percent of gross weight, and a rotenone recovery of 5 percent usually involves 20 to 22 percent of total ether extractives. Once processed the insecticide material becomes a most widely effective instrument of defense against hundreds of different species of insect enemies which sabotage our field and garden crops and injure or harass poultry, livestock and people.

At present a great deal of experimentation is in progress as regards the medicinal status of rotenone, particularly its use in the treatment of scabies. Long used as "skin medicine" by various South American Indians, United States and British dermatologists now heed the substance as a particularly promising treatment of scabies. At long last and on many scientific fronts rotenone is beginning to be identified as the world's most versatile insecticide, of immediate protective and curative value to people, animals, plants and fowls. The perennial and unwon global war is between man and insects and man and fungi. Rotenone is a forceful, if still a more or less secret, weapon in this ever-continuing war.

4. THE VALUABLE TROPICAL OILS

In terms of domestic needs, edible oils and fats are in perennial shortage throughout the American tropics. For generations and centuries the nations of Middle America have imported fats. On the whole such imports are and have long been both uneconomical and paradoxical. Tropical sea fronts are the natural home of the enormously valuable and varied families of palms which through all the ages have remained a premier source of edible oils.

Most palm oils are edible and many have unique chemical qualities which have kept their value far in excess of the market range of animal fats or petroleum by-products. Many palm oils are lather oils which are almost, if not entirely, indispensable in the making of toilet soaps, shampoos and numerous cosmetics. Since about 1880 the United States has been importing hundreds of millions of pounds of these palm oils every year, the great bulk of which has originated in tropical lands of the Far East. The proportion obtained from the other side of the world has increased through the years, until by the time of Pearl Harbor all lands of Oceania and areas of Africa provided practically all the palm oils consumed by the United States, which uses more soaps, more shampoos and more cosmetics per capita than any other nation.

But most of the palm oils are also food, which is at once a primary weapon in war and a basic insurance for peace. The perceptive historian has learned that a nation's supply of fats and oils has much to do with the nation's survival, because countries without enough fats and oils are likely to suffer crippling economies and serious inadequacies in nutrition. That many nations and millions of acres of Middle America are capable of growing palm crops is common knowledge. The fact that these basic crops have not been adequately developed or sufficiently produced during bygone years is equally common knowledge.

The current renaissance of American tropical agriculture is spotlighting several of the great tropical palm crops, some indigenous, others being imported from the far corners of creation for planting in richly responsive Middle American soils.

The African oil palm is an outstanding example of the latter. This is an ancient species of palm—what botanists call a "lingering" species. Its native habitat is tropical West Africa where the local name is rather poetically "Prince of the Palms." This great crop was brought to the Americas during the earlier decades of the African slave trade. Slave-traders had introduced it to the headlands of the Amazon as early as 1800. By 1850 Dutch planters had introduced the palm into Sumatra and other Far Eastern tropics. In the Netherlands Indies the crop thrived under deft and capable sponsorship of the Queen's Colonials. By 1910 more than 100,000 acres of the palm crop had been planted in Sumatra alone, and only Liberia had larger orchards. In time the Netherlands Indies became the world's stronghold of African palm oil.

The African oil palm is a magnificent tropical tree which rises to an eventual height of fifty or sixty feet and usually begins to produce fruit during its fourth or fifth year, raising mature yields by its eighth or ninth year. The fruit is borne in huge, pendant bunches, at least two, and sometimes as many as six of the heavy clusters to a single tree. A cluster weighs from 10 to 40 pounds and contains as many as 700 fruit kernels, each about the size of a small plum or a medium-sized raspberry. Where cultivation is efficient and planting sites are well chosen the yields are heavy. Sixty of the stately trees planted to an acre usually yield somewhere between 1,000 and 1,800 pounds of the oil-bearing kernels.

The kernels are crushed to produce the basic oil, which is usually extracted chemically by means of solvents. Since the oil is a superior source of margarines, it is frequently refined for that specific use. After the oil has been drawn from the kernels the residue is pressed into a mealy cake which is outstandingly rich in proteins and carbohydrates and is, therefore, an excellent livestock food. The low-quality cake and residue can be used valuably as fertilizer ingredients.

In chemical and physical qualities this palm-kernel oil is closely similar to coconut oil. Like the former it is both an edible oil and a lather oil, ideal for the manufacture of toilet soaps and shampoos. As a rule, palm-kernel oil used for making soaps and shampoos is the part that melts at a low temperature. This is called "olien." The part that melts only at a high temperature is called "sterin" and is best for making butter substitutes and similar products. The sterin, also characterized by quick-lathering qualities, has numerous specialized uses in soapmaking. From various derivatives produced in the course of separating and processing come valuable ingredients for paints and varnishes, waterproofing and specialized lubricants.

Clearly the oil palm is important to all the Americas. It is impressively necessary to the United States because United States consumption of oleomargarines grows persistently— from 230,000,000 pounds (about 1.9 pounds per capita in 1931) to 366,000,000 pounds (about 2.7 pounds per capita in 1941). Of the latter production more than 80 percent was made from palm and other vegetable oils.

The use of African palm-nut oil in the manufacture of quick-lather soap is likewise in the ascendancy. For example, in 1940 the United States soap industries used only 197 pounds of the refined kernel oil; in 1941 the quantity grew to 1,113,000 pounds. At present the latter demands cannot now be filled, but the use is proved and the demand continues to increase. In Honduras, Costa Rica, Haiti and other areas of Middle America this African palm is being introduced and grown successfully. As yet only limited numbers of the palms have reached bearing age. But the crop can be grown in Middle America, and in the years immediately ahead it probably will be grown extensively.

Unquestionably, various other oil-producing palms still unexploited and in many instances indigenous to the American tropics are destined to vie with African palm oils as commercial crops. The over-all demands for fats and oils appear to increase unendingly as population expands, as buying power arises, as cleanliness and nutrition continue to draw a more just and studied consideration. In terms of gross acreage the native palm reservoirs of the American tropics as a whole are unquestionably the largest in the world today. The exploitation is barely begun.

Another important palm oil source is the cohune nut, the oil-bearing seed of the manaca palm, which in turn is another member of the vast and still little known family. In general the manaca flourishes in the deep northerly tropics, particularly along the Caribbean coastal regions which extend from Mexico into Colombia. Here in low, wet lands, usually in the valleys of rivers and creeks, in virgin forests and along thousands of miles of coast lines, these graceful trees cover untabulated hundreds of thousands of acres. They are abundant in the spreading flood plains of Guatemala, and the Caribbean fronts of Panama, representing in some districts as much as a fourth or a third of all the crowded vegetation. But Honduras, Nicaragua, El Salvador and Costa Rica also have important treasuries of cohune nuts. At least temporarily Honduras is the number-one supplier of this particular oil nut now being collected from indigenous forests of manaca, at least one of which covers some 600 square miles. The same palm grows extensively in southern Mexico, and from southern Mexico came the first use of its great, though still little known, product.

The oil of the cohune nut has been used in these Americas for unknown centuries. Long before the coming of the Spaniards, native peoples of Middle America were familiar with the oil and its practical uses. In Mexico, where the nut is commonly called *coquitos de aceite*—"little oil coconuts"— pre-Columbian Indians used the oil to light their homes and in some instances to prepare their food.

The story of the industrial exploitation of cohune oil covers the past seventy-five years. The early attempts failed because its nut is difficult to process. Its hard, dense shell blocks the way to easy recovery of the oil. A pressure of around 1,800 pound is needed to crack the nut. Evidently, pre-Columbian Americans with powerful muscles used heavy stones to break the kernels, but in so doing lost a great deal of the oil. Also, transportation from deep jungles to convenient shipping points has long remained a principal deterrent, for there were no roads or trails, and by tradition the kernels had been brought out of the jungle on human backs. During World War I, United States chemists proved that the shell of the cohune nut when converted to charcoal is a superior filler for gas masks, since the charred shell is unusually absorbent. Thus, the cohune nut came to the attention of the United States. Our mechanical engineers hastened to perfect equipment to crack the nuts and to recover the oil efficiency, and the cohune became an industry that invited, at least temporarily, both enterprise and capital. Unfortunately, the commercial importance remained centered in the manufacture of gas masks, and when World War I ended, the United States was sick of war and all the appurtenances thereto. But not all the work and money invested in the jungle-edge enterprise were lost. A few individuals continued to process and export the valuable oil which is commonly rated as superior to coconut oil, since it is highly edible and easily employed in the manufacture of fine soaps and nut butters.

The palm bears generously. The fruit grows in large pendant clusters, like huge bunches of grapes. Usually one palm tree produces three or four bunches, each cluster weighing 100 to 150 pounds. Even the tough fibrous cover of the nut contains considerable oil. Inside the cover is the shell, and inside the shell is the oil-bearing kernel, usually one to three kernels in each shell—kernels that contain from 65 percent to 75 percent hard white fat.

Agriculturally speaking, the crop remains another jungle grab bag. People gather the nuts and pile them along the nearest roadway or trail, or preferably at the banks of the nearest river large enough to accommodate barges or motorboats. Cracking plants are usually located downstream, preferably at a confluence of creeks or rivers. Here the husks are removed mechanically, and after a period of drying the nuts are dropped into heavily built rotary cracking machines, which in rotating crack the shells and deflect the kernels from the shells without crushing the kernels. The latter then travel along a moving belt where workers separate the whole kernels from any adhering bits of shell, then sack the kernels for market. The ultimate oil recovery is about 25 percent of the gross weight of the kernel, but this figure is being increased as the mechanical presses become more efficient. The residue is a valuable protein cake which is highly nutritious to cattle, while the shells are commonly used to fuel the machinery and thus supply steam power for the processing.

During the last year of World War I, United States con-

sumption of cohune oil increased more than 900 percent.
Then came the doldrums. But the cohune of the American
tropics is of great potential value. It flourishes on lands that
could have no other use. The tree reaches bearing in from five
to seven years, and as a rule the nut is harvestable at least
twice a year. The oil is exceptionally nutritious and digestible,
and it fills several continuing needs. But unfortunately the
scientific literature on cohune is sadly lacking. There have
been virtually no new publications since 1918. Whatever else
it may be the cohune is surely a distinguished challenge to
men and women of science who desire to learn of the interminable resources of the American forest and the American
jungle.

Thus far we have noticed only two of the palm oils. There
is also palm wax, chemically decidedly different from the oils.
The assured source of vegetable wax is the carnauba palm,
which is also indigenous to the American tropics, though principally to Brazil. Eighteenth-century explorers in Central and
South America named it rather poetically the tree of life,
because there is hardly any fundamental need of mankind
which this magnificent palm does not supply. It is food, it is
shelter, it is raiment and commerce. For many centuries the
carnauba palm has furnished wood to build the walls and
floors of native huts, wood for crude furniture and for fuel.
The fronds are a staple source of thatched roofs and of
mats upon which the earlier Americans slept, as well as the
woven nets with which they fished. The tender shoots of the
palm are edible. Certain juices from the palm are described
as valuable medicines, and from the palm juices tropical
American Indians learned to distill a purely alcoholic beverage called *nenpethe*. For more centuries than we can
surely name, man and the carnauba palm have lived, as they
say in college, in economic equilibrium.

The uses for the palm seem almost interminable. The wood is valuable in power building because it withstands the action of salt water. The wood is impervious to most insects and presumably to termites, which makes it immensely valuable for building bridges, wharves and fences. The edible young shoots also provide the bases for fine wines and palm vinegar. When crushed the dried fruit produces an excellent cooking oil, and when roasted and ground the same fruit provides a brown and stimulating drink which is flavored considerably like coffee. Cattle fatten on the roots of the palm, and the ground roots produce a richly flavored drink somewhat similar to sarsaparilla. Through the years the uses of the tough fibers have grown and multiplied. From the fronds can be made baskets and hammocks, mattresses, frames, floor coverings and shades for windows and doors. When the stalks are burned there appears an alkaline ash which is valuable in soapmaking.

But the really decisive resource of carnauba is its wax, the only important source of a true vegetable wax in the world today—wax which is used in the manufacture of solid and liquid polishes, floor and furniture waxes, in shoe polish, certain types of lubricating oil and numerous other uses.

Carnauba wax is used in the manufacture of phonograph records. It is used to insulate electric wires, to seal dry batteries, to waterproof cloth, in the manufacture of carbon paper, in the various types of soap, and as a basic ingredient in salves and ointments. In wartime picric acid made from carnauba is a staple ingredient of explosives. In war or peace it is a valuable unguent for burns.

New uses appear almost every year. United States imports of carnauba wax grow persistently: from 12,500,000 pounds in 1936 to 16,626,000 pounds in 1940, and to an estimated 23,000,000 pounds in 1943.

Brazil is the great producing stronghold of carnauba. The

United States normally consumes about half of the entire Brazilian production, which has doubled during the past decade. We have never yet been able to buy as much of the wax as United States industry needs. Epidemics of malaria and other virulent diseases frequently impede the harvest to a point where even the most urgent orders cannot be filled. We have permitted the current war and the sorely scrambled management of merchant shipping to retard the otherwise needed imports during the frantic years of World War II. But at long last American industry realizes the peculiar consequence of what has now become another indispensable tropical commodity.

It is a strange sort of commodity. The carnauba is a tall, straight palm which grows slowly to a maximum height of twenty-five to thirty feet. Its bark is scaly. Its fan-shaped leaves grow out from the petioles in serried conformations around the trunk. The palm perpetuates itself by seed. As the ripe seed falls to earth new trees grow closely around the parent tree, forming a dense clump and a sort of fortress against the ever encroaching jungle.

The wax is formed during the dry season or, better said, during the four or five months of the year when the rainfall is at a minimum. The leaves and the petioles exude a sticky liquid which dries into wax, nobody knows just why or how. In the old days botanists suggested that the exudation of wax was nature's device to prevent rapid evaporation of moisture by the fierce tropical sun, but this theory was long ago discarded for the explanation that the leaf wax results from certain salts in the soil or that the wax is a "natural characteristic of this particular palm species." Neither explanation is particularly satisfying. Nature's chemistry is fantastically involved with the still unsolved puzzle of chlorophyl and leaf structure.

Roselle Fiber Placed in Irrigation Canal to "Rot"—Santa Rosa, Honduras

amous Bamboo Grove near Kingston, Jamaica

African Palm Oil Trees, Lancetilla Experiment Station, Honduras

Harvesting Mahogany in the Jungles of Honduras

Lemon Grass, Source of the Essential Oil by that Name, a Tropical
Grass Being Grown in Honduras and Guatémala

Harvesting Citronella Grass in Honduras

Usually the wax is exuded during August and September. The harvesting process consists of clipping off the medium-aged leaves and then drying the leaves in the sun—taking care to prevent the light wax dust from being blown away—then threshing or beating the leaves in unventilated enclosures. Before the beating or flailing begins, the ribs of the leaves are split apart, the webs torn open and the leaves ripped apart. Diligently the wax taker shakes loose the hardening protector, permitting it to settle on spotlessly clean floors. He then sweeps up the particles and pours the wax dust into heavy iron pots or caldrons for melting. The melting is slow and exacting work. When the wax is properly cooked it must then be strained and molded into cool hard cakes or blocks for export to market. Thus far, no machinery has been used to extract the wax. To date it is a manual-labor job, which places tremendous accent on skill. A fleet and diligent worker can "dust" 3,000 to 4,000 of the leaves in a long-hour day.

We are not sufficiently well informed about the natural habitat of the carnauba. Its principal commercial source, at least for the time being, is the comparatively dry lands of the vast Brazilian northeast, particularly the State of Ceará—which incidentally in 1935 formally prohibited the export of carnauba seed in order to control the market for this uniquely valuable product. The latter effort, however, was not particularly successful, for the growing range of carnauba is far-spread. It grows in many lands of the American tropics, throughout a considerable range of altitude and mean annual rainfall. Little is known of the crop's horticulture. It remains another gracious donation from the mysterious treasury of the open world of the tropics. Carnauba is superbly important, and there is good reason to believe that it can be grown commercially in Middle America.

5. THE CASE FOR SPICES

Spices are also decisive crops of history. During the centuries before metal cans or other air-sealed containers and during the greater number of centuries before the invention and development of what we now call modern refrigeration, spices were the staple preservative of meats. They were used to save most of the world's meat supply from rotting and, further, to make palatable the meats which in the more fastidious contemporary reckoning would not be rated as edible.

Nowadays mechanical refrigeration is once more in urgent scarcity. There never was enough of it, and hundreds of millions of people have never yet had opportunity to benefit from what there is. During the global-war era, when most metals and alloys used for the manufacture of freezing or refrigeration equipment are in desperate shortage, when home butchering, at least temporarily, regains its place as a classical farm-home function, the more ancient role of spices begins to regain distinguished importance. Spices are of enormous importance now in getting meats and other foods distributed about an impoverished and war-blasted world. Accordingly we begin somewhat dazedly to awake to the importance of spices, most of which are venerable crops of the tropics.

Within comparatively recent times, spice wars have been fought. Any historian knows that Portugal became an empire principally by way of spices; that repeatedly Britain and Holland and even Russia have survived because of spices. More than any other factor, the need and lure of spice sources prompted the great era of exploration which brought about the discovery of the New World. The story of India and the Far East, of Africa and the Middle East is closely interlaced with the world-spanning epoch of the spice. At least 2,000 years before Christ the Egyptians had carved the virtues and values of spices in enduring stone. In the New World the ancient Mayas and the succeeding Aztecs have done the same. The Pharaohs ordered the burning of spices at state spectacles. Ancient China was strongly spice conscious, and a great part of early Chinese law deals with the transport and proprietorship of spice. When the Goths conquered Rome they stated ransom terms in pounds of spice.

The term "spice" fits rather loosely. Conceivably it could include all native herbs and aromatic plants. Practically speaking, the term suggests a comparatively limited group of the staple spices, practically all of them ancient crops, practically all of them native to the tropics. More important to our interest here, practically all the staple spices have been grown, or certainly can be grown, in the American tropics and on the enormously varied land surfaces of Middle America.

For example, there is the clove tree, whose dried flower buds provide one of the most popular of all the classic spices, a flavor-odor ingredient widely used in foods, cosmetics and soaps, candies, ointments, cigarettes and medicines; also in baiting traps and effecting the destruction of certain injurious insects.

Botanical history tells how the stately clove tree was first discovered in the Moluccas Islands by roaming Portuguese; how a French botanical expedition later succeeded in transplanting clove seedlings to the islands of Zanzibar and Pemba, where the trees flourished. The latter islands, now British protectorates, have been producing about 80 percent of the world's supply of cloves. But the same tree was long ago transplanted and successfully propagated in the American tropics, particularly the Caribbean islands. The principal stronghold of the Western Hemisphere is now the island of Santo Domingo. Before World War II, Dominican planters had been unable to compete extensively or successfully with

European importers. High duties had been levied against the Dominican product and the Dominican growers had learned, to their sorrow, that the spice trade in some of its components is unfortunately tinted with cartels and other collusive enterprises designed to choke minor competition, and in all events to soak the consumer.

But the fact stands that given any reasonable encouragement in the way of horticultural direction and moderate tariffs, thousands of small farmers of Middle America could unquestionably grow clove trees. Many of the soils and climates seem to be particularly well suited. The tree is a long-term resource. It reaches bearing age in from seven to ten years after a seedling is planted, but frequently remains in bearing for seventy-five or even a hundred years, and almost invariably outlives its planter. The usual stand is about fifty mature trees to the acre, and the average yield of each tree is around seven pounds of the dry spice each year. Thus, a comparatively small grove can be expected to yield a ton of spice per year, which should be a sufficing cash crop for the small farmer.

A comparable situation holds for the so-called twin spices, nutmeg and mace. The walnut-sized nutmeg kernel contains a lacy membrane which provides the mace of commerce. (Incidentally, the word "nutmeg" is an Anglicized corruption of the French *noix muscade*.) Presumably this tree is also a native of the Moluccas or other tropical islands of the South Pacific. More than 200 years ago the *noix muscade* was carried to the British West Indies and later to coastal Brazil.

The nutmeg tree is peculiarly adapted to ocean-front locales. Usually it grows best within sight and sound of the sea. However, it is now proved by experimental stations in various tropical areas, including the distinguished Lancetilla Station of Honduras, that the tree thrives at considerable distances inland so long as it has a rich and moist soil. There are a great many fables about this particular spice crop, but the limited experimentation indicates that its so-called exotic qualities are largely imaginary.

The recovery of nutmeg is forthright and simple. One simply picks or otherwise collects the heavy wood-filled kernels. The recovery of mace is intricate. The membrane that produces this costly spice is actually a gauzelike filament which must be separated from the shell by skillful handwork. Thus, the harvesting of mace is minute and patience-trying work. As a rule, between 100 and 200 pounds of nutmeg yield only one pound of cured mace.

Cinnamon is another comparatively hardy spice tree. It is thought to be indigenous to Ceylon, which still supplies some of the finest grades. The spice is derived from the sweet inner bark of the cinnamomum tree, which is another stately and relatively hardy tropical native. It is one of the oldest of the spices. In ancient Roman days it was used as an incense, and through the centuries it has remained among the first three or four condimental materials.

Cinnamon grows in scores or hundreds of tropical lands. It was introduced into the Caribbean at least 200 years ago and prior to that time the tree had been grown commercially in French Guiana. There is no doubt that many Caribbean lands could produce this valuable tree now and in the future. But there is considerable doubt as to its feasibility as a commercial crop. The problem of box shipping and curing makes it a "labor crop," since the harvest has not been mechanized and therefore remains a matter of matching work hours and prevailing wages of one growing area against those of another. In Ceylon, still the foremost commercial stronghold of cinnamon, wages are notoriously low and farm living conditions are notoriously bad. From this it would appear that substantial protection in tariff advantages would have to be given the possible and probable cinnamon crop of Middle America.

The same applies somewhat less emphatically to allspice, which derives its name from the fact that it combines the taste and fragrance of its three principal competitors—cloves, cinnamon and nutmeg. Spain introduced the allspice to Europe and to the commercial world generally almost five centuries ago. The tree is hardy and flourishes even on shallow inland soils, particularly those with limestone bases. Undoubtedly allspice could be made a successful Middle American crop, at least in so far as its horticulture is concerned. Species of the tree are native to various Caribbean areas.

In Jamaica allspice seedlings have already been planted extensively in otherwise unprofitable brushlands. The trees have flourished, and in some instances have proved to be a profitable crop. They reach bearing age in from six to ten years after planting, and a hearty, mature tree yields as much as a hundred pounds of dried spice per year. The bearing life is long; forty to fifty years is average. The spice is particularly valuable because of its versatility in flavor and fragrance. Shallow limestone soils known to be suited to developing the crop are common throughout much of Middle America, particularly in lower Mexico, in many of the British West Indies, in British Honduras, and in substantial areas of Cuba.

Ginger is another crop well proven throughout the Caribbean lands and in limited areas of continental Central America. The plant was first brought to the Western Hemisphere in the middle of the sixteenth century. Before the seventeenth century began, an extensive trade in ginger root had risen. Botanically ginger appears to be a native of the Far Eastern tropics, in particular some of the lesser Netherlands Indies. But the plant has readily adapted itself to the soils and climates of various Caribbean countries. It is a nourishing crop and its cultivation is comparatively easy. Yields are high. In suitable soil and with good cultivation, harvests range widely from 700 to 1,200 pounds per acre yearly of the dry root.

From the standpoint of international volume demand, the common peppers are the most coveted of all spices. Great wars have been fought for the possession of pepper sources, even as for the possession of oil fields, diamond mines or rubber plantations. In early colonial days in the Far East, particularly in the Netherlands Indies, taxes were paid in pepper, and Imperial soldiers were frequently paid bounties or bonuses in the same good. At present, United States consumption of black and white pepper—which, incidentally, are harvested from the same tropical vine—averages in the neighborhood of 50,000,000 pounds per year.

The common pepper vine is one of the hardiest of tropical crops. It bears heavily, sometimes yielding as much as a ton per acre of the bell-shaped pods whose seed provide commercial pepper. When ripe, the harvest is common black pepper; when immature, the harvest is the so-called white pepper. Vine peppers could be profitable to the American tropics.

The experimentation is, unfortunately, inadequate so far as the Caribbean lands are concerned, but there is no real doubt that the common market peppers can be grown economically. Many of the important vegetable peppers and tree peppers are native to the American tropics. Early Spanish explorers noted that Mexican and Central American Indians used a pod-shaped harvest called capsicum as a flavoring material. The capsicum pepper was presently introduced to Europe, and intermittently throughout four centuries it has been grown and exported by Middle Americans.

Strangely enough, the preparation of this rather loosely named group of spices was largely perfected by Europeans, who never saw the producing plant. A good example of this is paprika, made from the core of the capsicum fruit and developed commercially in Hungary, though the plant could never be grown in Hungary or any other mid-temperate-zone area. A great many edible peppers are native to the American tropics. The pimento bush was first discovered growing in the sheltered limestone soils of Mexico; green peppers, bell peppers, cayenne, and many other important vegetable peppers, some of which are now securely adapted to our own gardens and fields, are native to Mexico or other Middle American countries. It is entirely probable that other great spice crops could be developed in the ever challenging soil laboratories of the Caribbean.

There are many reasons why our nearest southern neighbors have not as yet been able to profit adequately from their illustrious spice resources. As already noted, Imperial Spain, Portugal, Holland and Great Britain were the pioneer exploiters and developers of the great spice trade in west Europe. Favored Eastern tropics, such as the famous Spice Islands, were early developed as sources for continuing supply of the ever strategic spices. Shrewd imperialists fought for advantage, control and monopoly of the spice trades. In particular, the Dutch set out to establish basic spices as a lush monopoly of empire.

Spain and Portugal did little or nothing to improve the cultivation of spice crops, and the United States, which in terms of proved cash markets is the world's foremost consumer of spices, has long bought from a world market without any particular heed or study of possible and desirable American sources for our principal spice imports. That is a rather sad and repetitious story, but it is a continuing challenge. Momentarily Far Eastern spice supplies are gravely reduced and in some instances totally blockaded as a result of Japanese aggression.

After the war it is entirely evident that without conscious effort on the part of the United States Government and without the deliberate co-operation of the United States spice trade, the markets can again be flooded with Far Eastern spice grown by coolie labor, exploited by trusts and otherwise

at variance with that noble document called the Atlantic
Charter.

6. OILS FROM GRASSES

Since Pearl Harbor essential oils—distilled from tropical
grasses—are beginning to win an important place in Middle
American agriculture and trade.

Again Japan is largely responsible. During the first ninety
days of 1942, which netted the little yellow men almost a
quarter of a billion square miles of tropical lands including
the established sources of about 85 percent of all tropical
crop tonnages in international trade, the Nipponese also
grabbed a momentary world monopoly on grass oils. The
grass oils include the distilled essences of citronella or "sereh"
grass, lemon grass and vetivert—special and valuable oils
which are meeting urgent war needs and durable peace
needs. For these grass oils are now the staple sources of many
important aromatics, such as geraniol, citronellol esters, synthetic menthols and other ingredients or starting materials
used in the manufacture of soaps, cosmetics, perfumes, pharmaceuticals and synthetic flavors, as well as in dozens of
technical preparations such as insecticides, sprays, polishes,
and weather surfacing, particularly for aircraft.

United States industry now requires more than 3,000 tons
per year of essential oils which, until recently, were grown
and processed almost entirely in Java, Ceylon, Malaya, Madagascar, India and other eastern tropical areas which are now
held outright by our enemies.

For many years tropical agriculturists have known that
these valuable oil grasses can be grown in the American
tropics, particularly in the lowlands or medium-altitude areas
of Central America, northern South America and the Caribbean islands. Before Pearl Harbor a few profitable grass-oil
plantations had been developed in neighbor nations, particu-

larly in Guatemala and Brazil. But for several reasons the developments were limited. Most or perhaps all of the native "essence grasses" of the American tropics are low in oil content. Also, United States needs for large quantities of grass oils are comparatively recent. And until Pearl Harbor the production and distillation of oil grasses were principally coolie-labor enterprises.

Particularly in India, Ceylon and Madagascar, desperately poor people, eager for the chance to earn a few pennies a day, harvested the wild grasses with hand sickles or knives, distilled the oil in crude home-built mud vats, then sold the poorly graded and badly polluted recovery to native buyers for a few cents per gallon. Only in Java was the agriculture of oil grasses well developed.

As early as 1899, with the help of the Netherlands Government, citronella grass imported from Ceylon was planted in the Dutch Far East colony of Java. By 1934 that lush island was producing about 1,800 tons of citronella oil per year as compared with 600 tons for all of Ceylon, the original home of the crop.

At the time of Pearl Harbor, Java had about 50,000 acres of citronella grass in bearing and about 100 commercial distilleries, in addition to about 80 comparatively primitive home distilleries, practically all of them in western areas of the island. The Dutch leadership of Java had established the accepted routine for processing grass oils. The grass is mowed like hay and left to dry in the sun from one to three days. Before distillation, the grass is usually chopped to pieces with a mechanical ensillage cutter. Usually the stills are fired with "spent" grass or bagasse, supplemented with wood.

Direct fire stills and steam-kettle stills are most commonly used to extract the valuable oils. Direct fire stills, commonly used by small growers in the Far Eastern tropics, are usually primitive clay vats imbedded in stone hearths and provided with a grid on which bundles of the grass are stacked. The water beneath the grid is heated by direct fire. Grass is stowed or tramped into the still from a top manhole, and discharged from a side vent. During firing, the crude condensation liquids are collected in jugs placed at the bottom of the still's "crater."

The steam must rise through the packed grass with sufficient force to penetrate the entire grass load evenly. Uniform temperature and pressure must be maintained throughout the distillation period, which averages three or four hours. Oil recoveries average between ½ and 1 percent of the original weight of the grass.

More recently large farming companies in the Far East developed "battery" stills in which the steam is generated in a central boiler (fueled with wood or spent grass). The chopped grass is placed in batteries of giant kettles, each holding from 1,000 to 2,000 pounds. The kettles rest on revolving platforms, discharge the extracted oils into filter jugs, and dump their contents of spent grass into catchcars when the operator pulls a lever or turns a spillage wheel.

After Pearl Harbor it was obvious that if the United States got any more essential oils, these would have to be grown and distilled in the American tropics. It was equally obvious that the United States must have essential oils to fulfill many strategic war needs and to carry on flavor, pharmaceutical, cosmetic, soap and spray industries, and other essential enterprises. So Yankee ingenuity now joins hands with Central American farming skill to supply at least part of the essential oils that United States industry needs so badly. Independent farmers of Central America, such as René Keilhauer of Guatemala and José Ramirez of El Salvador, have taken the lead in introducing essential oil grasses into the American tropics; citizens with enterprise and with the willingness to experiment and to risk. The story of this introduction is a repetition of the adage about mighty oaks growing from tiny acorns. For example, during June, 1941, Dr. V. C. Dunlap of the United Fruit Company succeeded in importing 65 "mats" of citronella or sereh grass into Honduras and divided these into 596 new plants. In four months this first handful was increased to half an acre. In another year the planting grew to 200 acres —principally in Honduras. Increase of acreage is definitely possible.

The story of lemon grass is similar. From a first tiny planting begun in 1939, Dr. Dunlap developed a seedbed of 1½ acres. By 1942 this provided planting stock sufficient for 35 acres—in furrows 18 inches apart. Experimental harvests yielded about 13 tons of green grass per acre yearly. In 1942 the planting was expanded to 200 acres, and may be expanded further. Tests in distillation showed first recoveries of about 97 pounds of lemon-grass oil per acre. The oil now in harvest has an unusually high citral content, and otherwise is far above market specifications. Citronella-oil yields average about twice those of lemon grass, or from 195 to 210 pounds of oil per acre yearly from three or four cuttings of the grass. Already the essential oils grown in the American tropics have won premium market gradings. Further, the practical ranges of these valuable grasses are being rapidly expanded. For example, the United States Sugar Corporation has recently completed extensive plantings of lemon grass—at least 1,200 acres—in the vicinity of Clewiston, Florida. For the first time this particular grass is being grown and processed within domestic boundaries of the United States. Probably lemon grass is the only one of the essential oil sources that can be propagated that far north. But the accomplishment is particularly significant because it indicates that the oil can be distilled in or with the help of sugar-cane mills. Fuel is a principal overhead cost in the distillation, and in "sugar-cane country" sugar-cane refuse or bagasse is the cheapest imaginable fuel. For this reason the inter-American centers for producing the essential oils may tend to gravitate toward the sugar-cane centers—which means, in a word, Cuba.

Current developments in the distillation of oil grasses grown in the American tropics are an even more impressive proof of Pan-American ingenuity. Since the new agriculture began, producers of essential oils in the American tropics have not been able to buy the necessary stills or the materials with which to build the distilling plants. In every instance they are being forced to improvise by employing any usable junk or scrap metals, wood or building materials that can be found close at hand.

One of the larger grass-oil distilleries, recently constructed and put into operation near La Lima, Honduras, by the Tela Railroad Company, a subsidiary of the United Fruit Company, is entirely a flotsam factory. The first attempts at distilling the grass employed an old-style copper-vat still with a capacity of only a few hundred pounds of the dried chopped grass. Next the ingenious tropical neighbors began building wooden stills of 200 cubic feet capacity each, and pivoted them on home-forged iron frames, then salvaged old boilers and discarded iron pipe, therewith establishing a steam-distributing system. The rather remarkable fact is now proved that the flotsam stills are working—perhaps more efficiently than the Javan stills that are now stolen by the Japs. As already noted, the United States Sugar Corporation has established the first large planting of lemon grass within the United States and reports that this particular oil grass can be grown in Florida's subtropics.

Four years of World War II have further accentuated the fact that the grasses are the most numerous and valuable of all the immense roll of the "vegetable kingdom." Besides the great pasture crops that are basic to our supplies of meat, milk, butter, eggs, poultry, leather, and most other livestock products, the grass "families" include all the cereal grains (which are still the number-one foods of people); also sugar cane (which supplies about four-fifths of mankind's sugar supply); and corn or maize, which is by far the biggest volume and most valuable farm crop grown in the United States or the Western Hemisphere. In addition to the production of grains, sugar, starches, livestock feeds, cellulose and other manufacturing and building materials (such as thatched roofs and grass-striated adobe), the practical uses of grass are now greatly expanded by the varied uses of essential oils in the manufacture of perfumes, soaps, scented toilet goods, synthetic flavors, aromatics, insecticides, sprays, varnishes, and many pharmaceuticals.

Though essential oils represent a comparatively small percentage of the value of the total United States prewar imports (around $10,000,000 a year) they are key products that are more or less essential to many great industries—perfume and cosmetics, which represent a normal turnover of $350,000,000 a year, and at least $150,000,000 in other United States manufactures.

In all there are more than 100 essential oils of market value. Also on the list are: petitgrain, derived from the leaf of bitter orange and normally produced in Paraguay and southern Europe; geranium ordinarily from Algiers; lavender from southern France; neroli from the flower of the bitter orange produced in Italy; jasmin, cinnamon cassie and the tuberose, all three from southern France; rose oil from Bulgaria; ylang-ylang from Madagascar; and bergamot, produced from oranges in southern Italy.

All these requirements of the cosmetic and perfume industries can be produced in Middle American terrains, as current experiments are beginning to prove. The Jewish refugee colony at Sosua on the north shore of the Dominican Republic plans to specialize in essential oils and has made extensive plantings of citronella, lemon grass and ylang-ylang. The United States Agricultural Experiment Station in Puerto Rico is now experimenting in the production of citronella grass for the manufacture of menthol. The station is also growing lemon grass, jasmine, gardenia, cassie and mimosa, and is further studying the possibility of obtaining an essential oil from the fragrant blossoms of the coffee tree. Pine and eucalyptus oils can unquestionably be produced in Middle America, if price and tariff standards permit. The same may hold for various medicinal and spice plants, including pyrethrum, coriander, white mustard, poppy seed, goat's-rue, marjoram, sage, rhatany root, and soapbark.

Also the pimienta or allspice and the laurel or the bay tree of the West Indies; the balsams of Peru and Central America and the tolu of El Salvador and Colombia; the copaiba which grows on the shores of the Oronoco; the linaloe of southern Mexico; and the palorosa of the Guianas and Brazil. Like the great palm crops, the essential oil crops are not yet sufficiently explored or sufficiently known.

7. DRUG AND MEDICINAL CROPS FOR MIDDLE AMERICA

For generations low wages have decided the places where the staple drug crops are grown. It is common knowledge that the American tropics, and indeed many areas within the United States, have climatic conditions well suited to many of the staple medicinal crops in international trade. But because of wage differentiations the great drug crops such as senna, ipecac, ergot, aconite, and many others were heretofore grown in southern Europe, northern Africa, Spain and Portugal, Madagascar, Ceylon, and other areas wherein manpower was plentiful and exorbitantly cheap.

Not long ago the Agricultural Division of the Co-ordinator of Inter-American Affairs made a study of the possibilities for growing these great crops within Middle America and adjoining areas. The report prepared during 1942 was definitely encouraging. It pointed out, for example, that such staple drugs as belladonna and stramonium can be grown effectively and advantageously to all American interests in Mexico, Guatemala, or Haiti. Ipecac grows wild in most of the Central American countries and presumably can be obtained in sufficient quantities without cultivation. Senna leaves, harvested from a tree of the cassia species, are known to thrive in dry-land areas of the Caribbean republics. The trees grow particularly well on hillside lands in Mexico, Guatemala, Honduras, Haiti and the Dominican Republic. The Haitian-American Corporation, in co-operation with the United States Government, has expressed interest in the commercial development of stramonium, belladonna, and senna as accredited Haitian crops. Botanists on the scene report that many lands of Mexico are well suited climatically to grow the roots of ergot and aconite.

A persisting difficulty in the establishment of valuable drug crops in Middle America has been the lack of basic experiment and research. Comparatively few Americans, regardless of the particular country in which they live, know enough about the primary botanical features of the great medicinal crops that are in continuous use throughout the far-flung pharmaceutical industries and sciences. Stramonium, for example, is taken from the dried leaves and flowering tops of the common Jimson weed (*Datura stramonium*) which grows wild in most areas of the temperate zone. This drug is a valuable sedative and antispasmodic. It is also used in the treatment of asthma, and the crude drug produces such valuable medicinal alkaloids as atropine and hyoscyamine.

This particular drug crop could obviously be gathered wild in large quantities within the United States. But high wage levels and acute labor shortage have joined in preventing its domestic recovery, and the product that we formerly imported almost entirely from Central Europe is now being imported in limited quantities from Mexico, Argentina and even Canada. Normal United States consumption of the drug is about 350,000 pounds per year, which figure is considerably raised by military needs. Practically all the established sources have been thrown under the Nazi yoke, that is, Hungary, the principal source, and Italy, Yugoslavia and Belgium, which have long been the minor European sources. At present Guatemala exports about 20,000 pounds of the crude drug per year, and Argentina's production since 1941 has climbed to more than 100,000 pounds yearly.

The dried leaves and roots of the belladonna plant are another indispensable drug, for belladonna is used by opticians for the dilation of the eye pupil and by surgeons as a preoperative defense against excessive secretions in pulmonary areas. Certain ingredients of belladonna are used extensively as sedatives. The plant can be grown within the United States. Trial plantings have recently been made in California, Michigan, Pennsylvania and Indiana. Before World War II, practically all the United States requirements—which average 130,000 pounds of the dried leaf and 55,000 pounds of the ground root—were imported from Central Europe. Though limited quantities of the drug are now being imported from British India, the current deficit is estimated as 80 percent of established United States requirements. In prewar times Bulgaria was the largest European exporter of belladonna, with Yugoslavia second and Hungary third. After 1940, British India produced and exported almost the entire world supply, which is still, unfortunately, below the proved needs. Plant experts are well aware that belladonna can be grown effectively in Mexico and probably in other Middle American countries.

Ipecac, which is made from the root of a plant indigenous both to Central and South America, grows wild in abundant quantities. It is a staple emetic and purgative drug which is also used effectively as a remedy for certain types of dysentery. Before the war considerable quantities of ipecac root were imported to the United States from Germany and Japan. But since 1930, or before, our decisive supplies have come from Nicaragua, Costa Rica, and Brazil. Ipecac is a valuable drug plant. During 1941 and 1942 prices of the crude root averaged about $19.20 per pound. Since 1914, recovery of the wild roots from Costa Rica has climbed to more than 75,000 pounds per year, from Nicaragua about 50,000 pounds a year, and from Brazil about 150,000 pounds yearly. The established demands are still not sufficiently fulfilled. But ipecac is one staple drug whose production seems permanently tethered to the rich earth of Middle America.

Senna is a botanical drug in leaf form and is one of the principal cathartics of medicine. There is no commercial production of crude senna in the United States. Most of our 4,000,000 pounds per year have come from Egypt and India where senna is an important cultivated crop.

However, British Indian production and Anglo–Egyptian Sudan production are heavily dependent on favorable rainfall conditions. Both producing centers suffer severely from droughts. At present India's 10,000 acres of commercial senna include approximately 5,000 acres of irrigated land which yield an average crop of half a ton of the leaf per acre, which is at least double average yield from unirrigated land. Immediately before Pearl Harbor the Defense Supplies Corporation was authorized to purchase 4,000,000 pounds of the leaves as a stock pile for emergency purposes. The future of Indian and Egyptian senna culture is definitely uncertain. Current yields are said to be about one-half of the established United States demands and a little more than one-fifth of previous world demands for the drug. The plant grows splendidly throughout much of Middle America, particularly in foothill areas with rainfall in excess of forty inches annually. The value of senna as a crop is as yet undetermined. It could conceivably be an important Middle American export, though it is not yet proved a "practical crop."

Ergot is a fungus growth that occurs on most grains and grasses but particularly on the rye plant. The commercial ergot is carefully dried, stored in airtight containers and otherwise processed to meet various medicinal uses, such as prevention of hemorrhage and in obstetrical practice. Since 1935 the principal United States supply has been imported from Portugal, prior to that time from Italy and southern Europe. United States requirements average about a quarter of a million pounds per year, which is substantially the entire exportable surplus of Portugal and half of the Spanish exports. Shortage has recently been accentuated by shipping losses. The importance of ergot to Middle America is not yet accurately estimated. It is probable that the beneficial fungus would thrive in the summer dry-land areas of Mexico, Guatemala, and other countries to the immediate south. That is for time and experimentation to prove.

The story of aconite root is comparable. This drug—which is likely to be a grayish-brown powder, prescribed for quieting overaction of the heart and otherwise valuable in treatment of inflammatory fevers and diseases of the circulatory system—is produced from a specie of the crowfoot family, also known as monkshood and wolfsband. These are common hardy plants which grow throughout the temperate climates and well into the tropics. Before the war the principal source was central Europe, particularly Italy, Germany, and France. The root is valuable in terms of price, and the plant has been successfully cultivated in Europe, especially in Italy. According to the United States Department of Agriculture, experimental cultivations in the United States are not outstandingly promising. At present our source of supply has failed almost completely. According to the Defense Supplies Corporation, no country except Spain holds any substantial exportable surplus. According to plant experts of the Department of Agriculture, aconite could probably be produced economically in Mexico and perhaps in other Middle American countries. Mexican climate and soils are unquestionably suitable for the crop.

In all, the future of drug crops for Middle America is exceptionally bright as regards soil, resources and agrarian geography. Research, risk, and hard work are the initial admission to the long-important international drug trade. The demands are almost certain to remain comparatively steadfast, in many instances to increase. Wage considerations are inevitably important. It is noteworthy that current wages in Spain and Portugal are generally comparable to current wages in Mexico, Guatemala and various other Caribbean nations. The prevailing Spanish wage level is a meager but living wage, that is, $.50 to $1.25 per day in the equivalent of United States money. Such wages may be termed tolerable in certain areas of Middle America because of relatively favorable buying power. If the crops were once successfully established, it is at least possible that the accompanying wages could be increased. That, too, is for time and practice to prove or disprove.

8. CHEWING GUM BECOMES SIGNIFICANT

Here, briefly, is the story of an ancient wilderness crop that has been reborn and raised to international importance through the somewhat ambiguous birth of airplane freight.

The primary ingredient of chewing gum is chicle, the congealed sap of a tropical tree which is indigenous to the jungle forests of upper Central America. Our near southern neighbors pronounce it "cheek-lay," and for centuries or more men and mules of Guatemala, British Honduras and far-south Mexico have intermittently toiled, sweated, risked and given their lives to perpetuate the more or less attractive saliva coaxer.

For the United States, chicle is become a virtually indispensable import. In the United States about 1,500,000 stores, shops, and miscellaneous counters sell chewing gum. Probably no other product is sold by so great a number and variety of retail outlets. Chewing gum is an international commodity. But chicle is not. It is probably the world's closest approach to a local, "natural" monopoly of a valuable harvest. Apparently the chicle tree, *Achras chicle pittier,* does not thrive under cultivation or grow extensively beyond its native range which is largely limited to the Department of Petén, northmost subdivision of Guatemala and smaller areas of adjacent British Honduran and Mexican frontiers. Most of the best yielding chewing-gum trees grow in the wild Caballo country, a wet jungle land about twice the size of the State of New Hampshire. Here the human population is perhaps 8,000—roughly one person to two square miles; while the insect population would seem to be hundreds to the square foot.

The dog-saturated villages of Flores and Paso Caballo are official outposts of chicle lands. By plane the towns are about twenty minutes apart. By foot or mule train they are a hard and dangerous week to ten days apart. The wild lands of Petén are dotted with deep swamps where mules sink belly deep and sometimes drown, where drivers, while praying for safe delivery from sandfly fever, ruinous dysenteries or malaria, spend feverish nights in high-swung hammocks wrapped heavily with mosquito bars.

During pre-Columbian times these chicle lands were peopled with Mayan Indians and presumably were sites of many towns and shrines of the Mayas. For in the black-green jungle one can still find remnants of hand-carved pillars and statues, and the wood most commonly used was this same chicle or, locally speaking, *chicozapote*. Among the recently discovered ruins of Tikal were heavy, richly carved beams of chicle wood which had lasted through wet tropical centuries. It is therefore a safe bet that the diligent, inventive Mayas were chewing chicle gum centuries before Columbus saw the Caribbean; more centuries before hurrying commuters began to drop round coins into the maws of mechanical venders.

Petén lacks railroads. Its highways are pestiferous foot trails. Apparently that is the reason why the chicle tree has survived. Certainly it is the reason whereby chicle harvest has incubated and successfully launched a brilliant, world-spanning industry of airplane freight. Yet the actual work of chicle recovery remains one of the most primitive enterprises of man. The traditional harvester is the *chiclero*, a tree-climbing lumberjack of the tropics. His working equipment is forthright and simple: a ball of small rope, an outfit of rubber bags, a sharp knife, a hand adz or other cutting instruments, and sometimes a pair of heel spurs similar to those used by telephone linemen.

The harvest is largely confined to the rainy season, which usually covers ten to fifteen weeks between April and November, the period of maximum sap flow. It is the chiclero's job to form a highly intimate acquaintance with every eligible tree within his beat, paying greatest heed to the stately achras tree of the Lake Petén Itzá area. South of this badly lost lake and along the left bank of the Pasion River in the neighboring Guatemalan state of Vera Altapaz grows another variety of chicle called *chicubull*. The resin of this tree is red instead of white, hardens more slowly and melts more easily than the standard chicle, and tends to ooze away before it can be carried to market. Sometimes the two types of resins can be mixed.

The chiclero begins the harvest by making a herringbone-pattern incision close to the base of the tree. This cut or "wound" drains into a bag or bucket. Nowadays the rubber bag is the most used receptacle, a heavy "wallet" about a foot long and six inches wide which is anchored to the tree trunk with two sharpened wooden pegs. Having set the bags the chiclero is ready for climbing. He stretches the rope about the tree trunk and ties it slip-noose style about his own waist; then with deft use of his climbing spurs he mounts the trunk, and with both hands free for knifing he begins to shape spiraled incisions into the inner bark.

This is real tree surgery. It can't be hit or miss, for the tree must live to bear another year. Present conservation laws of Guatemala specify that only the main trunk may be "bled." Limb gashing frequently kills the tree, or makes the sap flow *concada*, or dormant. When the cutting is finished and the "bleeding" begun, the next job is to collect the resin, mix it with equal parts of water and boil it. "Cooking" is also a skilled avocation. The fire must be slow and the brew stirred continually until the gum becomes moldable. The usual refinery equipment is a fire-blacked, three-legged iron kettle and a scattering of wooden box molds, both operated in the shade before a shack built of bamboo or brush and roofed with palm thatch. It may be a coincidence, but this reporter has repeatedly noticed one or more lean darkish pigs walking in or out of the doorless doorway of the chiclero's shack.

When the brew is properly cooked the chiclero pours it into wooden molds where it cools to form solid blocks or *marquetas* of chicle. He then sews the blocks into canvas or burlap wrappers and the product is ready for export.

The standard price received by the chiclero is ten dollars per quintal or hundredweight at the *hato,* or specified delivery point. Usually the first transportation is by mule pack. But in the rougher stretches or areas where sparse forage or lean purses prevent the ownership of pack animals, the chiclero carries his harvest by shoulder pack, for ten, twenty, or even fifty miles, following fearful trails through thorny jungle and sunless passes, sometimes with a shoulder burden of two hundred pounds or more.

Generally the chicle chaser is a hard worker, a kindly natured hombre who smiles a great deal, speaks colloquial Spanish with many nouns and few (if any) verbs, and garnishes his speech with gestures and postures that are unmistakably Indian. His work regalia is usually rags or nothing, his face is frequently sooted and gummed, and sometimes just for variety's sake his head is covered with a smug, dentless Wall Street style derby.

Usually the chiclero is a habitual borrower and a loyal repayer, and during the "season" he works frantically to repay old debts and maintain future credit. From the day he pours his first marqueta of chicle to the day he dies, he is rarely if ever entirely out of debt. He is much inclined to wheedle cash advances from his "contractor," whose work agreement, though prescribed by local government authorities, is one of the most complicated contracts ever entered into by man.

In return for a cash advance in quetzales (Guatemalan dollars) the chiclero gives his word of honor that he will deliver a specified amount of chicle—one ton per season is a good average—at a specified point by or before the end of the season. He usually understates his capacity in hopes that he can conclude the season with a few blocks of chicle to the good, in which case he happily trades it for liquor, perfumes, Woolworth jewelry and other pleasantly useless merchandise.

In Petén practically all the domestic trade is born of chicle. At the beginning of the season exporters and concessionaires advance money to local contractors in the form of I O U's or *vales*. Contractors then cash the vales among jungle-edge merchants, and distribute the advances so that the release of a comparatively few thousand dollars actually propels the entire harvest operation.

This is possible because Petén-style trading is not done at conventional stores. Practically all the stores are kept in private homes and usually consist of glassless counters and midget shelves loaded with cloth, groceries and trinkets. Most of the permanent homes of Petén villages are built of adobe. Frequently a household store and a family of eight or ten are quartered in the same and only room. Usually the womenfolk are the merchants, and chicle-country women generally hold the purse strings. By old and persistent tradition most cash advances go directly to the chiclero's wife or woman. The contractors prefer it so. So long as the alluring sex holds the money, the gum-tapping husbands are more inclined to come directly home when their season of work is finished.

Chicle begets a unique frontier economy. Its exploitation is nonagricultural, and like placer mining it is primarily a free-lance enterprise. In Guatemala a provincial government employs public servants to enforce chicle-conservation laws and to issue licenses to contractors and concessionaires, in return for which they collect severance taxes. Like El Salvador's balsam, or Brazil's carnauba (vegetable wax), chicle is one of the few crops of this hemisphere which one particular government can control absolutely if that government so decides.

United States capital—in particular Wrigley, Adams and American Chicle—continues to head the parade of chicle exploitation. But without the unique chiclero, there wouldn't be any parade. Unlike the fantastically romanticized United States cowboy or lumberjack, the chiclero has not passed from real life to Hollywood. He remains the patiently productive tapper of green hells into which plush-lined *Americanos del norte* cannot enter via highways, railroads, delicatessens or de luxe motion-picture houses. It is true that the gringos of the gum trade have studded Petén with concessionaires, "contact men" and other species of middle men; also that the majority acreage of the more valuable chicle-bearing forests are now leased by United States chewing-gum manufacturers or their agents. But the chiclero is still indispensable to chewing gum.

The chiclero is rather clearly aware of that fact; also of the proved truth that from first harvest to final purchase by the gringo gum maker the price of crude chicle increases about 500 percent more or less. Before airplane freighting came into the chicle lands and before Guatemala firmly closed its chicle frontier to British Honduran export, Señor José Tercero of the Pan-American Union compiled an itemized account of costs of a hundredweight of chicle delivered aboard ship at Belize (see p. 155).

That approached an all-time high for initial transportation costs of a staple vegetable commodity. The tariff and excise levies were and to some measure remain the motivation for smuggling. Particularly during the 1920's, while the United States rotted with bootlegging, Petén was visited with a comparable era of chicle bootlegging. On the whole the chicleros were innocent or comparatively so. Opportunistic contractors and free-lance runners, sometimes in collusion with local of-

Paid to the chiclero	$10.00
Municipal taxes and extraction permit	2.80
Overland transport from hato to Lake Itza-Petén	10.00
Boat transportation on lake	.50
From Lake Itza, Guatemala to Cayo, British Honduras	10.00
From Cayo to Belize	2.20
Transit toll through British Honduras	1.50
Export duty at 7 cents per pound	7.00
Wrapping materials	.50
Total transport cost	$44.50

ficials, conspired to cheat the governments of Guatemala and British Honduras of their severance fees. Frequently they would bootleg the chicle into Mexico, and sometimes they employed Mexican chicleros to invade the Guatemalan wilds. It was a bad situation. Individual chicleros were not licensed or officially counted. Their numbers range widely, from 3,000 to 6,000 or more. Twenty years ago the chicle bootleggers (like our own Al Capones) were operating in gangs, terrorizing frontier guards and frequently persecuting or even murdering chicleros. Guatemala officially closed its British Honduran frontier to chicle. In 1933 when aggressive General Jorge Ubico became president of Guatemala he promised a house cleaning for chicle and resolutely fulfilled that promise. But when he had shut and locked the chicle gates through British Honduras the transportation problem became acute. For then Guatemala's own Puerto Barrios became the official export point, and the shoulder-pack or mule-train portage from Caballo or Flores through hot relentless jungle to Barrios required from four to eight weeks of painful and dangerous tramping. If the luck were good a train of twenty mules with drivers could portage a ton of block chicle in five weeks. But frequently luck was not good. Mules died of heat and exhaustion. Men also suffered and died. Sandfly fever, malaria, blackwater fever and dysentery took on new emphasis and menace. Chicle supply became imperiled and chicle prices began to skyrocket.

Then men and wings made to the rescue of the hard-pressed chewing gum. Today one Ford trimotor type of freight-cargo plane carries two tons of chicle from Paso Caballo to Barrios in about an hour and a half. First ventures in air freight for the chicle jungle began in 1934. One of the distinguished first flyers was Sam Penry, a Montana cowboy who took to flying, so he says, because the bulls on the Montana range were too damned noisy. Today virtually every pound of commercial chicle is flown out of Petén—most of it to seaboard at Puerto Barrios. Air transport across the jungle costs from $20 to $45 per ton, or about one-third of previous land-portage expenses. Thanks to aviation the chicle industry is convincingly saved, and airplane freight is well inaugurated as an all-American institution.

During the harvest season commercial airline Transportes Aereos Centro-Americanos—TACA—formerly flew an average of three planeloads or six tons of raw chicle per day, for a season's total of about 2,000,000 pounds. And today the principal buyers of chicle stipulate by contract that the product must be flown from hato to port. For this and other reasons the great wilderness of Petén and its adjoining highlands are becoming dotted with jungle airfields; not the elaborate, cement-paved, gauge- and beacon-studded saucers which we know as commercial airports, but narrow clearings, sometimes no bigger than football gridirons, frequently bumpy and soggy, and thickly surrounded with giant forest trees. The chewing-gum pilots circle mud-splattered planes above these dots of fields, bank and maneuver to slip planes smoothly into port, even though wing tips and landing gear frequently glaze the tips of mahogany, vitae, and other tall jungle trees. Wide-opening side doors allow field attendants to pack the freight holds and bellies of the planes with tight-fitting cargoes of chicle blocks. Then doors and belly holds are shut, and planes charge frantically and lift at roof-pitch angles to clear the tall fringes of forest.

Thus chicle becomes the hemisphere's first significant harvest to be carried to market almost exclusively by plane. And today the expeditious practice of air freighting spreads fast and far to become one of the brightest omens for survival and increase in inter-American trade and American tropical agriculture.

9. OUT OF THE WILDERNESS

Chicle is a classic instance of an isolated and, until recently, rather casual jungle resource which proceeds to gain decided moment and significance with the coming of the era of air transportation. Thus chicle holds its place as an illustrious, sweat-provoking enterprise in trail blazing; also as an ancient henchman to an air age. In terms of Middle America today and tomorrow this is particularly important. The air-transport age is here to stay. Roughly half the land surface of all Middle America is still generally untenanted and inaccessible to land travel. But the freight plane can take goods out of the wilderness; and for this reason it can establish value and wealth in such lands. Now that the plane is proved the working comrade of the tropical frontiersman, it is good time to begin to view the real or possible wealth sources of the Middle American wilderness.

When and if one launches into such a study he will observe immediately that the hillsides, forests, and lowland jungles of the ten Caribbean republics probably lead the world in their treasuries of native fruits, and that on the whole these native fruits of Middle America are little known; that through the centuries they have been consumed and enjoyed by Indian and other first citizens of the American tropics—usually as raw fruit, and without benefit of recipes or methodical harvest or export.

A few Middle American fruits such as the avocado (native to Mexico) are in process of becoming important United States foods—current market consumption of avocados in the United States is about 70,000,000 pounds per year. United States consumption of the West Indian cashew nut now exceeds 8,000,000 pounds yearly, and our domestic markets sell a similar volume of papayas (the magnificent tree melon which is native to Cuba).

Middle America's foremost fruit export, and the world's largest export of fruit, is the banana. But bananas, as we shall shortly notice, are native to the hot wet valleys of India or possibly Indo-China, and came to Middle America circuitously—via Africa, the Canary Islands, Hispaniola and Panama.

Today, almost within sight of the world's most productive banana fields, bizarre and delicious indigenous American fruits bear and ripen—many still without takers. But first we might notice some of the tropical wonder fruits which are, to some measure, known.

For one, there is the valuable cashew or *marañón* nut—borne by a smallish tree (*Anacardium occidentale*), which usually grows on the dry bushy hillsides. Immediately back of the tree's rather scraggly reddish blossom grows its two-part fruit—a long grayish kidney-shaped nut which hangs from a red or yellow spongy mass about the size and shape of a pimento pepper. The pepper-shaped fruit can be eaten raw, but the nut is poisonous unless cooked or roasted until its oil is dissipated.

Yuca or cassava—commercially named tapioca (*Manihot esculenta*)—has long been a staple food crop harvested from the abounding tropical wilds. Like yams or sweet potatoes, yuca has edible roots. It is a hardy bushy plant with large stalklike leaves that are divided into pointed sections. The roots can be boiled and eaten like potatoes or they can be grated or powdered and made into nutritious bread. One variety of yuca root can be eaten raw; another is highly poisonous when raw and requires long heating and steaming before it is safely edible.

Bejuco de agua (water vine) is a tropical vine which bears small sour grapes—apparently the only grape crop indigenous to the American tropics. For jungle roamers the vine is a godsend because its stem is filled with clear, drinkable, and frequently lifesaving water. Many of the wild fruits of Middle America are vastly more appetizing than the grapes of bejuco de agua. For example, there is ciruelo or jungle plum, the delicious fruit of a small, heavily leafed tree which thrives in open fields or bushy hillsides. The ciruelo looks and flowers like common orchard plums of the United States. The plums vary considerably in size and color—some are red and some are orange. The larger varieties, called "golden apples," average about one and a half inches in diameter and are truly delicious.

The yellowish-brown, nispero or sapodilla (*Achras sapota*) is edible only when raw. This fruit is ball-shaped, about two inches in diameter and luscious. The tree is large, standing fifty feet or higher, and is distinguishable by its peculiarly shiny leaves. Similar is the star apple or caimito (*Chrysophyllum caimito*). This tree, which frequently reaches a height of sixty feet, is also common to hillside forests. The fruit looks like a small apple—with smooth greenish or purplish skin. The meat is soft and milky, and pleasantly sweet. The dark-brown seeds make starlike figures. Cooking destroys their delicate flavor. Pleasing in flavor, though more heavily crowded with seed, is the guanábano torete (*Annona purpurea*), another forest fruit with brown, feltlike skin and orange-colored flesh which is heavily crowded with large flat seeds.

Many other wild fruits of Middle America are deserving of notice: coconut, the greatest food palm of the warmer Americas; the wild-growing naranja or sweet orange; the guava, native to the American tropics but now established in many other tropics. Guava is a small tree, usually ten to fifteen feet high, and is common to the dryer pasture lands and hillsides. The tree's bark is smooth and scaly, and the fruit, about the size of a small apple, is usually brownish yellow outside and yellow to deep pink inside. The raw fruit is entirely edible but the ripe fruit makes one of the most delectable of jellies. The name guava is shared by another tropical fruit tree (*Inga spectabilis*), whose fruit is sometimes called the "ice-cream bean." There are several species of this smallish tree which are readily identified by the large leaves—eight inches or so long—dark green on top and decidedly hairy on the underside. The fruit pod is a huge, greenish-brown bean, frequently a foot long. The seed grow in a thick juicy pulp. This sweet pulp is the edible portion of the strange but worthwhile fruit.

Mamey (*Mammea americana*) is the jungle peach. It is borne by a tall handsome tree indigenous to the West Indies islands and sometimes findable in the Central American lowlands. The tree bears a large roundish fruit, frequently four inches or more in diameter. The brown leathery skin, about an eighth of an inch thick, covers a rich yellow pulp, sweet and rich and flavored like a clingstone peach.

And there is sapote (*Calocarpum mammosum*), a big ball-shaped fruit, four to eight inches in diameter, with rough brownish skin and reddish flesh which encases large brown seed. The raw ripe fruit is well flavored and has considerable food value.

There are incidental and unique fruits, such as the soursop

Abacá Fiber Newly
Removed in Panama

Mechanical Removal of Abacá Fiber, Middle American Style

Sundrying Henequen Fiber in Campeche, Mexico

Young Abacá Plant, Age about 90 Days, Costa Rica

Clearing Jungle for Planting Abacá in Panama

Loading the Peeled Strips or "Junks" of Abacá into a Mill
Shed at Almirante, Panama

or guanábana, a huge spiny fruit frequently weighing as much as ten or twelve pounds, containing a head-sized load of juicy whitish pulp which provides a commonly used base for beverages, fermented and otherwise. Soursop is not an epicure's food. But in terms of flavor, texture and size the luscious pineapples of Middle America are easily the world's best.

The same is generally true of the cultivated mangoes and papayas, those delectable green-skinned "tree melons" of Middle America, with their juicy, superbly flavored meats and well-proved nutritive merits. Like the common melon, both the papaya and the mango are best eaten raw and full ripe. But the green papaya can also be cooked and eaten like squash.

Middle American jungles hold many food crops besides fruits; among them is the water chestnut, the highly edible thumb-sized seed of a smallish, swamp-loving tree, which bears a large pod shaped like an oversized serpent head. Another is the forest yam or *yampi*, a wild-growing sweet potato with large, brown-skinned, white-meated roots which when thoroughly cooked (they are inedible when raw) are a good substitute for sweet potatoes. Another potatolike root of the Middle American wilds is badu (*Xanthosoma violaceum*) which must be cooked before the food can be rid of its high contents of toxic crystals.

Another great tree crop of the American tropics is bread-fruit, *fruta de pan*, or, more formally, *Artocarpus communis*. It is native to the East Indies, but it flourishes widely throughout many of the lands of the Caribbean. The mature trees are ordinarily thirty to forty feet high. The broad leaves are dark green and lustrous. The varishaped and yellow-greenish fruit —usually three to six inches in diameter—is dry, starchy and a generally satisfactory substitute for white potatoes which are altogether too scarce in the American tropics as a whole.

We have already noticed a few of the more promising palm crops of Middle America, but here it may be well to note briefly at least a few of the lesser known palm fruits that grow in the countries immediately south of us. Among these are the closely clustered fruits of the black palm, *Astrocaryum standleyanum*. The reddish or orange-colored fruit, roundish and about an inch and a half in diameter, has a well-flavored sweetish meat that can be eaten raw—and only raw. Then there is the heavily clustered purple-black fruit of the *caña brava—Bactris minor,* borne by a tall slender palm that is crowded with thorns. The corozo (*Scheelia zonensis*) is among the more conspicuous palms of the warmer Americas; a sturdy palm with huge leaves, sometimes as long as thirty feet and five or six feet wide. The drooping fruit bunches—four to six feet long—are crowded with orange-colored fruit pods which look like undersized coconuts and have meat, husks and milk cavity closely similar to those of the coconut. The meat provides an excellent cooking fat. The folded young leaves near the top of the tree taste a great deal like crisp lettuce and make an excellent salad green, indigenous to countrysides where green vegetables are chronically scarce or nonexistent. The corozo colorado nut, the egg-shaped fruit of a stubby and vigorous swamp palm, is another valuable source of edible and cooking oils.

There are many other palm oils of possible export and well-proved domestic values. Two kinds of edible oils are obtained from the red corozo, a palm tree—one derived from the red hull of the fruit and the other from the kernel. The fruit is called "red butter" and the second "dark butter." Both can be bleached and purified and kept indefinitely. The corozo de gunzo provides similar oils, which have medicinal properties as well as keeping qualities. The *pixbae* is a palm which is sometimes cultivated; it was grown by pre-Columbians; *pixbacilla* is a similar palm which is not cultivated. The pulp and the kernel of both species yield oil. The *palma pacora espinosa* is also a source of oil, and its fruit is used for making *chicha*, a fermented beverage.

Not all the fruits of the Middle American forests and jungles are of value. A few are poisonous—fruits such as the green, crab-apple-like manzanillo. Messrs W. R. Lindsay and M. F. Ward of the Canal Zone Experiment Gardens point out that "the early Spanish explorers upon meeting with this tree believed they had found crab apples in the New World, and ate the fruit, in some cases with fatal results. It is said that the sap was used by the Caribs for poisoning their arrows." The poisonous thorns of the *ortiga* nettle are another herbaceous nightmare widely prevalent throughout the American tropics. Pica-pica, a tropical thicket weed, menaces the passer-by with the shedable and poisonous hairs that garrison its beanlike seed pods. The forest shrub called Strychnos (*Strychnos toxifera*) is one of the world's most poisonous plants—the source of one of the deadliest of poisons.

Happily and in terms of totals the lethal plants are greatly in minority. But the fact remains that while the forests and jungles of Middle America are bountiful, and in many respects almost fantastically generous, their fruits are not invariably safe.

But some of the better proved tropical fruits also have distinguished nonfood values. This is true of the papaya. Cuba is taking steps to reintroduce the commercial cultivation of this immensely valuable tree and to take over some part of the task of supplying the United States with papain, which is the dried latex from green papaya fruit. Papain has a digestive enzyme resembling pepsin, and it has numerous commercial and medicinal uses. The latter include the treatment of diphtheria; the former the chemical capacity for making tough meat tender. (In 1941 the United States imported about $453,000 worth of papain, most of it from Ceylon and other Far Eastern sources, which are now cut off by the war.)

The harvest is simple. Commercial papain is obtained by making cuts in the skin of the green papaya fruit. The latex then drips out into cups and when dried is ready to market. Haiti, Puerto Rico, Jamaica and Trinidad also are producing small quantities of papain, and there is a good chance that the output will be substantially increased.

Stated generally the jungles or tropical wilderness remain the great and eternal reservoir of valuable crops. One after another, they have given to curious, explorative man the great crops of the world—the grains, the principal fruits, fibers, vegetables and drugs; rubber, strategic timbers, oils and gum. In past decades and centuries, most of the ultimate bases of wealth were given to man from out of the jungles. The jungles continue to give.

10. NATURAL RUBBER

The United States and most or all other industrial nations need and will continue to need natural rubber.

This statement is respectfully presented—respect for the dazzling if not too accurate press-agenting bought and paid for by taxpayers' money in behalf of certain minor public officials; respect, also, for the classic synthetic rubber publicity field days staged by several rubber manufacturers and paid for in considerable part by taxpayers' money; also respect for the fact that so much printed and spoken confusion about the rubber crisis has appeared that extremely few Americans have any clear idea of what the score really is.

Altogether, the well-intentioned citizen has been imbued with the vague, hopeful idea that "everything is going to be all right," that "good old Yankee ingenuity will find a way," which may become so. But the instant truth stands that we are paying and will pay dearly for our rubber shortsightedness. No doubt Yankee ingenuity will find a way. It found a way long ago when it learned that the milky latex of the hevea tree, a tropical native of the Amazon Basin, is the best, cheapest and most consistently reliable source of a large-volume rubber supply for the Americas.

Yankee ingenuity was on this trail as early as 1820, when Yankee merchants on clipper ships first began to import rubber shoes made in Brazil by Amazon Indians. These shoes, modeled for tiny Indian feet, were too small for North Americans. Yankee ingenuity went a step further in 1825 and began sending properly sized wooden lasts down to the Amazon. Jungle Indians modeled rubber shoes on these lasts, and thus began the world-decisive industry of rubber manufacture. Certainly there was, and is, Yankee ingenuity. Charles Goodyear, a frail, jaundiced, ex-preacher from New Haven, Connecticut, invented vulcanization, which finally launched a big-scale rubber manufacture. A century ago Goodyear had patented or clearly envisioned practically every principal use to which rubber is now put. Charles Goodyear, still rubber chemist number one, used hevea rubber, which has to this date supplied around 95 percent of all the rubber used by mankind.

Yankee ingenuity has had most to do with bringing the manufacture of natural rubber to its present brilliance and excellence. It has produced about twice as many tons of rubber as all the rest of the world combined. It has kept 32,000,-000 automotive vehicles on rubber tires and developed many thousands of other valid uses for rubber. But Yankee ingenuity has been both witless and lazy to allow the source of rubber to drift to the East Indies and Malaya. There in the hands of the British and Dutch cartels, it has permitted the fixing of prices, the monopoly of supply and the logical source of rubber—the Amazon Basin and Middle America—to get out of its hands. Our rubber manufacturers have done a marvelous job of manufacturing, but they have been guilty almost to the point of treachery in passing on price rises to the public and letting the supply of crude rubber fall into the hands of a greedy cartel control. Today, Yankee ingenuity, greatly intensified, knows that the huge reservoirs of natural rubber which already grow in the forests and fields of Latin America simply must not be neglected. In these good-neighbor countries, easily accessible by ships, planes and the coming great Inter-American Highway, natural rubber can be grown cheaply and in great quantities. The gallant Brazilian hevea tree is an easy and ideal small-farm crop whereby women and children can also work and earn. Its latex, or tree milk, is harvestable any day of the year and can be cured and processed on the spot with simple and inexpensive equipment. When not harvested, it can be stored in the tree, without cost or deterioration. And Yankee ingenuity knows that when rubber is scientifically grown and harvested in South America and Middle America, the United States will never again be abjectly dependent on Dutch and British cartels or on any coteries of would-be monopolists who have set out to subsidize themselves from the United States Treasury.

Our good neighbors to the south have millions of acres of rich, cheap land ideal for the best proved rubber crops. Hevea trees, Castilla, guayule and other valuable rubber plants can be grown on land unsuitable to any other important crops. That is doubly appropriate; land is there and tropical land for this greatest of tropical crops which is not competitive to crops grown within the United States.

Granting that many nonrubber elastomers or "synthetics" have valuable specialized uses—such as strategic resistance to cold, sunlight and various chemicals, the truth remains that natural rubber has that peculiar facility of bounce or stretch and retract, which engenders its distinguished value for making pneumatic tires, which account for about three-fourths of all rubber used.

A bomber or heavy freight plane traveling at 100 miles an hour touches the ground; the tires are suddenly required to turn at terrific speed at a split-second's notice. Grinding, shearing, tearing and scratching begin. An ultra-slow-motion camera reveals the bomber tires badly distorted—bagged down heavily at the touch point. A microscope shows tiny fibers of rubber hugging the runway, and yet clinging together so viciously that only a few are torn away. Then, the instant the strain is released, the plane tires miraculously resume their usual shape, the fibers mesh together again, and the tire is ready to take the grueling punishment again and again. That is real rubber at work in war or peace. Nobody can clearly explain this bizarre magic of its stretch and bounce, and nobody has yet succeeded in duplicating it.

Since we live in a rubber age, each one of us has a right to his own views and estimates about rubber, whether his main interest is centered in rubber tires, rubber dolls or rubber dollars. We need some quantity of synthetic to meet specialized uses that help the entire rubber industry. We also need natural rubber in ever greater quantities for the years and the world that lie ahead.

The case of natural rubber is based on known performance and proved averages, on the fact that natural rubber is long proved to be the nearest ideal material for auto and aviation tires and tubes which combinedly require around three-fourths of all rubber actually used. We know positively that natural rubber will do this job, and we are still not sure that any of the synthetics will give us consistently good and economical tires—now or ever. In 1943 we were being told that the synthetic plastomer called thyikol would do the job. Now thyikol has been tried and found wanting. In 1944 the main hope in synthetic has been Buna S., which may also be found wanting.

As already noted, the case for natural rubber is based on proved science and known industrial performance—and on the right of tens or hundreds of millions of tropical peoples to live from and earn from the earth that is mother of us all.

For our own good, maybe for our survival, we will require natural rubber, and this reporter contends that a reasonable part, eventually a third or more, of our natural rubber needs should be grown in the Western Hemisphere. A recent survey made by our Department of Agriculture indicates that the hevea rubber tree, which is native to Brazil, can be grown as a valid orchard crop in at least sixteen American nations from lower Mexico to Bolivia.

This same hevea tree has been and is being grown by the millions of acres in such Far Eastern tropics as Malaya and Sumatra. The goal of wisely directed planting of hevea rubber in the American tropics is not to filch a great established crop of one hemisphere and grow it in another, to the lasting injury of the first. I believe that rubber is one of several vital tropical crops that should be produced in this hemisphere, not to the exclusion of importation from other sources, but enough so that in time of emergency the Americas will not again be whacked off from sources of such vital materials. This very day good, high-yielding strains of hevea trees are growing in Central America, which, of course, is part of our own North American continent. If the United States could buy even one-fourth of its proved needs for natural rubber from the nations of Central America, it would profoundly help both these near neighbors and the Central American markets for United States goods. Comparable gains and advantages could be realized by our allies and friends in tropical South America.

For natural rubber is not divinely ordained to remain a

crop for the profit of the cartel and the sweaty toil of the downtrodden coolie. Natural rubber, particularly the hevea tree, is also a valid, proved, yeoman crop for the self-respecting citizen farmer. At world prices of crude rubber current since 1936, hevea is a soundly profitable crop, when grown by independent farmers in Sumatra, Indo-China or in our own nearby American hot lands.

Certain would-be wise men have a way of implying that synthetic elastomers are the new way and natural rubber is the old way. This is bunk. In Germany, Buna S., the momentary white hope of our would-be synthetic "program," has been in manufacture for more than twenty-five years. When Germans began the routine manufacture of Buna S., average yields of cultivated hevea rubber were under 300 pounds per acre yearly. Even during the querulous lifetime of Buna S., tremendous progress has been made in the agronomy of natural rubber.

Selective breeding, bud grafting and advanced nursery practices and orchard management methods are combining to increase average yields of hevea trees from the old level of under 300 pounds of sheet latex per acre yearly to present levels of 1,200 to 1,500 pounds, with a record harvest as high as 1,970 pounds per acre. Most of the new hevea orchards and nurseries that are now being planted in Central and South America are from these high-yielding strains planted with knowledge born of proved agronomy and sound research.

The American tropics hold much of the richest soil on the earth. It is not easy for any factory, or advertising writer, to produce tangible goods in direct competition with the age-old firm of rich land, plentiful rain, and hot sun and a great crop that is growing and in harvest 365 days of every year. Just to talk cold turkey about a hot subject, the great new age of rubber is actually growing out of the soils of many nations, including those of at least six nations of Middle America.

11. TIMBERS

The forests of Middle America remain among the most versatile, valuable and least exploited on earth. At least thirty of our most needed tropical timbers are indigenous to the Caribbean countries. Certain of the forest resources of these nearer American neighbors have recently climbed to the first ranks of war essentials. One of these timbers is mahogany (practically all of our supply comes from Central American forests south of latitude 20), now used for making the hulls of hundreds of light-fleet submarine-chaser craft so ably employed by our Navy; another is balsa, a very light tropical wood used widely in the manufacture of gliders, life rafts, plane models, and various other war and peacetime manufactures.

But the rich and varied forests of Middle America are supplying many other war essentials and peace essentials. Among them is lignum vitae, "wood of life." Its most important use is for making bearings or brushing blocks for lining the stern tubes or propeller shafts of steamships. The wood has exceptional strength and tenacity. These qualities, combined with the self-lubricating properties resulting from the resin content, make it outstandingly resistant to water. Lignum vitae is also used extensively for the manufacture of mallets, pulley sheaves, caster wheels, bowling balls, masthead trucks, stencils, chisel blocks and so on.

This timber has been in trade since 1508 when it was introduced to the medical profession of Europe as a specific for various mortal diseases. The name "lignum vitae" originated from belief in its remedial powers. It was almost two centuries before the medical claims were questioned, and eventually disproved.

There are several species of the tree. Colors of the heartwood vary from olive brown to dark brown or near black.

The sapwood is white or yellowish, sometimes with blue or greenish vessel lines—waxy or oily in appearance. All are medium-sized trees with short trunks: diameters ranging from ten to twelve inches and occasionally from eighteen to thirty inches. The most common commercial lignum vitae (*Guaiacum officinale*) now comes from Cuba. Besides Cuba and other West Indian islands, other lignum vitae grow extensively in Venezuela, Colombia, Panama and Honduras.

Several related timbers grow in Middle America. From the island of Jamaica and other lands of the West Indies comes the *Guaiacum sanctum*, or "bastard lignum vitae," an evergreen tree, usually less than thirty feet high and twelve inches or more in diameter. Haiti exports a species which flourishes on the dry plains to the south side of the island.

Also of distinguished value is the ceiba or "silk cotton tree," common throughout the West Indies and much of Central America. It is a massive tree, frequently 80 to 100 feet high, with a heavily buttressed thick trunk. The ceiba is imposing. The spread of its crown is frequently 100 feet or more. It is deciduous and blossoms immediately after the shedding of the leaves. The seeds are packed in the white kapok, a light cottonlike fiber which ancient Indians of the West Indies used for weaving cloth; a fiber exquisitely soft and almost unbelievably light, and therefore increasingly valuable for padding pillows, cushions and furniture. The timber is also valuable.

When freshly cut, it is heavy but it becomes light (about twenty-seven pounds per cubic foot) when dry. Long used for making dugout canoes and rafts, its proved commercial uses include the manufacture of paper pulp, slack cooperage, packing cases, toys and hundreds of other articles that require a soft, easily worked wood. It cannot compete with balsa for buoyancy but it is by all odds the most plentiful light timber of Middle America. Its kapok or "tree cotton" continues to meet increasing demand as a stuffing material, all the more so since the United States supplies formerly imported from the tropics of the Far East are now lost to us.

Balsa, one of the world's most important light timbers and widely distributed throughout Middle America, is the Spanish word for raft. Early Spanish immigrants dealt the name when they saw the Indians hollowing the logs to make boats. Balsa is sometimes pinkish white or pale reddish, and sometimes brownish with a rather silky luster. The tree is easily identified by its large simple leaves, solitary flowers and very conspicuous fruit, which resembles a huge cotton boll. Its mature fruit looks considerably like a rabbit's-foot, and presumably from this originated the scientific name *Lagopus*. When fully ripe the fruit pod bursts and a mass of furlike down falls to the earth. The seeds which look like small grapes are enveloped in this fur.

In the global war, as in World War I, large quantities of treated balsa were used in the manufacture of buoyancy and insulation products, such as life preservers, submarine mine floats, also for parts and fixtures of lifeboats, hydroplanes and pontoons; also for streamlining of struts and braces in airplanes and for commercial refrigerators for which the open porous structure is particularly well suited. The role of balsa in aeronautical manufacture and refrigeration equipment assures its continuing value.

The botanical classification of mahogany is somewhat involved. The staple or *Swietenia candollei* consists of five known species: (1) *S. Mahogani (L) Jacq*, (2) *Shumilis Zucc*, (3) *Macrophylla King*, (4) *Candollei Pittier*, and (5) *Cirrhata Blake*.

The first species and the longest used grows in the West Indies and southern Florida. The second, in common use since about 1836, grows along the coast of Guerrero and Oaxaca, in Mexico, and in northwestern Guatemala. The third, now the most widely used, ranges from southern Mexico through Central America into Colombia and Ecuador, with maximum stands in the great forests of Honduras. The fourth is apparently limited to Venezuela. The fifth is found in Sinaloa, Michoacan and Oaxaca, Mexico, and in El Salvador, Nicaragua, Honduras and perhaps elsewhere. These five known species are the only source of true mahogany, the premier cabinet wood of the world.

Mahogany was one of the first timbers to come to the attention of European explorers, and its merit for ship construction and repair was early established. Cortes employed mahogany, probably from Santo Domingo, to build the ships for further voyages of discovery after his conquest of Mexico, and it is not unlikely that mahogany timber from the West Indies or Campeche, Mexico, was requisitioned by the government of Spain for use in building the proud, ill-fated *Armada*. Sir Walter Raleigh is credited with introducing mahogany into England—and presenting a mahogany table to Queen Elizabeth.

All true mahogany is necessarily of the tropical Swietenia family. Regardless of the particular species, the mahogany tree is a king of the forest and jungle; a stately and beautiful tree which frequently reaches a height of 100 feet or more, with a straight symmetrical bole four to six feet in diameter. Sometimes the body logs are free of branches to heights of from forty to sixty feet. The pinnate leaves have several pairs of leaflets that are smooth and shining from above and slightly brownish on the under surface. The flowers are small and white striped with purple, and the fruits are light chestnut brown pods—one to two inches in diameter and two to six inches long—which split open when ripe and liberate numerous maplelike seeds. It is a far-scattered timber which grows at rather unpredictable intervals in Florida, the Bahamas, Cuba, Haiti, Jamaica, Mexico, Honduras, British Honduras, Guatemala, Nicaragua, Costa Rica, Panama, Colombia and Venezuela—only a few trees per forest acre, but the valuable trees can be identified easily from low-flying planes.

For good reason we hear considerable of Middle American resources of "dyewood." It should be "dyewoods." They are an extensive list of Middle American timbers. One is chlorophora, which grows from forty to a hundred feet tall, with thick trunks about three feet in diameter. The wood is much like United States black walnut. The sawdust and bark are used both locally and in the United States as a source of dye which colors cloth a rich coffee brown. Of the various species, chlorophora, generally known to the dye trade as "fustic" or "old fustic," is one of the most important dyewoods of commerce. The bark is a brownish gray; the crown is open and spreading; the flowers are small and beadlike; the fruit is a tiny rounded nut. The tree grows abundantly in the lowlands of the Tampico area; along the lowlands of both the east and west coasts of Central America; also in the lowlands of Colombia and Venezuela.

Another tropical cousin of black walnut is *Phoebe porphyria,* also a beautiful tree. It grows fifty to eighty feet high and from two to four feet in diameter. It has a black fissured bark and lustrous ever-green foliage. The dark heartwood resembles walnut, though its color is richer. The wood is highly fragrant, finely textured, easy to work, takes a glossy polish, and so long as it is not exposed to sunlight it is usable, like walnut, for various kinds of civil and naval construction, carpentry, cabinet work and furniture. Its deep violet dye, usually made from the sawdust and bark, is commonly used in the manufacture of fine leathers.

Logwood (*Haematoxylon campechianum*) is a comparatively small tree with a gnarled and fluted trunk, rough grayish or brownish bark; clustered flowers that are small and ill odored; and thin flat seed pods. The tree is abundant in southern Mexico (Tabasco, Campeche and Yucatán) and throughout much of Central America. It also grows in Colombia, Venezuela and the Guianas. Early attempts to use logwood dyes in England were not successful and further importation of the timber was prohibited by British law. But presently chemists learned how to make a fast dye from the extract. "Brazilette" is the name commonly applied to the heartwood of a Middle American tree similar in habitat to the logwood and often confused with it. The color of the fresh heart is a rich orange, turning to dark red on exposure to air and light. The wood supplies a bright or so-called "fancy" red dye of outstanding beauty.

The *Eysenhardtia,* consisting of eight or nine species of shrubs and small trees, is distributed from western Texas and southern New Mexico and Arizona to southern Mexico, Lower California and Guatemala. The Mexican plant is a shrub or tree ten to twenty-five feet high, with a hard, dense, reddish-brown wood. The dye is a pleasing yellowish brown.

The *Cabralea* genus consists of nearly forty species of shrubs and trees and grows throughout most of the tropical Americas. The bark, especially that of the root, is used medicinally as a febrifuge; the wood is used in furniture making, carpentry, wharf and dock construction and shipbuilding. A red dye is extracted simply by soaking the shavings and sawdust in water, and the bark is employed in tanning. Similar are the *Comocladias,* a group of about twenty-five shrubs and small trees, which grow in Mexico, Central America, northern South America and even more abundantly in the West Indies.

These are only a few of the valuable woods that are yielded by the great and still little known forest lands of Middle America. Skilled foresters and forest surveys and fire protection are badly needed in all these tropical wonderlands. The huge majority of the timber wealth of this hemisphere is south of the Rio Grande, and most of it remains unharvested; much of it not even surveyed. During my various travels in Central America and the Caribbean islands I have never ceased being impressed by the magnificent abundance of timbers or the lushness of the ever-verdant forests. Nor have I ceased being disturbed and disgusted by the flagrant waste and perpetuated ignorance of timber resources, which include a great deal more than lumber and structural woods. For forest lands and granges of these ever-marvelous Caribbean lands hold other great gifts—lush ranges and grasslands, much of which is still unused; and great treasuries of valuable tannin plants—probably enough to supply all United States leather industries for decades or centuries.

Mangrove is Middle America's foremost source of tannin. Its particular use is in curing shoe soles. Mangrove is one of the most abundant and generally invincible of all jungle flora. It is a strange, weird sort of growth; a dense, blockading tree which makes for those dark, impenetrable forests that frequently fringe the tidal estuaries, spread over salt marshes and fortify hot, muddy coast lines. Frequently the tides wash in and out among the densely grown trees, sometimes covering them partly or completely in high tide, and at low tide exposing the weird masses of interwoven, gnarled roots and incredible aerial roots that grow out from the trunks and branches to droop and swing earthward in wide arcs, finally taking root some distance from the parent tree, promptly to become the trunk of the new growth.

Mangrove is native to every country of Middle America and many other tropical countries as well: northern South America, the Philippines, East Africa and many islands of the Netherlands Indies. The processing of the tannin is comparatively inexpensive, and the recovery of the tannin therefore increases year after year. The species most common in Middle America include those known as rhizophora or red mangle, whose inner bark is deep red. The harvest consists of felling the tree and stripping off the bark. Mildly stated this is a terrific job. Mangrove jungles are likely to be feverous and ill odored, and the dense growth provides ideal protection for unassorted tropical snakes. By tropical tradition the harvesters work in small boats in which they penetrate the forests at high tide, strip off the bark and paddle back to the collecting spot. The bark must be dried, broken into small pieces and bagged for market. The tannin content is high, from 20 to 35 percent of the dry-bark weight. The feat of changing mangrove from a jungle nuisance to a valuable export crop requires the establishment of extraction mills within the immediate area.

In the past East African and Madagascar mangroves have supplied the greatest quantity of commercial tannin. This trade was developed before World War I largely by German chemists and German jungle traders. Shortly thereafter Dutch enterprise in the Netherlands Indies began to develop a Far Eastern tannin industry from mangrove. Then British Malaya became interested, and some of the less favored plantations, particularly those unable to develop available hevea rubber properties, began to harvest the free-growing mangrove bush which previously had been rated as a foremost nuisance of the hot countries.

Mangrove tannin exports climbed rapidly after 1921. The Strait Settlements delivered to market some 3,600 metric tons yearly. Dutch Indian exports climbed to almost 4,000 metric tons per year; Madagascar and East African exports continued to increase. By 1930 Philippine production loomed important. In 1938 the United States imported 12,000,000 pounds of crude tannin from the Philippines alone, and imported, all told, approximately $389,000,000 worth of tannin materials of all types.

But still no capable American source was developed. During 1940 Philippine production dropped to less than half of the 1938 figure because of disrupted labor supply and profound uneasiness. After Pearl Harbor the Philippine, Madagascar, Malay and Dutch East Indian supplies were cut off entirely. At long last it was up to the Americas to develop American sources of tannin necessary to the manufacture of shoes and other indispensable leather goods. Today, though this enterprise is still in the beginning, despite extremely difficult shipping problems, labor shortage, and acute shortage of processing machinery, mangrove is becoming a noteworthy Middle American crop. It can very well become a valid and lasting forest harvest of distinguished importance to United States industry and of continuing benefit to the Middle American nations.

12. BANANAS

In terms of progressive agricultural industry, the banana is by far the best developed, and in terms of the hectare or acre the most valuable of Middle American crops. In any "normal" year, more than 100,000,000 bunches of bananas are exported from Middle American fields. That is more than 3,000,000 tons; an average of 150 bananas per bunch; a total of some 15,000,000,000 bananas.

To carry 100,000,000 bunches of bananas at one time would require a fleet of 1,600 refrigerated steamers, each one loaded with more than 60,000 bunches. But banana production is rather evenly distributed around the calendar. Ordinarily, in peacetime, about 200 ships, large and small, are

engaged continuously in the trade. Most of these are refrigerated steamers, some of the best maintained merchant
shipping in the world. Time and time again banana ships have
been proved of first value in war transport.

The sources of bananas are comparatively widely scattered.
During the past twenty years Honduras, Guatemala and Jamaica produced and exported about 20,000,000 bunches each
per year as compared with 10,000,000 each from Costa Rica
and Panama. Mexico has grown about 12,000,000 bunches
per year and Cuba about 6,000,000. Recently the latter totals
have fallen drastically—to less than one-fourth of the usual
totals. There are several reasons: the lack of concentrations
of good banana lands, poor shipping, weather losses and,
more important, the difficulties encountered by Mexican and
Cuban growers in protecting their banana crops from major
fungus diseases.

Ordinarily, over 250,000 acres of Middle American lands
are planted to bananas. Temporarily, war conditions and ship
shortages have reduced the total. But direct investments in
banana properties remain at about $500,000,000. In normal
times the banana industry pays more than $6,000,000 per
year in direct revenues to the Middle American governments;
also about $30,000,000 in cash wages to the citizens who
work on or for banana properties, and some $30,000,000 for
local merchandise and products incidental to production.
The operation and upkeep of thousands of miles of railway
and tram lines are also a part of the banana picture; as are
about 40 seaports of the hemisphere.

The United States and Canada together consume nearly 60
percent of all Middle American bananas. The British Isles are
the next most important market. The nations of Scandinavia
and Central and Southern Europe are the major secondary
markets, with the temperate regions of the South American

continent among the newer consuming areas. Today Middle America provides most of the world's supply of what may be the world's oldest cultivated crop.

The cultivated banana is certainly not a native of the Americas. Chinese writings of more than 3,000 years ago mentioned the fruit. More than three centuries before Christ was born Alexander the Great found bananas growing in the valley of the Indus. Later, history records its further journey westward to East Africa, then to the Holy Land and northern Egypt. In 1482 the Portuguese found the fruit growing along the African west coast, where the natives gave it the name "banana"—African dialect name for an Asiatic fruit now securely adopted by the tropical Americas. When Columbus sailed on his first voyage of discovery the banana was growing abundantly in the Canary Islands—yellow bananas, though most of the earlier Central American plantings were of red bananas. As men and nations moved westward, banana rhizomes were brought to most of the tropics. In 1516 Tomas de Berlanga, a Spanish Dominican, carried with him roots of the banana plant when he sailed to Santo Domingo as a missionary.

But export commerce in the fruit is a comparatively new development. The first bananas to arrive in New York came from Cuba in 1804. By 1830 occasional clipper ships were bringing small cargoes from Cuba and the Bahamas. From 1857 to 1880 this trickle gradually developed into a small but steadily increasing export stream. At the Philadelphia Centennial Exposition of 1876, bananas were offered for sale —wrapped in tinfoil—at ten cents each. Even then this was an exotic curiosity, since the commercial range of the banana was limited principally to tropical lands. It was not until the development of large-scale cultivation on the Central American mainland and the introduction of the refrigerated steamship around 1900 that the unique crop began to realize major importance. Before the turn of the century the eastern coast lines of Middle America, all the way from Tabasco to Panama, were for the most part of uninhabited and economically worthless swamps and jungles. Concentrated along the cool highlands of the central plateau, with very little access to the sea except for a few scattered ports on the Pacific coast line, the native populations were almost completely isolated from the remainder of the world. In one brief generation the advent of the banana industry has changed this.

Along the fertile river valleys hundreds of thousands of acres of this swamp and jungle land have been cleared, drained and planted to the ever amazing *Musae*. New seaports were opened, and railway lines were built to bring out the fruit to the ports. In time the railroads were extended inland, breaking the ancient isolation of the highland cities of the interior and bringing them into direct communication with the Caribbean coast. With the railroads came telegraph and telephone lines and the first network of radiotelegraph stations. Around the new ports and along the right of way of each of the new railroads, towns sprang up, and hundreds of plantations rose from the wilderness. One after another "divisions" of these plantations materialized, to keep pace with an apparently measureless demand for the number-one tropical fruit. Production for export doubled by the decade. In Jamaica, Honduras, and Panama bananas ordinarily account for 55 to 70 percent of the total value of all exports. In Guatemala, Costa Rica and Nicaragua, where bananas are second to coffee, they ordinarily account for 15 to 30 percent of all exports. What is decidedly more important, the banana industry, with all its complexities and despite its many faults and fallacies, has been and may long continue to be the open-sesame of Middle American communications. Further, it has served greatly to increase tropical wage scales and to train citizen workers in scores of valid trades and professions. It has provided both the incentives and the means to thousands of Middle American youths to find careers as doctors, engineers, chemists, accountants and superintendents—both within the framework of the industry and in other newly created fields made possible by its existence.

For the banana industry is carried on by skilled workers; it is by far the most specialized and the most highly mechanized of all major agricultures. The crop requires the installation and deft management of at least two tons of mechanical installations per producing acre. It requires incessant routines of spraying and highly mechanized irrigation. It requires a speedy and elaborate distribution setup: a basic business for at least 2,000 banana jobbers in the United States—an item of revenue for about 400,000 retail merchants.

In terms of fundamentals, the banana is a land-reclamation crop. It grows and bears best in hot, wet valleys where the soil is rich but usually more or less uninhabitable. The first endeavor of the banana industry becomes the job of changing lowland swamps and jungles to productive farms and livable communities. This transformation of tropical wilderness is a feat and responsibility for which there is no temperate-zone equivalent. During the pioneering era of the United States, for example, our own forefathers were usually able to claim homesteads and begin farms with no particular resources except ax, hoe, team and plow, strong bodies and willingness to work. Thus equipped a man could select a few acres of suitable land, build himself a log cabin, fell trees and brush during the winter, plant a first crop the next spring, then gradually extend and develop his holding.

But in wet, tropical lowlands a man can rarely stand alone against the jungle. That is why, through the centuries, so much of the most fertile lands of the American tropics have remained in swamp-pestered jungle. Usually the few people of such lands live along the river banks, since only the narrow fringes of river banks are sufficiently well drained to

permit field crops to grow. Away from the river banks the
jungle reigns; sometimes wildly luxurious and wildly beautiful; rarely profitably productive, frequently harboring ruinous diseases, and/or perpetuating severe isolation.

The banana industry's primary job is the development of
valid farm sites from the unproductive wilderness—not the
exploitation of fertile lands that are ready set for profitable
use. The best proved procedure for changing valueless jungles to valuable banana farms begins with elaborate surveys
of topography, soils, and possible railroad and drainage sites.
Then river ports, airfields, hospitals, work camps, workmen's
quarters, field clinics and supply depots must be built in the
wilderness. The next indispensable task is that of establishing drainage systems. Seaports must be made ready and
railroads must be built to link them with each developed
plantation. Reliable supplies of drinking water must be developed. Scores and hundreds of permanent buildings must
be raised. Field sanitation must be instituted, farms located,
drainage systems completed, bridges and roads made ready,
churches, schools, and other public buildings raised and put
to use.

When the time comes to change the jungle tracks to farms,
the dense brush is first cleared away and the jungle fields are
spaced for banana rows—as a rule the plantings are "squared"
at fourteen-foot intervals. Then "bits" or selected cuts of the
bulbous roots or rhizomes are planted in hand-dug holes and
carefully covered with a few inches of soil. Finally the trees
and giant vines must be felled and the litters cleaned away or
burned.

When first lusty shoots appear, immediate cultivation is
required, usually with the machete or all-purpose working
knife of the tropics, since the young plants are easily killed
by the crowding vegetation. As the plant begins to grow,
additional investments and services become necessary or at
any rate advisable. Nowadays the new plantings must be

protected against destructive fungi, such as *Cercospora musa zimm,* a virulent leaf-destroying round spore that causes sigatoka, a disease that has recently threatened the survival of all the Middle American banana industry; a disease that has long since destroyed the banana industry throughout most of the eastern tropics. ("Sigatoka" is a corruption of "Singatoka," the name of a once famous but now demised banana valley area of the Fijis.) Protection against ruining fungi and insect commandos calls for the permanent installation of elaborate spray equipment which requires that the banana fields be permanently girded with pipelines and dotted with heavily powered pumping stations, and manned by numerous spraying crews who have the job of making the rounds of every banana plant once, twice or even three times monthly (a capable two-man spray crew if well equipped can ordinarily cover about five acres per day). Finally, nowadays the banana crop usually requires irrigation, for otherwise the harvests may slough away or vanish entirely during the dry season, and the nature of banana marketing is such that the fruit must be harvestable every day of the year, Sunday and other holidays included. The crop requires heavy irrigation. Overhead irrigation is superior to the surface type, due to the immense leaf surfaces and other botanical peculiarities of the crop—hence elaborate and costly overhead irrigation has come to be still another prerequisite of banana agriculture; systems of spray towers, each topped with a revolving nozzle which throws hand-tailored rains over a circle of two or more acres of banana plantings; the equivalent of an inch or more of rainfall each day with no allowance or charge for the myriads of rainbows.

Much money must be spent, frequently millions or even tens of millions of dollars, before a single stem of bananas can be harvested. The cost of bringing one acre of jungle land into valid banana production is not easy to compute. But the cost is inevitably high; greater than that of any other principal crop.

In any case the cost is too great to warrant the casual or arbitrary abandonment of banana lands. When planted and brought to bearing, every diligent effort is made to keep the crop in bearing. But sometimes this is impossible. Occasionally climatic changes or the ruinous frequency of hurricanes or storms force the cessation of the banana crop. Sometimes, too, banana plantings succumb to the one still incorrigible disease enemy—the Panama disease, caused by a virulent root parasite which, being below the soil surface, remains inaccessible in terms of fungicides.

Today the banana industry is, and must be, a well-correlated enterprise. In order to survive and serve its sources of supply, its distributive channels and its customers, operations of a banana company need to be sizable, spread over a large area of land and capable of coping with natural and economic exigencies inherent to the industry. Such natural phenomena as plant diseases, hurricanes, floods, tropical storms, the time and place of whose occurrence in any one area cannot be foretold, can be met only by widespread operations. Some years the banana crops over a wide area are reduced or wiped out by natural calamities, while other areas produce bountifully. But at all times the life of the banana industry depends on producing and delivering regular and ample supplies of the fruit to the developed markets.

To transport Middle America's decisive banana crop to its many distant markets requires large merchant fleets of fast, specially designed and equipped refrigerated vessels, capable of handling the peak production of all banana-producing countries. The shipping service must be supplemented by widespread sales and service organizations and facilities throughout the consuming countries. The necessary merchant fleets must be so composed and operated that the needed complement of ships can be diverted easily to any port where they are required to move the maximum banana harvest of any producing area at any time.

When climatic disasters or other ruinous natural enemies destroy the harvest of one producing region, other banana-producing areas take up the slack. When ships cannot load banana cargo in one country, or can secure only a part cargo, there are other banana supplies with which the ships can load or fill out a load to maintain the necessary flow of marketable fruit. It is only by this wide diversification of source of supply that the banana industry survives. Fortunately the banana-producing organization in any given country can, and for the most part does, adjust its work policies to comply with the laws, the specific needs, the social and traditional usages of a particular country.

The correlation between the banana crop and other great crops of Middle America becomes ever more apparent. The banana crop remains the productive spearhead of man's stand against the wilderness. Middle America's former banana lands can be, and today by the tens of thousands of acres they are being, planted to other crops. Particularly along the north coast of Honduras thousands of acres of former banana lands are being returned to citizen farmers. Throughout much of Central America railroads, towns, hospitals, schools and various other facilities—built originally to foundation or otherwise carry the banana industry—are now being used directly in the introduction and establishment of more diverse crops for greater numbers of citizen farmers. This is apropos of principal needs that are certain to remain and to continue. The term "banana republic" is sorely outdated. In Middle America, as elsewhere, a one-crop agriculture is almost certainly a tragic fallacy. Diversification of crops is a prime fundamental of solvent agriculture in the tropics or out.

CHAPTER SIX

❧ ～～❧

FROM EARTH GROW THE PEOPLE

First and above all else Middle America is agricultural. The decisive majority of its people live on and from the lands—in the low valleys and jungle edges, on plateau lands, mesas, mountainsides and mountaintops. In the Caribbean world of today and tomorrow, as in the Mayan world of 1,000 or 5,000 years ago, the real and decisive history of Middle America is written on the varied faces of producing fields, forests and range lands.

There is no good reason to believe this will change markedly. As agriculture is stabilized and improved, as and if the proprietary citizen farmer can be made more secure and more productive of salable goods, local manufacturing, air, ship and rail transportation, labor fronts and home services of governments can be expanded and improved. But agriculture remains the great denominator without which all talk of a better life for the Caribbean countries is sheer academic theorizing.

Therefore, I here repeat the belief that no appraisal of the Caribbean nation which neglects the past, present and future agricultures can possibly be sufficient. But the good earth of Middle America, however fertile and versatile, cannot of itself erase all the persisting problems and dangers that are common to the Caribbean countries. For these nearer American nations are also warring nations in a war-shocked world. They face many ominous forces which if unopposed can enslave them economically, if not politically. One of these premier enemies is that rather insidious word "cartel."

An unusually capable summary of this particular scourge of tropical peoples was offered by Mr. Robert Reuben, of the Washington staff of Reuters Agency, who recently wrote:

Unless there is a radical change soon, the people will win the war on the battlefields but will have neither the opportunity nor the understanding to build a people's peace. The peace will be built, not by the people, but by individuals who have dominated it in the past, the only ones who are scientifically and in detail preparing for the re-establishment of a world economic order. These are the international industrialists who through their cartel agreements in the past have already established a "super-government," an international organization that dominated the common man as much as any political super-government can in the near future.[1]

The previous chapter offers a summary of certain proved or potential crop exports from Middle America. Separately and as a whole these crops are enormously important to the present and future of Middle America and all the American tropics. But inevitably, other crops are needed for enduring agrarian balance: food and subsistence crops and most particularly livestock.

Gardens, home orchards, and fields of corn and beans and other edible annual crops have been and will be grown. But livestock population is one of the most urgent challenges now facing the American tropics. The issue is not one of theoretic clashes between vegetarians and meat eaters. Rather the issue is simply the well-proved fact that meat-eating people and a people adequately supplied with milk, butter, cheese and other dairy products—also with leather and wool—are definitely healthier and happier than the habitual victims of the

[1] *The New Republic*, Vol. 109, No. 15, October 11, 1943, pp. 476–8.

starch-cereal diets that provide no wool for clothing, no leather for shoes and no other of the many valuable products derived from livestock establishment. Furthermore, livestock farmers are almost invariably better farmers than are those who do not grow livestock, since animal husbandry and livestock resources are at the same time creative attributes and fundamentals to the conservation of human health and productive soil.

Middle America today does not have nearly enough meat to fulfill minimum nutrition needs. Domestic supplies of milk and dairy products are tragically insufficient. There is a perennial shortage of leather and wool. Routines in basic agriculture have been gravely hampered by lack of sufficient livestock. The supply of milk and beef cattle, chickens, hogs and sheep is most inadequate, and has always been so. To make matters worse the breed standards of existent livestock are unfortunately low. But love for the animal emerges as a significant motif in this new age of Pan-American work. In a basic sense of the word, man has always been "animal-minded"—from Old Testament days when citizens measured wealth and political importance in terms of flocks, through the Middle Ages when titles and ownership of lands were strongly pegged with animal properties, to our own frontier days when the pioneer's prosperity waxed or waned in terms of cattle, horses, sheep or swine.

Today about half of the entire farm income of the United States is animal money—from beef, pork, dairy products, poultry, mutton, wool or other animal materials. In Middle America only 10 to 15 percent of farm income is from animals. As United States soils grow poorer the proportion of animal income grows greater, since an animal crop represents the minimum drain on land fertility. But the new age of the animal cannot be appraised as cold economy. It is also broadly social. It involves the inveterate creative urge of most Americans. If one writes a great poem or story, or paints a superb picture, or organizes a great and successful business, or perfects some worthwhile service to mankind, he is entitled to the premier reward of creator's satisfaction. Nowadays more and more millions of Americans are beginning to realize comparable delight and adventure in directing the mysterious pigments of blood and the magic clays of chromosomes toward developing a more perfect living animal than ever walked before.

Throughout these Americas more and more millions of acres of the less productive field lands are on their way toward becoming grazing lands. Great spheres of the cotton-ridden United States South now look to livestock for agrarian salvation. Mexico, Cuba, Costa Rica, Guatemala and the Dominican Republic all show distinguished progress in the raising of purebred or good-grade cattle—beef breeds and milk breeds. Here in the United States, Iowa, once the greatest of our grain states, now becomes the greatest of our hog states. The once great cattle empire of Montana, Idaho, and Wyoming is returning to life as a great sheep empire.

As continuous field culture saps the fertility of soils, good farmers of many of the Americas are drawing on livestock as a means of saving the precious tons of soil chemicals. Doubly important to Middle America is the fact that practically speaking the livestock grower is a manufacturer as well as a farmer. Animals become his productive machines. Grains and grasses are his manufacturing materials with which he can produce beef, pork, wool, milk or other foods that are, generally stated, more nutritious and more valuable than the same weights of grains or other direct food crops. Thus livestock can atone in some measure for Middle America's scarcity of machinery. Also livestock is a perennial crop which serves to bring about a longer tenure of land by the individual farmer, which makes for a more secure farm establishment.

From a census standpoint, man is now the most numerous and commonplace of all "higher" forms of animal life—however sardonic the adjective "higher" may now seem. In the United States we have about twice as many people as cattle, about two and a half times as many people as sheep, three times as many people as swine, and ten times as many people as horses. In Middle America the ratio of people to productive animals is approximately three times that current in the United States.

The United States is the greatest livestock nation. Though Australia once had more than twice as many sheep as the United States now has, though China had formerly almost three times as many hogs, and British India about three times as many cattle, the United States is leader in livestock as a composite resource. The United States has a world-famed assortment of eight national breed record associations for beef cattle, six for dairy cattle, sixteen for sheep, thirteen for swine, five for draft horses, seven for light horses, two for goats, one for donkeys and two for ponies. For some years a beneficial trickle of purebred livestock, particularly dairy and beef cattle, has been proceeding from the United States to the nations of Middle America, particularly Costa Rica, Cuba, Mexico and Guatemala. It is now comparatively well proved that purebred livestock can be grown successfully in most areas of Middle America.

But there are several good reasons why livestock resources of Middle America are still comparatively poorly developed. The transport of breeding animals is costly and difficult. Inadequate developments of hydroelectric and other power resources perpetuate serious problems in refrigeration. Eating habits of the majority publics have been molded by stern deprivations. Millions of our nearer southern neighbors have never had the opportunity to learn to use and like milk. Millions have never seen a purebred milk cow. The imported livestock frequently meet serious problems in becoming adapted to tropical grasses and rain conditions, and are frequently stricken with parasitic enemies and microorganic enemies to which they have little or no immunity. Thus, the scarcity of desirable breeding animals continues as a key difficulty in the development of needed livestock within the American tropics. It is an impediment that must somehow be overcome. An earlier chapter mentioned briefly the impressive new argosy of animal fertility, which is called artificial insemination. Reliable records prove that artificial insemination has made possible the successful breeding of as many as 15,000 ewes from one ram, as many as 1,000 cows from the same bull, or several hundred mares from the same stallion, during a single year. This new expedience of animal propagation holds tremendous possibilities for benefiting Middle America.

Russia deserves the credit for having pioneered this great new development in the livestock industries, but United States contributions are also important. First United States experiments were begun as early as 1930 and were principally directed toward horse population, particularly on progressive ranches of the Far West. More recently United States interest in artificial insemination has been directed toward milk cattle. A first co-operative association for artificial insemination of milk cattle was established in New Jersey in 1938 by E. J. Perry, State Dairy Specialist with Rutgers University. The venture met with almost instant success, and there are now at least fifty of these artificial insemination co-operatives within the United States, with a combined membership of about 5,000 dairy farmers who register a total of at least 53,000 milk cows in 22 states.

Artificial insemination is of particular value to small farmers, to operators of small milk herds of no more than twenty head, to those farmers who are able to maintain only a few

Middle America Information Bureau

The Rhizomes or Seed Stock of the
Banana Plant

Middle America Information Bureau

Loading Bananas with Conveyor,
Honduras

Bringing Fruit by Mule to Loading Platform, Honduras

Middle America Information Bureau

Middle America Information Bureau

A Plantation Schoolhouse Maintained by the United Fruit Company

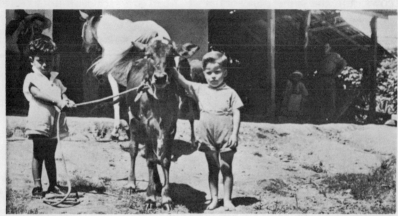

Photo by Iris Woolcock

Costa Rica's Younger Generation Helps Tend the Calves and Colts

Costa Rica Coffee Tree   Coffee in Bloom, Costa Rica

Photo by Iris Woolcock

dozen sheep and only one or two mares. It is noteworthy that about four-fifths of all milk farms in the United States keep fewer than eighteen cows, that approximately three-fourths of our entire sheep resources are produced on farms with fewer than thirty head of sheep, and that approximately 90 percent of the horse and mule population of the United States are on farms with fewer than four draft animals apiece. It seems probable that in Middle America as a whole 90 percent or more of all milk cattle are to be classed as family milk cows, and the same percentage of sheep are grown in flocks of fewer than thirty head. In all the Americas a permanent barrier to good livestock development is the costliness and scarcity of purebred sires for small farms. Many experts believe the only way the American tropics can ever develop competent livestock resources is by way of the family milk cow, the small flock of sheep or poultry or swine. By means of artificial insemination a minimum number of registered or otherwise superior breed animals can establish, improve and otherwise build up these modest holdings of livestock— throughout a community or country.

Animal breeding by means of artificial insemination substantially reduces the hazards of transferable disease of cattle and other livestock. It simplifies the mating of crippled animals that are otherwise valuable, also the mating of extremes in size. It avoids, or at least reduces, the cost and trouble of transporting breeding animals. In the tropics the transportation of breed animals is particularly costly and hazardous. The expedience of artificial insemination increases greatly the breeding range of a given valuable sire.

One experiment after another has impressively demonstrated the international possibilities of artificial insemination. It proved that mating of animals can be accomplished regardless of thousands of miles of intervening space, and that aviation is the indispensable transport medium for such insemination practice. It clearly indicated that by means of plane transport and low-temperature preservation of semen the great reservoir of livestock now existing in the United States can be used to improve livestock resources throughout our hemisphere and perhaps throughout most of the world. Since 1939 students of artificial breeding have perfected many improvements in the long-range transport of the life-creating fluid.

As war-pummeled agricultures seek refurbishment without which many nations cannot endure, livestock population is one of the graver problems in agricultural rehabilitation. If breeding animals must be developed for use on every livestock-growing farm, a costly lapse is certain to occur in re-establishing the production of meat, milk, wool and many other life-sustaining animal products. Livestock is not a seasonal crop. A cattle generation is five or six years; a horse or draft-animal generation eight to twelve years; a poultry, swine or sheep generation three to four years. Continued development and practical application of artificial insemination can certainly reduce these intervals of animal production—to three or four years in the instance of cattle; two or at most three years for sheep and hogs; and not more than five or six years for draft animals.

In any case the feat of refurbishing and reconstructing livestock population is of distinguished importance to all the Americas. There is vital correlation between animal crops and field crops; and nations frequently thrive when, if, and because their barnyards thrive.

Whether the locale be the United States, the Netherlands Indies or Middle America, successful and economic production also must be suited to the distinctive temperaments of the peoples who effect it. Inevitably human and emotional resources require consideration: the decisive races of Mid-

dle America; the Middle American lust for freedom from
alien interference; the essential place of womankind, the
church; indeed all the indispensable factors that go into the
Middle American way—an abstract resource that calls for indigenous interpretation, also specific recollections.

It was a hot day in Honduras and we were all sitting in
the shade gazing at the brims of our hats and waiting for the
sweet oranges to fall from the trees down into our laps.
Finally the doctor from Guatemala summoned energy to rise
and pick an orange. After considerable deliberation the engineer from Costa Rica did the same. But the señor from
the Dominican Republic said—no—that picking oranges is
woman's work. Then he conceded, graciously, and with many
and graceful gestures, that it is all very well to depend on the
woman so long, of course, as she understands who wears the
pants of the household . . .

Both the Guatemalan and Costa Rican smiled knowingly.
The latter patted the gran señor's shoulder and said: "My esteemed friend, it makes no enduring difference who wears the
pants. The important thing is who runs the home, the family
and the country. Here in these Americas of ours—in your
country as in my country—it is the women that do so much of
the running.

"Yes, Señor, first off our women run our homes. They teach
the daughters to work—even as the mothers learned to work,
for in our Americas it is most usually the women who learn
discipline." He yawned and stretched in the shape of a capital Y. "Then the beautiful sweet brides come forth from
cathedral doorways and begin to run their homes, the servants, the children, also their husbands. Having learned to run
all those so well, our women . . ." He gestured eloquently.
"Recall, your graces, that the great nation of Guatemala had
a woman governor more than four centuries ago—the great

Doña Beatrice de la Cueva who was proclaimed royal governor in 1541, some several generations before those solemn and graceless fishermen arrived at Plymouth Rock in the United States . . ."

The caballero from Costa Rica was growing eloquent. "When our women run our homes and our country they also run other great things such as our schools and magazines, and learned societies, and health services. Indeed . . ."

The Guatemalan doctor nodded understandingly: "The great United States is a man's country—that thinks and talks like a man. But our Americas here—they are thinking, talking, and planning in the way of women. In the United States men are usually happier than women because there the women are the more spoiled. Here women are usually happier than men, for here the women are less spoiled."

The gran señor from the Dominican Republic interjected: "Nevertheless, Señores, here in these Americas to the south we men are the masters. In my home, in your home, what happens? We can come home any hour of the night—and next morning nothing is said about it. If after midnight we begin to hunger in the stomach, or have merry friends with us, we have only to walk into the kitchen, open the what-you-call-it —refrigerator—and commence to nibble whatever appeals to our hungering stomachs. When morning comes, coffee is brought to us in bed, and our shoes are polished brightly, even though our womenfolk have already gone about their work in the patio, the washrooms, the nursery, or the sewing room. And as we walk out to converse in the plaza, my doña she smiles at me and says, 'Good morning, my great lover, I hope that your grace rises happily.'" The gran señor sighed with deep contentment and glanced at me. "Notice how the face of our esteemed North American visitor now begins to turn the color green with what is called envy." So we all sat in thoughtful silence until the deep cool shade began to slip away from us. Then one by one we sighed, got to our feet, and walked into the house for a bit of morning refreshment.

Most of America is still blessed with a great and old social structure wherein women do much of the relating, and men do their legitimate share of the ornamenting. There is graciousness and dignity in this continuing establishment, and there is the continuing reality that in Middle America, women and love are practically indispensable to successful agriculture or any other valid institution.

As a rule, love in the American tropics is a creative art played with dexterity and felicity. The climate, the tropical moon, the perfume of flowering trees and the wavery music of marimbas play their parts. But active flirtation usually begins it, as one notes from the illustrious tradition of window shopping for studied and traditional technique. A girl stands gazing into a shop window, watching her own reflection and the first image she perceives is of the approaching señor who, by an odd happenstance, is interested in the same window at the identical time. The man approaches, and for a time both stand together gazing into the window. Most probably neither has the faintest idea what is there being displayed—whether cough medicines, ladies' hats or horse collar. But presently the boy says something, bowing slightly, and the girl says something, making a slight curtsy. Then they walk together and look at the next window and the next one. Then presently they walk away side by side and all the windows be damned.

But this tropical romance has qualities of discipline. Chaperons are still standard and persistent fixtures. Engagements are relatively formal and long, and in contrast to United States standards divorces are rare. The latter item is worth noting. The prevailing religious faith of Middle America has much to do with it. But Middle American women also have much to do with it. Having once got her man the señora doesn't favor letting him go. She is definitely inclined to keep him as a husband and as a lover. She uses wiles and coquetries, but more important, she is a grand mistress of the art of management with the velvet glove and the endearing smile. This *Señora del Sur* is inclined to believe that men are necessary. In general she does not belittle or criticize her man in the presence of friends or in public, for that would be a confession of her own incompetence as a wife and homemaker; for this sister from points south knows her place and sees to it that her place is just about exactly where she wishes it to be. That is why every nation below the Rio Grande can boast a distinguished gallery of famous women and why the galleries are ever growing; why women are among the outstanding editors, poets, physicians and surgeons, lawyers, research scientists, clinic founders, chemists, mechanical engineers, storekeepers, stylists and a hundred other great careerists; why Middle American women are shapers of professions, of religion and agriculture.

The churches of Middle America, also rather definitely feminine in clientele, are deeply important to Middle America as stabilizers of people and establishments, and as living components of a great faith and several great cultures. No art form expresses the inner spirit of these southern neighbors so ably as the church, and no other institution demonstrates more clearly significant mergings of past and present.

With all their failings and villainies the Spanish conquerors who came to the New World were great builders. Aided by the millions of talented Indians they builded in Middle America more than 12,000 churches, many of which rival or exceed in age, beauty and impressiveness the European cathedrals. The Middle American church is more than an adaptation of cloisters or cathedrals of old Spain or the Mediterranean burying grounds. It is also an indigenous and expressive resource of the genius and faith of millions of Middle American Indians.

When the Spaniards first came to the Caribbean lands they built churches to double as fortresses. The Franciscans built such churches on the hilltops and terraces where ancient Aztec temples had stood, and frequently they used the very stones of the razed temples. But later, after the need for defense was abated, the architectures of the Spanish renaissance were combined with Indian genius to produce the celebrated Mexican churrigueresque, or florid baroque, with its gracious geometric patterns in lime mortar stucco and its glazed polychrome tile, and hieroglyphs born of Indian history and Indian community life. Saints, cherubs, religious figures, pagan forms, and myriad geometric designs are carved in high relief on stone, as in the church of Santa Maria Tonantzintla, or the church of Atlixco, Puebla, Mexico; and frequently the stone or stucco work is painted pink, blue, yellow and ochre in gayest Indian mood.

In Middle America's churches the New World becomes as one with the old. A classic example is the great Cathedral of Mexico City, a cathedral built on the site of the main teocalli, or house of the god, of the Aztecs, using the very same stones.

Middle America's churches are numerous—in some places almost unbelievably so. For example, the little town of Cholula, Mexico, with no more than 3,000 people, has at least 300 churches—at one time the village boasted a church for each day of the year. And all the churches were built on or among the ruins of the pre-Columbian temples. Antigua, the old mountain capital of Guatemala, had more than fifty churches before the building of New England's first meetinghouse. And all nations of Middle America hold their rich legacies of churches into which is built great history.

Of the thousands of Cuban churches best known to architects as well as tourists is the Church of Havana, which was the one-time burial place of the great Christopher Columbus. Nicaragua's massive, deeply impressive Church de la Recolleccion at León is rich with Spanish-borne durability—a massive, deliberate strength reckoned to stand and stand forever.

The amazing, blood-splashed history of Panama is best told by its churches. One realizes this when he sees in old Panama City the famous golden altar of San José, carved of native mahogany and lavishly gilded. The story goes that when Morgan and his pirates came to loot the town the local padre summoned his faithful and quickly smeared the altar with white paint, so that the British gold snatcher would not be too readily tempted. Also in Panama City, one can see the ruins of the ancient Church of Santo Domingo, now vanished except for its astonishing flat arch. Made of brick, tile and cut stone, this arch is so flat and its curve so extremely slight that according to all the so-called "laws" of physics it should have tumbled down centuries ago. Yet without a keystone it continues to stand, even as the rest of the great church has long since sunk to ruin and debris. Perhaps this particular arch is generally symbolic of the Middle American church which has risen to endure and to serve through the centuries and to prove that man's spiritual life, and the creative expressions thereof, can endure even as man dies and even as the sins of man blacken and impede the efficacy of his shrines.

Middle America is preponderantly, almost unanimously Catholic. That church is important, indeed basic, to the agrarian cultures of these distinguished agrarian nations. The essential strength of the church is centered in women—the women of Middle America who are indispensable participants in what is and has long been in substantial part a woman's world, perpetuated by woman's work in the home, the church and the cultivated field.

CHAPTER SEVEN

DESTINY BY AIR

AIR freight transportation began in Middle America back in 1931 when common public opinion generally supported the theory that the mission of the airplane was to serve as eyes for ground troops and as artillery in war; to carry passengers sufficiently reckless or hopeless to ride in planes, and, where space and politics permitted, to carry letter mail and, in extreme emergencies, small quantities of express.

Nevertheless, in many countries many new airlines were being foaled. Dr. Thomas B. Pounds, a United States optician living in Honduras, had failed several times to establish a commercial passenger plane service in that particular frontier. But during 1931 he made a last brave try which he called the Transportes Aereos Hondureños. It consisted of a five-passenger Stinson plane, no maintenance facilities, and no pilot. Dr. Pounds journeyed to Mexico, where he employed a barnstorming former World War pilot from New Zealand; a personable individual who had also taught school, herded sheep and headed what was called—in the giddy twenties—a flying circus. Nevertheless, with his trade limited to passengers and occasional mail shipment, Dr. Pounds found it impossible to take in enough money to pay his pilots and to keep the plane in repair even though Yerex, an above-average mechanic, managed all the general and emergency repairs.

Within a few months Yerex and his assistant, Jim Woodburn, took over the plane in lieu of back pay, and early in 1932 formed TACA—Transportes Aereos Centro-Americanos—

which lengthened the flights and continued to prove that mail and passenger service did not earn profits in rural Central America. Woodburn withdrew from the venture. Yerex bought out his interest in the plane and resolved to try out the then fantastic idea of commercial freight transportation.

The demand for such a service was immediately evident. An income of $3,600 from the first month's operations was plentiful encouragement to the one-man, one-plane airline which ranged somewhat at random over the unique republic of Honduras. Before the year had passed, Yerex bought three more Stinsons, hired pilots, and set up a well-ordered maintenance station at Tegucigalpa, the Honduran capital. By the end of 1935, TACA had branched out beyond the borders of Honduras and had acquired a newborn airline in Guatemala and two in Nicaragua. TACA continued growing, until today the company serves more than 200 airports in Honduras, British Honduras, El Salvador, Nicaragua, Costa Rica, and Panama, operates 34 radio stations and employs 36 cargo planes which make regular flights over more than 7,000 miles of air routes in Middle America and links the mainland United States with mainland Central America. TACA today is the largest nonmilitary air freight carrier in the world.

As already pointed out, TACA became the great champion of the industry of chicle—the basic ingredient of chewing gum, America's number-one jaw exerciser. Petén is wild jungle land for the most part, thickly blanketed with forests, jungle and swamps. The chicle trees stand in the midst of the wilderness, extremely difficult of access—except by airplane. From Flores one plane can carry six tons of chicle a day—in three trips to Puerto Barrios on the Caribbean seacoast. A few years ago it took three pack trains of twenty mules each and five weeks of travel time to carry that same load from Flores to Barrios. Hundreds of the Indians who work the chicle trees in Petén have never seen a train or an automobile.

Yet, they know airplanes, and they travel by plane willingly and eagerly. TACA held the franchise for the Petén chicle run from its inception (in 1935) until 1940 when the concession was given to Aerovias de Guatemala, a subsidiary of Pan American Airways. During its first year of chicle transport, TACA carried 1,350,000 pounds from Petén to Puerto Barrios. When the franchise was surrendered, the cargo had grown to as much as 1,000,000 pounds a month.

In the early days TACA depended almost exclusively on the old Ford trimotors. Fourteen of them are still in service; rugged, versatile and in many ways well suited to the needs of tropical weather, terrain, and cargo needs. Besides the aging Fords, TACA now has Lockheeds, two-motor Condors, Bellancas, Travelairs, a Hamilton, a Lockheed Vega, a Stinson Gullwing, and a Burnelli "Flying Wing." Most of the planes are now equipped with roll-top doors to facilitate freight loading, and plane flooring is reinforced to support the heavy mining machinery, tractors, and similar freight that TACA carries regularly. The "Flying Wing" has characteristics that make it adaptable to the job requirements in Middle America, particularly lifting power for quick take-off with heavy loads (as much as eighteen tons—the equivalent of two heavy truckloads and a creditable cargo for jungle transports), where landing fields impress the nervous passenger as being about the size of a victory garden. TACA is now a part of Inter-American Airways—a holding company headed by Yerex and including British West Indian Airways—which flies the Dominican Republic and various British West Indies, and Aerovias Brasil.

Yerex and TACA are distinguished pioneer names in international air freight. Actually Pan American Airways opened passenger and mail routes into Middle America—specifically from Key West to Cuba and the Canal Zone—five years before TACA became a reality. Since then Pan American Airways has grown to first place in international commercial air transport. Passengers continue to account for about 80 percent of its cargoes, and from 60 to 65 percent of the gross revenue derived from all its 18,000 route miles of airways in the Caribbean area. During 1942 "Pan Am" inaugurated a fast "Stratoclipper" passenger and mail service between New Orleans and the Canal Zone and Guatemala. The trip between New Orleans and Guatemala City, which takes six days by rail via Mexico, now requires barely six hours by air. Over this "run" was flown a first all-freight cargo of Guatemalan rubber bound for United States war plants.

Pan American began its cargo operations in 1929, and two years later entered general express haulage which totaled 4,075 pounds during the first year. With its affiliates, including Panagra, Compania Mexicana de Aviacion, and KLM (a Dutch Indies line), Pan American handled 5,963,550 pounds of cargo in the first three months of 1943. Most Pan American planes are twenty-one-passenger Douglas DC-3's and fourteen-passenger DC-2's. Panagra, the South American subsidiary, has refitted all its DC-2's for exclusive cargo use. According to Juan T. Trippe, Pan American's president, the company plans to introduce larger and faster clippers on many of its routes after the war.

William A. M. Burden, Special Aviation Assistant to the United States Department of Commerce, estimates the current total of commercial air cargo in Middle America as well over three times that of the United States. The comparison in the table on page 205 between express and freight tonnage of TACA versus all United States domestic air carriers combined gives striking evidence of Middle America's air cargo development.

Air cargo has already been proved a vitally important factor in developing Middle America's economy. What it will amount to in the postwar trade period is an exciting subject—

	TACA (pounds)	U. S. Domestic Air Carriers (pounds)
1937	11,347,000	4,294,000
1938	15,373,000	4,727,000
1939	20,034,000	5,851,000
1940	27,817,000	7,700,000
1941	30,161,000	11,160,000
5-year total	104,732,000	33,732,000

a subject that causes aviation enthusiasts to forget to eat and tropical tramps to forget to drink. There is no sufficient reason for predicting that air freight will replace ocean shipping between the many Americas, or between the Middle Americas and Europe. But there is good reason to believe that air freight will vitally supplement ocean ship traffic; that it can and will substantially overcome the chronic shortage of railway mileage that is common to much of Middle America; and that it will play a tremendously important or even decisive role in the transport of tropical fruits and other perishable edibles; also fashion merchandises, medical and surgical goods, repair machinery and untold thousands of tons of other important goods. The trend is already apparent in the inauguration (in September, 1943) of the first exclusively air freight service between the United States and Guatemala.

Several agencies of the United States Government are sponsoring a training program, financed by the Defense Supplies Corporation, which aims to develop pilots, mechanics, and administrative engineers for inter-American aviation. More than 500 Latin-American young men have already been enrolled since the program began in 1941. The objectives are to meet the immediate problem of transporting strategic war materials from Latin America's fields and mines, and to train flyers for the important roles they will have in the future development of Latin America's local transport systems.

Aviation is already part of the essential productive life of Middle America. It is already erasing boundaries, both commercial and political, and building these Americas into one. More effectively by the passing month it links each American nation with the score of other American nations, and it ties the individual community of one America into a hundred or a thousand individual communities throughout any one or all of the Americas. One realizes this best while visiting a terminal airport.

One night recently while at the Miami, Florida, international airport, I pondered on specific evidences pertaining to these immense generalities. The air express was running fair to medium. Uniformed baggagemen were loading cargo into the hatches and "belly" compartments of a Pan American clipper that roars through southern skies at 240 miles per hour to make Panama in 6 hours. This particular four-motored silver giant is primarily for carrying passengers. But its freight compartments can load between 6,000 and 10,000 pounds of merchandise. The port manager tapped my elbow. "Rio plane is coming in!"

The loudspeaker system began to announce the arrival. We heard the humming of many motors and to the southeast we could see a high green wing light. The Rio clipper glided in like a mallard settling on a pond. She landed sixteen passengers and ninety-seven parcels. I joined the ground crew and helped "count off" the latter. About half of them were farm goods. There were cotton samples from Brazil, wool and wheat samples from Argentina, barley samples from Chile, fourteen coffee samples from Brazil, Colombia and Guatemala, cocoa samples from various parts of Central America; also corn, Brazil nuts, tobacco, and divi-divi (a tree pod used for tanning leather).

The air express agent said, "This here is an age of business by samples. You can't haul a coffee crop, or a wheat crop or a million bales of cotton by plane. Not yet, anyway; not while you wake up every morning with your carcass snowed under with priority forms. But you can at least fly the samples that sell the crops. We fly around 150 tons of these samples into Latin America every year." I followed him into the express sheds where packages from all over the United States were being loaded out for south flying. "Here are samples of United States wool and cotton flying to Guatemala. Here's some Ohio corn and Dakota wheat going down to Salvador where the folks can't seem to raise enough grain. Here's a shipment of Mississippi cotton seed flying to Brazil 2,000 miles up the Amazon. Here's samples of canned goods, cured meats, and tinned syrups going to Panama . . ." Samples of flour and meal from our Midwestern mills are being flown all over the hemisphere. Rice samples from Arkansas, Louisiana and South Carolina are being flown to many market centers in the other Americas.

The big airports at Miami clear around 60 percent of our plane traffic to Middle America. Most of the rest goes south from Brownsville, Texas, and Los Angeles. But plane traffic has penetrated every nation of this hemisphere; every capital and, to a greater or less extent, every producing area. Some months before Pearl Harbor the Northern Ohio Food Terminal at Cleveland demonstrated this fact in a casual way when the manager cartoned a prize assortment of Ohio-grown garden vegetables, shipped it by airliner to San Francisco, then by China clipper plane to a home-town boy serving in the United States Legation Marines in China—14,000 miles away. Before the war New York department stores featured such plane-hauled food luxuries as kangaroo-tail soup from Australia, smoked oysters from China, Cheshire cheese from Montreal, and green turtle paste from Key West. God alone knows what brash Fifth Avenue merchants will be devising for the new world ahead.

Air freight is inherently a world story. The global war has obviously and hugely increased and expanded the institution of airplane transport of heavy cargo, hoisting its volume a hundred or perhaps five hundredfold in half a decade, and causing the proposition to become crystal clear that aviation will substantially set the pace and mold the destinies of post-war commerce.

But from a standpoint of origin, air freight is distinctly a United States institution. It began on a November day in 1910 when Orville Wright and his pilot, Phil Parmelee, fueled Mr. Wright's "chicken crate" biplane at Dayton, Ohio, and took off for the sixty-five-mile hop to Columbus. The first freight was a fifty-pound bundle of bolt silk valued at a thousand dollars. It was assigned to fly in the passenger's lap; but the passenger voted to remain grounded and so permit the silk to fly beside Pilot Wright. A "Big Four" express train was to show the plane the way from Dayton to Columbus. The plane got ahead of the train and flew the sixty-five miles in seventy-one minutes, to set a world record for fast haul.

The venerable Cincinnati *Enquirer* pointed out editorially that the feat of Mr. Wright was not entirely original. The *Enquirer* revealed that in Egypt of 1100 B.C. the caliph of Cairo had himself supplied with air shipments of lush, sweet cherries that grew 400 miles down the Nile. The pre-Christian ward heeler directed his flunkies to wrap each cherry in a tiny silk bag and tie the bags to the legs of carrier pigeons which promptly flew homeward to the caliph's palace. A few score of pigeons thereby delivered His Eminence a bowl of cherries. The *Enquirer*, ever able in matters of natural history, suggested that any good healthy passenger pigeon could have flown faster than Orville Wright's winged chicken coop, 1910 model. Certainly this could not be said of the Mosquito Bomber or the Hell-Diver.

Air express was officially introduced to the United States

back in 1927 when a fast plane could fly from New York to San Francisco in thirty-three hours. Since 1927 the domestic volume of air express has gained about 12,000 percent. In the United States during 1940, the final year of official releases, 1,083,016 shipments of merchandise traveled by air express in the holds of 265 scheduled airliners serving 269 domestic airport cities and flying an average of about 325,000 miles per day within domestic boundaries. The average weight of the shipments was between seven and eight pounds, though some shipments weighed several thousands of pounds each. In the United States today air express flies in every direction and includes thousands of commodities—from bridal veils, Brazil nuts, porpoise milk and newsreels to human blood and stuffed lizards.

Its cargoes are almost endlessly varied. For example, a famous apiary in Medina, Ohio, has pioneered in air-shipping queen bees and apiary supplies to customers in Middle America and northern South America. Stover Apiaries of Mayhew, Mississippi, specializes in air-expressing Italian-type queen bees to the American tropics—flowery lands wherein beeswax and honey industries are becoming increasingly important. They pack one queen and ten workers in a small wooden case with rations of sugared water. Airline attendants are inclined to treat the bees with great respect. Not long ago a Guatemalan customer sent the Stover's a radiogram that read: "Predict that continued buying of Italian queens from Mississippi will sooner or later give us bees with strong Southern accents and Fascisti tendencies to join whichever side is winning."

Not long ago the pilot of a California-to-Florida plane was handed a box of 50,000 selected ladybugs. These were grown by the California Insectaries which specializes in developing parasites that attack harmful insects. Dr. W. A. Morrill, founder and president of the concern, ships between 40,-

000,000 and 50,000,000 insects by plane each year to more than a dozen American nations. Wasps are being air-expressed from South Africa to fight the red scale of California citrus. Recently the Texas State Health Department imported by air express twelve shipments of Anopheles (malaria) mosquito larvae from Tallahassee, Florida, to the Texas Malaria Laboratory, where state patients are receiving neuro-syphilitic treatment by means of malaria injection. While Florida mosquitoes were being flown to Texas, Georgia minnows were being flown to Massachusetts to eat Bay State mosquitoes. Puerto Rico lightning bugs are being air-flown throughout Caribbean sugar-cane areas to fight a cane root parasite that could easily become a serious menace to the sugar crops. Entomologist J. G. Meyers has discovered that a deepwater grass fly of the upper Amazon is an effective parasite enemy to the sugar-cane borer. He directs collection and shipment of the rare fly by Pan American planes, and recently flew an even million, packed in cartons of 10,000 each, from a point 2,800 miles up the Amazon to the island of Saint Kitts, British West Indies.

Hawaiian farmers have successfully introduced a type of fig from south China, but for years they were unable to make the plants bear. The flower of this fig must be fertilized by a tiny wasp (*Fiscus pestura*), and it appeared impossible to introduce the wasp to Hawaii. Today the wasp eggs are imbedded in ripe figs, wrapped in wax paper, packed in ice and flown 6,000 miles from Hong Kong to Honolulu.

Formidable pamphlets of statistics tell that at least 1,000 different merchandises are now being flown to market. There are such entries as 300 pounds of cholera serum carried by plane from Washington to Caracas for use of the Venezuelan Government; tens of thousands of tons of essential military supplies; thousands of pounds of blood plasma contributed by United States citizens to fighting men on a score of battle fronts; hundreds of tons of medical supplies; auto and engine parts and machinery repairs; not to mention live humming-birds flown from flowery Cuba to the Zoological Park at Washington; or Hawaiian plane shipments of ti, palm lily leaf for making grass skirts for hulu dancers in New York; boxes of snow recently flown from New Hampshire to Havana—the first snow that many Cubans ever beheld; mangoose livers, human ashes, millions of doses of vaccines; strawberry plants to Central America; live snails; Panama pearls; millions of dollars' worth of gold flown from mines and smelters in Cen-tral and South America; and, most touching of all, a plane shipment of artificial eyebrows from New York to Hollywood where the motion-picture industry was still again needing.

This reporter has been particularly impressed by aviation's place as winged mercury to agriculture—strategic seeds and planting stocks; young trees and tender seedlings; staple and emergency foods. To the immensely productive agrarian lab-oratory of Middle America, air transport harbingers a better and more plenteous world. For the airplane is the friend and champion of the tropics and tropical people; a champion which the countries of Middle America have accepted ea-gerly and without hesitation—without waiting the slow and toilsome sequence of horseback to covered wagon, to stage coach, to train, to auto, and finally to plane. Quite literally the people of the American tropics have begot and proved air transportation. Bravely and eagerly they have changed from burro back to hedgehopping, rough-flying aviation.

Thus, they have earned a place and right in this superb resource which is both a protective and a creative asset. Capa-ble transport aviation is a pre-eminent defense against the blights that have been wrought by international cartels, whose productive strategy is that of holding people and crops and seeds immobile, thus creating crop monopolies in fixed locales. Transport aviation is equally the enemy of that cankerous disease of ethics that expresses itself as would-be "nationalism" or "supernationalism." Also, the birth and the brilliant growth of transport aviation are a valuable immunization against another would-be economy called "super-Americanism," which would preach that the Americas alone should prosper even while the rest of the world starves and rots. This mighty new age of air transport thwarts this caliber of lunacy. Practically speaking air hauls can no longer be limited solely to the Americas; for no habitable point on the earth's crust is now more than sixty air hours from the farthest distant habitable point, and the air mocks all boundary lines.

One is almost constantly reminded of this fact as one reads the newspapers. This writer recently gained a still more vivid realization of the cosmopolitan genius of air transportation while visiting the great new Douglas factory near Oklahoma City. This giant plant, the newest and biggest of its kind, is devoted to assembly-line manufacture of heavy transport aircraft for use throughout the world. On the mile-long assembly line, which is temporarily manned by two women for every man, one watches the transport craft begun with a single steel beam and built by a forthright series of time-clocked "move-ups" to a complete, three-motor or four-motor, eighty-ton aeronautical colossus, devised from warerooms crammed with more than 400,000 different structural items and from huge furnaces, electrical shops and tooling lines all beneath the same roof and within the same windowless infinity of "breathing walls." Test pilots wait at the factory doorway; as soon as a giant transport plane is pronounced complete the test pilot climbs to the controls and the tractor man drags for the vast cemented fields which eighteen months before were growing corn; the pilot warms the stiff new motors, taxis, then lifts for the initial and decisive test flight.

He returns the plane for final conditioning and for "special equipment," such as specially built landing gears for the miry hills of China or the sodden valleys of India, or special hot plates for the British crews who will inevitably require a spot of tea. Within easy distance of this great factory are a major base for ferry transport to and from all the continents of the earth and a major repair and overhaul station where bombers and heavy aircraft from all fighting fronts of the earth are flown in for overhaul, alteration, or repair of battle injuries.

On the latter field I viewed two of the bombers that General Doolittle led on the first heroic attack on Tokyo. Near them were battle-scarred heavy craft that had bombed Berlin; others that had survived forty or more combat missions over Europe; still others that had flown and fought over India, Burma, the Solomons and various other South Pacific spheres. In most instances the monstrous battle planes had been flown directly from theaters of war to this remote, far-inland spot which until so recently had been a parched cornfield in a tranquil midland of Oklahoma.

As one views the salty hieroglyphs of combat missions, the records of enemy planes destroyed and ships sunk, the plane guns and artillery, the huge and deathly efficient bombracks, the surprisingly expansive cargo maws, one sees the sky fortresses as peaceful carriers, serving the scores of nations, providing the goods of trade, knowledge, health, and the happier life for peace which is so infinitely more forthright and rational than war.

The changed cornfields of Oklahoma and the many other newly built war plants now more or less discernible from Maine to California and back again; the hundreds of thousands of young men of the Americas who fly in war and would much rather fly in peace; the ever astonishing American genius to build and to move; the tens of thousands of magnificent war planes that can in some measure be adapted to peaceful transport; the magnificent new factories that have built for war and are doubly eager to build for peace—all merge into an impressive if still vague montage of a world without boundaries and with the realities of peace and justice that are born of plenty.

Middle America, like aviation, belongs immutably to such a world, for come what may, Middle America and aviation belong together. This is no theorist's dreams. TACA and Pan American Airways, and their varied and respective associates, have provided history-making proofs. Other great business firms now follow suit—United Fruit, American Export, Braniff Airways and many other builders and dealers in the absolutes and tangibles.

Both commercial and military history have proved that air transport needs Middle America. There is no shadow of doubt that Middle America needs air transport: the planes to link the lushly productive fields and the magnificent tropical frontiers that are otherwise destined to remain shrouded in isolation; air transport that can effectively join seashore and mountains, which railroads and highways (for good and varied reasons) could never join; aviation that creates value where value never existed before and otherwise could never be. For Middle America, aviation spells the valid distribution of both the seed and the tools of production; the road to market which is also the way to peace.

While helping to pioneer and develop the vast productive resources of Middle America, air transport furnishes the strongest and surest defense resource for the Americas. Potentially the Pan-American jungles, bushlands and mountains are among the best natural defenses that God ever gave people. The nations of Middle America are not and most probably can never be uniformly settled by people. A great part of the jungles and mountain lands are destined to remain as such.

That a hundred miles of jungle can stop any army afoot or awheel is an old tropical proverb.

With good reason, the sixteen nations of the American tropics are more than ever anxious to place secure handles on their jungle shields, which are also protective shields for the United States. Practically every American, literate or otherwise, has been reminded lately that the Natal-Pernambuco coast front of Brazil is only about 1,800 miles—5 or 6 hours by bomber—from the Dakar coast of Africa. During the busy World War II years Brazil, Colombia, Venezuela, Peru, Ecuador and most of the Middle American governments have worked and planned brilliantly to make more maneuverable and profitable their defense resources in interlocking jungle, wastelands and great untenanted mountains.

Time and time again during past centuries the Pan-American jungles have blocked the course of ruining invaders. From sea, land and air these same jungles continue to serve as strong shields against attack. With the probable exceptions of the Soviet Army and the horseback legions of Genghis Khan, the greatest masters of mobile warfare were the Spanish conquistadors. With no more than a few thousand horsemen and foot soldiers their ranks swept across two-thirds of the Western Hemisphere and established lines of forts and administrative outposts stretching from Tierra del Fuego to Panama, through Mexico and far into our own West, including the ever strategic California coast line. Spain's conquerors of the New World were great masters of "war of motion." Again and again they spread their audacious handfuls of men into nipping claws which vanquished the Indian defenders of millions of square miles; and many of the Indians were great strategists in their own right.

But even the most skilled and ruthless of conquistadors could never really conquer the jungles. When they tried they either met hidden death or ruin from disease or found themselves hurled back by resilient and powerful jungle walls. They learned at first hand that men and beasts can starve in the jungle and that great armies can be wiped out by flood, thornbush or invisible but ever deadly microorganisms of disease. The political and military leaders of present-day Middle America know these stories well. And they also know the danger of armed invasions which are ever possible during the years ahead. They are well aware of the virtual impossibility of sea defense for their incorrigibly long Pan-American coast lines. They know, too, that many hundreds of thousands of square miles of the Pan-American jungles and adjoining frontiers still wait to be charted, manned and made useful; and, more important, that effective use of the jungle shields calls not only for a new all-hemispheric defense strategy but also for a new school of productive economy—both heavily dependent on this new age of air transport.

Obviously the best and surest way to fortify a jungle is to make it fruitful and livable, or at minimum effectively accessible to those who hold and cherish it. In the past we have been inclined to picture defense outposts as more or less sterile territory. As a rule potatoes do not grow on parade grounds, and corn and hogs do not thrive on artillery ranges. But the global war has already delivered some impressive lessons in competent and incompetent jungle warfare—the decisive strategies of verdant waste spaces. In particular our enemies the Japs have wielded jungle shields with impish skill to seize nearly 3,000,000 square miles of tropical earth—adding about 120,000,000 new subjects—and temporarily making Nippon the second largest empire of the earth. Japan's conquests have demonstrated that jungles without shields' value are pitiable liabilities to incompetent defenders. Our American neighbors have observed and absorbed the several morals of this terrific lesson. They know that the effective use of their jungle shields requires that the said shields must have firm handles in the form of strategically located towns and cities; health centers, airports and capable aircraft; also railroads, highways and trails, river shipping and ocean shipping. Those are big, hard orders, but they are indispensable to the broad view of hemispheric security, and they were ably stated at the 1942 Conference of American Ministers at Rio by the great and then Undersecretary of State Sumner Welles, who said in part:

My Government believes that we must now begin to execute plans vital to the human defense of the hemisphere, for the improvement of health and sanitary conditions, the provision and maintenance of adequate supplies of food, milk and water, and the effective control of insect-borne and communicable diseases. The United States is prepared to participate in and to encourage complimentary agreements among the American republics for dealing with those problems of health and sanitation.

This is a superb approach to the validation of jungle shields. But aviation is the number-one co-ordinator and supplementer of that ever-present hyphenated need of the American tropics—transportation-communications.

CHAPTER EIGHT

~~~~~~~~~~

CARIBBEAN DANGER ZONE

ONE bright Saturday several thousand persons sat in the stands of the arena at Tegucigalpa, mountain capital of Honduras, waiting for the bullfight to begin. It was a glorious occasion. Not only were they to see four good bulls dispatched, but also by paying the price of admission they were helping to erect the nation's first tuberculosis sanitarium. Sponsors of the fight were the doctors of Honduras and the editorial staff of the Honduran medical magazine.

The day started well. The banderilleros flung their darts. The picadors drove their spears. Then—catastrophe! The matadors, whose job it was to slay the beasts, fled. The crowd began to boo and stamp, and finally to clamor for the return of their money. In the box, where the doctors sat unhappily watching their sanitarium vanish in this storm of popular disapproval, a broad-shouldered young medico, Dr. Ricardo Aguilar-Meza, stirred and then suddenly sprang to the railing. An older doctor grasped his arm and shouted, "Idiot, you can't fight bulls."

Dr. Ricardo bowed. "In this case," he said, "fighting bulls is the same as fighting tuberculosis." With that he leaped into the ring. A moment later another young doctor, Augusto Monteroso, followed.

The crowd roared its applause. This was a show rarely vouchsafed an audience—doctors operating on bulls in the arena with cape and sword. The operation was successful and the crowd carried them off on its shoulders in triumph. Dr. Ricardo explained his triumph by saying: "It's safer to fight a bull than to run away from him . . ."

The story of the bullfight is the keynote to the character of a great Middle American doctor, a man who has repeatedly demonstrated his ability to accomplish the impossible.

When as a young man he expressed a desire to become a dentist, the wiseacres chorused, "Impossible! You are too poor." He became a dentist.

As a dentist, he looked beyond the teeth and beheld disease-worn bodies; he swore he would become a doctor. Again the chorus spoke: "Where will you get the money? Where will you get the time?" He became a doctor.

Again as a doctor, he felt the need of surgery. And once more he climbed the wall of the impossible, traveling to New York to acquire an art which he has employed in thousands of cases—some of them near miracles of surgical dexterity.

His greatest triumph, however, arose out of his love for children and his desire to see them cared for properly. One day when the physician was still a young man, a farmer from a remote hillside brought in a sick child. Dr. Ricardo made the conventional blood test and found the concentration of malarial sporozoa frighteningly high. The physician caressed the dying child, opened his medicine bag, and resolved that some day he would establish an institution to help these poor country children of the tropics who consider malaria unavoidable.

Today, twenty years later, at Tiquisate in western Guatemala, Dr. Aguilar-Meza has founded a hospital for little ones, which is proving that excessive sickness and death among children in hot countries can be prevented.

When Dr. Ricardo first proposed his children's hospital, the so-called practical people branded the idea as fantasy. And not without a measure of justification. In all of the tropical

Americas there were only a handful of children's hospitals, most of them in cities. The doctor wanted a country hospital for country children.

From long experience Dr. Ricardo knew that child health is the real keynote of preventive medicine in the tropics. In hot countries the bodies of children are the usual reservoirs for malaria, tuberculosis, leprosy and other diseases. Adult health is likely to be decided during the first six years of life. He also knew the hospital business at firsthand.

It was his job to plan, equip, and superintend a 250-bed United Fruit Company hospital at Tiquisate, one of the best rural medical centers in the hemisphere. Primarily an adults' hospital, there was unused space on the ground floor, and here Dr. Ricardo announced one day he proposed to establish his hospital for infants and minors. His assistants murmured that hospitals cost money, that government requirements are hard to meet. The doctor frowned, got out notebook and pencil, and began figuring.

He had saved a few thousand quetzales from his practice and out of royalties from his medical books and translations. That much was ready cash; enough for a beginning. He invaded the vacant basement much as he had invaded the vacated bull ring twenty years before. He divided the space into four big wards and several bathrooms and playrooms. He called in painters and told them: "Make this room look bright and happy. Make it look like a good place to live in— not to die in." He bought fifty attractive cribs and high chairs, play pens for young children, several crates of assorted toys, an oversized ice-cream freezer, and a good supply of quinine and honey. He directed the laying of gaily colored tile floors. He selected four superior nurses and a good dietician.

Finally Dr. Ricardo discovered a native house painter who is a Walt Disney addict. With typical Latin-American dexterity the painter began producing beaming Mickey Mouses and Plutos to hang above every crib and in every wall space. The bathrooms he splattered with Donald Ducks.

The "impossible" children's hospital was almost ready. But practical operation called for still more money—too much to be raised by a bazaar, a fiesta, or even a charity bullfight. "A children's hospital is not charity," said the doctor. "It is the world's best investment. It builds the future and makes the physician's work ten times more valuable!"

The biggest employer and investor in the Tiquisate area is the Compania Agricola de Guatemala, Guatemalan division of the United Fruit Company. Dr. Ricardo proceeded to the manager's office. He described his idea of a free hospital for children, took a deep breath, and raised his request by $5,000. The boss gazed at the ceiling philosophically and said: "God helps those who help themselves. I'm not God, but . . . we'll raise the ante $5,000 more."

Late in 1941, Dr. Ricardo opened his children's hospital. Little Alberto Gomez, age six, was the first patient. Like little Hijo Gaitan, twenty years earlier, Alberto suffered from a virulent type of malaria, and, like Hijo, Alberto believed that everybody has malaria. The fact that Hijo died and Alberto is now well is no accident. Malaria is curable and, with proper facilities, it is preventable.

The children's hospital has these facilities. To the limit of its capacity—fifty children—the refuge is free to all sick children of the Tiquisate area of about 400 square miles. It has already helped make hundreds well. Youthful patients— the usual ages are six months to nine years—come by train, by burro, often on the back of a father or mother too poor to own pack animals. The greatest number are Indian or of mixed blood. The people who first labeled the idea of such a health center as impossible now praise the hospital as a significant step forward.

When you visit the children's hospital, you notice an almost incessant exchange of smiles between Dr. Ricardo and his very young patients. The doctor turns to you and gesticulates with his rather large muscular hands: "Note the eyes, Señor! Windows to souls. Also gauges to sickness or health." He stoops to poke a cookie into a small mouth. He assists with solving a jigsaw puzzle. He lifts a tired little one to its crib. "Watch them play, Señor! The best therapeutic." A section of floor is reserved for a ninejack tournament. Farther on you hear the snap of bright blue marbles striking other bright blue marbles. In a corridor, an Indian nurse squats Guatemala style within a circle of tiny nightshirted figures. All are laughing heartily. The doctor also laughs. "Good nurse. Good medicine." The doorway is momentarily blocked by another nurse who is wrapping a miniature serape on a mamma doll. Dr. Ricardo tells you in a hissing whisper audible for at least twenty yards: "A fine surgery nurse. Also good at dressing dolls. So I had to promote her—to here."

Not all the wards are for play. There are isolation rooms for contagious cases. There are "bad-sick" rooms and an observation ward for the g.o.k.'s (God Only Knows).

Dr. Ricardo pauses beside the crib of a child who does not play. He touches the child's forehead, examines eyes and tongue, and instructs the nurse to call him after evening surgery. In another crib a tiny Indian boy is wailing with toothache. Dr. Ricardo crosses himself. "Just one small look, Chico!" You notice the doctor's fingers close upon the miscreant tooth. A lightning-quick motion of his hand and the tooth is gone. The doctor produces a stick of candy from his bulging coat pocket and puts the candy into the child's mouth. The nurse intervenes: "No sugar . . ." The doctor's expression is one of deep remorse. "So sorry. Completely forgot." You strongly suspect that he will forget again.

Dr. Ricardo describes the opening of this children's hospital as the "happiest phase of my life." He calls it a "step."

He knows that the battle for child health is still far from won. Somewhat more than fifty years ago at Heredia, Costa Rica, he was born to firsthand knowledge of poor and sick children and to defiance of the word "impossible."

He was the eleventh of fifteen children, including two pairs of twins and one set of triplets—all born within eleven years. His childhood home at San José was a two-room house with dirt floors, no windows, and no illumination unless neighbors donated a candle. There was no bed for Ricardo.

At fifteen, with both his parents dead, Ricardo resolved to follow in the steps of his illustrious grandfather, Dr. José Meza Orellana, one of the first great plague fighters of Central America. Ricardo had no money for schooling, but a cousin helped him through two years of high school at San José and two years of college at Cartago, where he led his class. Graduated and broke he scrubbed schoolhouse floors to earn his railroad fare to Puerto Limon. There he stowed away aboard a German liner, was hauled before the captain, and signed on for a two-year term as fireman's helper.

One night in Havana a friend gave him a steamer ticket to the United States. Ricardo landed in New York penniless, and spent his first night in Battery Park covered with newspapers. He found jobs as dishwasher, janitor for a cigar factory and messenger boy, and after completing a night course in an installment-plan business school, he became secretary in a newspaper office.

By 1915 he had a diploma in dentistry, one good suit, a set of forceps, and no money. He returned to Costa Rica on borrowed ship fare. Unable to raise the 300 colons for his license, he found a job as a dentist's assistant in San José. One afternoon he fell asleep while molding a set of uppers. He was awakened by a beautiful girl who introduced herself as his distant cousin Angela. She, too, was an apprentice dentist. A few months later, boy dentist married girl dentist. The couple promptly set out to drill, fill, and scrape Ricardo's way to a degree in medicine. Friends and relatives thought them deranged. But the couple moved to Tegucigalpa, where Ricardo entered medical school and with his bride set up dental practice. The couple's first son, little Ricardo, was born just as the influenza epidemic of 1918 struck Honduras, dealing death rates two or three times those of the United States. Ricardo, although still a student, was dispatched to minister to the sick.

Not long after Ricardo became a full-fledged doctor of medicine, revolution broke out and the young M.D. went to the battle front, where he became surgeon to both government and revolutionary forces. To anybody else that might be impossible. One can't be chief surgeon for two opposing armies at the same time. But Ricardo felt that such formalities as banners or insignias should make no real difference to a physician.

With a suitcase dispensary and a new stethoscope dangling from his smock pocket, he climbed on a burro, trailed through arroyos and jungles, and treated as many of the sick and wounded as he could find, directing a muleback dispensary, digging out bullets, doctoring the sick, and amputating mangled limbs. He estimated that he got ten years of medical experience in six weeks, also the resolution to become a master surgeon.

When the revolt was ended, Dr. Ricardo discarded his blood-smeared uniform, donned workingman's clothes, and wore out his last pair of boots walking home. He promptly became a member of the Honduras National Faculty of Medicine, editor of the medical magazine, and a private practitioner. That was more work than any one man could possibly do. So Dr. Ricardo did it and took on still other jobs.

He returned to Costa Rica, first as physician to the poor, then as physician and lecturer for the San José schools. He

Photo by G. W. Romer

Loading out Plane Cargo to Latin America. Hydroplane Port of
Pan American Airways, Miami, Florida

The United States Now Has
a Nation-wide Air Express
System that Flies More than
a Million Shipments per Year

Airport at San José, Costa Rica. Throughout Latin America the Airport
Is the Keystone to Trade

Photo by Iris Woolcock

Middle America Information Bureau

Study in Automatics via the Junk Pile. Grass Oil Stills Newly Put in
Operation at La Lima, Honduras

Middle America Information Bureau

Locally Constructed Cutting and Loading Machinery for Processing
Lemon and Citronella Grasses, La Lima, Honduras

Middle America Information Bureau

Crusher for Castor Beans Now Being
Planted in Guatemala

liked the work and the people. He liked being a physician. But he was keenly conscious of the crying need for surgeons. He opened a private hospital that featured free surgery for the poor. That was unprecedented and impossible. But Dr. Ricardo did it and charged the well-to-do accordingly. He bought a home, which an earthquake promptly razed. He pulled his family out of the rubble and got to the hospital just in time for three emergency operations.

He became chief surgeon of the Limon Hospital in Costa Rica, then went to Guatemala as surgeon for the famed Quirigua Hospital. It is highly unusual for a man to gain surgical eminence in three Latin-American countries, but Dr. Ricardo didn't stop at that. Ten years ago he was made a fellow of the American College of Surgeons, and was granted membership in five other honorary medical groups in as many different countries. His roster of major operations has climbed far into the thousands.

Recently he took a train trip and as usual rode in the cab with the engineer. Just as the train pulled into the station one hombre shot another. The doctor sprang out of the locomotive cab and administered first aid. An onlooker shouted: "There's a doctor who gets to the shooting before the trigger is pulled!"

The resilient medico barely had time to wash his hands when he was called back to his hospital to look after two particularly troublesome surgery cases. Case A, a youth with a badly injured foot, urgently needed a large-area skin graft. Case B, with a badly injured leg, required several inches of bone graft to save the leg. A few minutes after the doctor's arrival, an ambulance brought in a suicide—a young man who had thrown himself in front of a speeding train. The latter hombre died in the emergency room. Dr. Ricardo rushed to the operating room and promptly grafted skin from the suicide's foot to the foot of Case A, and bone from the suicide's leg to the leg of Case B, thus making two well men from one who thought himself of no further use. Though theoretically impossible, that feat, like so many others of Dr. Ricardo's, became proved fact and surgical history.

One day a terrific hurricane pretty much ruined the city of Belize and left the old British Honduran capital littered with dead and maimed. Dr. Ricardo and Dr. Nutting, of the Rockefeller Foundation, were directed to fly to the scene of the catastrophe and take over. Their instructions were to direct minor first aid and seek to prevent contagion. Major surgery and attention to fractures would be impossible until the necessary supplies could be dispatched.

Once more, this time in company of a distinguished colleague, Dr. Ricardo accomplished the impossible. Since the water-supply system had been wrecked, he ordered drinking water flown in from Nicaragua. Then, arming himself with hand ax and machete, he chopped splints from debris of wood and proceeded to set broken bones. He performed amputations and other emergency surgery in the open, and with excellent results. To the amazement of the storm victims he topped emergency surgery with emergency dentistry.

"So long as there is life and a tomorrow, nothing is impossible." That is Dr. Ricardo's favorite proverb. He is certain that younger doctors will appear to continue and extend the work. He points proudly to his secretary and business manager, who is his daughter Angelita. "That child is a dental surgeon, Señor, and a good one!" He speaks of his young son, Ruben Andino, who was graduated recently from a British medical school and has joined his father in Guatemala. Dr. Ricardo stops abruptly: "That little boy—this hijo of mine! To think that he is a doctor already! Fantastic! Señor, it is absolutely im—" The doctor's teeth snap together. He is silenced in the nick of time.

Disease and poverty are premier enemies of Middle America. They are closely related; to a considerable measure they are as one. Diseases create poverty and extreme poverty begets and perpetuates diseases. Generally speaking, in temperate climates people who believe themselves in good health usually are. But in the tropics a man may live the "everyday" life for years on end. Yet when and if examined, he may be found to harbor malaria and perhaps several other major infections. Frequently he sickens and dies from tuberculosis, pneumonia, dysentery or some other disease entirely out of the fold of the initial diagnosis.

A great many maladies of the American tropics are relapsing. Their victims may be gravely ill in June, apparently recovered in July, and again desperately ill in August. Certain races or communities show inexplainable immunity to certain diseases, and inexplainable susceptibility to others. Time and time again lowered vitality caused from malnutrition baffles the most expert diagnosis.

The ways of tropical-American diseases remain dark; less dark than they were a century ago or even a decade ago but dark nevertheless. Great work has been done; greater work is being done by the many thousands of Middle America's able physicians, surgeons, researchers and technicians. But dark ways wait. Millions of our southern neighbors are dying prematurely. More millions are needlessly sick. The average life span in Middle America as a whole is still under forty years—about a quarter of a century shorter than the average life span in the United States.

Defending the Americas involves fighting a bloodless war against diseases which lurk and flare to destroy the Americas. And we cannot fight the diseases well until we know them better. We cannot finally curb them until the living standards of Middle American publics have been drastically raised. The challenge is squarely evident. Death will not wait, nor take a holiday.

Good health for Middle America is a continuing challenge which confronts all the Americas alike. It calls for integrated, ever-persistent work. It calls for government, business and institutional support. And perhaps most important of all, it requires individuals, in medicine and out, men or women who dare to stand alone and work creatively.

Dr. Aguilar-Meza is such a man of medicine. Others, outside of medicine, also serve and save. For example, here is the modest epic of one Joseph A. LePrince, pioneer sanitary engineer of the hemisphere, and one of the premier benefactors of Middle America.

Not long ago, at Memphis, Tennessee, a rookie patrolman came puffing into police headquarters, leading a lank elderly man dressed in a red bathrobe and muddy bedroom slippers. It was around four in the morning and the patrolman shouted triumphantly: "Sarge! I caught this thing down at Oakmont Place—flashing his light around basement windows."

The dozing police sergeant frowned, blinked and noted that the suspect was carrying a flashlight, a cloth cage about four inches square and a glass tube partly filled with cotton; also that the prisoner was extremely tall and narrow, wore gold-rimmed spectacles, had a cropped gray mustache and stood with knees slightly bowed, as if in readiness to sprint or jump.

When the sergeant asked: "Who are you and what's your business?" the suspect fingered the little cloth cage: "I'm out catching specimens. I have to be up early to get what I'm after. But I caught three . . ."

"Three what?" the patrolman demanded.

"*Anopheles quadrimaculatus.* You know . . ."

The rookie nodded sarcastically. "Oh sure! I have 'em every morning with sliced peaches!" The sergeant smiled sadly, began making circulatory gestures in the area of his right ear and spoke condescendingly to the rookie: "All right, stoopid! Leave the old gent go catch quadricam— Well, *scram!* He's nuts, but harmless."

So Colonel Joseph A. LePrince returned to his perennial hobby of applied entomology—catching, dissecting and otherwise learning about mosquitoes. The colonel did not explain to the policeman that the *Anopheles quadrimaculatus* is one of the most common and destructive malaria mosquitoes that infest the United States and the nations immediately south. He failed to say that Oakmont Place is his home; or that his career in studying and fighting mosquitoes has had a great deal to do with making Western Hemisphere history. He neglected to say that he was the same Joseph LePrince who directed the cleanup of Cuba after the Spanish-American War; who spent ten memorable years making the Isthmus of Panama sufficiently livable for Americans to dig the big ditch; who did most to protect our Army from malaria during World War I—Colonel Joseph A. LePrince who is still playing an important part in the losing fight against that foremost enemy of tropical man, malaria.

But Joseph LePrince is not inclined toward boastful recitations, and he is more or less accustomed to being arrested for poking around windows immediately before dawn—the best time and place to catch certain species of malaria-carrying mosquitoes, and for rousing the darkest suspicions of night-beat patrolmen. Joseph LePrince has nabbed mosquitoes in this fashion hundreds of times in a dozen countries. He has been arrested repeatedly; and also called crazy on three continents and several islands in at least four languages.

That began back in 1900 when he first left New York for Havana, which was then a city of death. Mosquito-transmitted diseases were consuming Caribbean peoples like a furnace takes tissue paper. At that time a great many Cubans believed that the fevers were being blown in by damp winds. The word "malaria" is Italian for bad air, and in 1900 the mosquito-born diseases of yellow fever and malaria had not been clearly segregated. Other Cubans strongly suspected that the brass buttons on United States Army uniforms were carriers of the yellowing death.

But the United States Post Office Department had ordered that all letters leaving Cuba for the United States be perforated so that the poisoned air could not be exported.

The United States "triumph" in Cuba had been short-lived. Our occupation troops were taking yellow fever, spouting black vomit, turning yellow and dying; or chattering and shivering with malaria and wishing they were dead. Havana then had about 300,000 people of whom at least 100,000 were sick with "the fever." The most needed job was one for an engineer who could double as physician, undertaker and politician.

Joseph LePrince proceeded to qualify even while Havanans branded him stark mad. His medical commandant, Dr. William Crawford Gorgas, a handsome, slow-talking Alabaman who later became surgeon general of the United States Army, had also come to believe that mosquitoes carry yellow fever and malaria, from which most of the American tropics were then languishing and rotting.

In Cuba, Gorgas undertook fighting the fevers and LePrince set out to fight the mosquitoes that transmit the fevers. His title was "sanitary engineer." In 1900 there was no such trade. "I had to dig it out of a fog of doubt." Out of the fog of doubt LePrince has successively organized and led anti-mosquito crusades that have saved hundreds of thousands, or perhaps millions, of lives.

Blood-poisoning malaria appears when an anopheline mosquito bites a person suffering from malaria, contracts the disease, then spits the cell-bursting parasites into the blood of a healthy person. Both human carriers and anopheline mosquitoes are therefore indispensable to spreading malaria, which again flames as an international menace.

Our fighting men are inevitably bringing malaria back to the United States. There is no vaccination against the disease, and most of the inhabited world and all of the Americas are within its proved range—forty degrees north latitude to forty degrees south. Our Army and Navy medical corps have learned about malaria on fighting fronts and at home. As lay testimony of the former, here is how the United Press, on April 17, 1942, told of the downfall of American defenses on Bataan:

In the last desperate showdown, the Battle of Bataan ended because the quinine pills ran out. Ten thousands of our troops lay in two field hospitals, most of them with malaria. . . . Another 10,000 were confined to camps with lighter cases of malaria. . . . There was no quinine to fight that deadliest of our enemies. It was malaria—not Japanese tanks, or dive bombers or bayonets —that told the final story.

Joseph LePrince fully appreciates such a report. In Cuba he saw about 90 percent of the United States occupational forces put out of action by malaria, and the other mosquito-borne terror—yellow fever. In 1900 and 1901, after our troops returned from Cuba, they brought back malaria epidemics to home fronts as far north as Greenwich, Connecticut, and Buffalo, New York. Yet only a few thousand fighting men came home from the mosquito flats of Cuba, whereas millions will be returning from malaria strongholds of Africa, India, the Mediterranean, Italy, the Balkans, the Far Pacific islands and Asia. Therefore malaria blitzes can happen here.

During the eighties and nineties of the last century, the LePrince family lived in the Victoria-style Belmont House at 169th Street and Broadway. All the neighborhood, including

the cow pastures that are now the site of the Columbia Pres-
byterian Medical Center, was a notorious malarial area, and
little Joe was fortunate enough to survive an extremely malarial childhood.

Joe's ex-schoolmaster father, Louis Aimé Augustin Le-
Prince, swatted frantically at mosquitoes while he invented
the first motion-picture camera which he patented in 1888,
five years before Thomas Alva Edison of New Jersey first
patented a penny-in-the-slot peep show which ultimately
grew into commercial motion pictures. But the elder Le-
Prince suffered direly from inventor's luck as well as mosquitoes. In 1890 he returned to his native France to show his
method and apparatus for producing "animated pictures of
natural scenery and life." On the night of September 16,
Louis LePrince boarded a Paris-bound train but never reached
Paris. The inventor, his patent diagram, business papers and
luggage—all vanished from the face of the earth. Foul play
was evident but never proved.

Meanwhile Louis Aimé Augustin's widow and the five
young LePrinces were back on Broadway among the mosquitoes. During an interim between chills and fever Joseph
entered Columbia University to study engineering. When
the Spanish-American War broke he volunteered for Army
duty, was rejected on grounds of poor health, whereupon he
joined the Ludlow's Engineering Reserves and finished his
course at Columbia.

Cuba and the Philippines had been won from Spain and
were being lost to mosquitoes. The foremost military ambi-
tion of those times was to get the hell out of the tropics as
speedily as possible. When Joe LePrince boarded a sugar boat
en route to Cuba his best friends called him suicidally insane.
Nevertheless, Joseph went to the tropics for sixty days and
stayed for fourteen years. During the first three, working

frenziedly with Colonel William Crawford Gorgas, he saw Cuba's malaria rates fall 90 percent, while the ruinous scourge of yellow fever was beaten for the first time in more than three centuries.

Thereupon Gorgas and LePrince elected to take over the vastly more formidable job of clearing up the Isthmus of Panama and the green hells beyond, which were poisoned and rotting with malaria and most other diseases. The first would-be canal builders, the French de Lesseps Company, had collapsed in the pyres of man-killing fevers. LePrince's first sight of the fabled isthmus was revealing. He tramped down the gangplank at Colón, which was a highly temporary town slopped upon a low-lying island spotted with green scum and peopled with a desolate flotsam of squatters. Besides green scum, vile diseases, and unemployment, Colón suffered from real-estate speculators. After LePrince had led his sanitation gangs into action, inaugurated sanitary inspection, established a safe water-supply and drainage system, paved some roads, reduced the terrific stenches and the gray clouds of mosquitoes, and won the local acclaim of being stark, ranting crazy, the rents in Colón promptly climbed 2,000 percent. When Joe LePrince protested, the real-estate speculators chortled: "You're crazy! But we ain't!"

Rough-and-tumble canal workers clung to similar views. They said: "Hell, we ain't afraid of the fevers nor the skeeters!" They kicked holes in screen doors, shunned quinine and otherwise refused to obey sanitary regulations. Hundreds of them died of the fevers. The indoor politicians who directed the early stages of canal building also classified LePrince and his helpers as imbeciles. The bureaucrats doubted the capacity of mosquitoes to carry disease and explained that natural enemies could solve the mosquito problem.

"Such as what?" Le Prince queried.

"Bats," answered the high command. "*You* ought to know

about bats." By more than happenstance LePrince did. He and his twenty-four sanitation laborers had set up working headquarters at a canal-side village called Paraíso, where they had taken quarters in a ramshackle old house called La Papote. The mayor of the village warned them that the house was haunted. The ghost turned out to be an anteater. But the garret in the old house was occupied by hundreds of bats and the citizens of Paraíso reported merrily: "Crazy men living in the bat house!"

LePrince proceeded to learn about bats as mosquito killers. He found that nearby tubs of water were scummed with mosquito larvae and that many of the mosquitoes were anopheles—malaria carriers. The mosquitoes were stuffed with bat blood! The bats were not destroying the mosquitoes, though the mosquitoes were doing their utmost to destroy the bats.

LePrince's consuming aim was to kill the mosquitoes wherever, however and whenever possible. Results were soon apparent. Within two years, or by 1907, the sick rate among canal workers, which had been as high as 670 per thousand, had fallen to 20 per thousand. (That of New York City employees was 27 per thousand.) LePrince led his workmen into the far jungle edges of the canal strip to destroy mosquito breeding places. Along came Sir Savage Landor who in native disguise and without a companion had successively walked across Africa and South America. In Panama Sir Savage proposed to walk into jungles—which no other white man had ever seen. He followed a stream bed far into the Chiriqui wilds to a point where he felt certain no other white man had ever set foot. "At that point I found one of LePrince's bloody old oil drippers—killing off the blarsted wrigglers!"

But malaria persisted. LePrince noted that mosquitoes showed great fondness for the stately rows of palms that graced the Central Plaza of Panama City. There, as in many other tropical cities, palms are herbaceous royalty. But sometimes they harbor the most villainous mosquitoes. LePrince felt confident that if the palm trees were done away with, their tenant mosquitoes would be forced to take shelter in houses or buildings, where the pests could be erased by fumigation. Accordingly, one very dark night in Panama City, LePrince and a picked posse of his workmen entered the Plaza, dug up the palm trees and hauled them away.

That was dastardly; also illegal. But it thwarted malaria. The isthmus warfare against mosquitoes became still more ambitious. The cleanup boys put up millions of yards of copper screening. They installed double screen doors at every hospital entrance. They ordered all malaria sufferers confined in mosquitoproof cages. They distributed quinine at every mess table. The health of canal workers reached world highs. LePrince worked on and wrote with sweat and muscle grease the ten commandments of mosquito fighting which he presently saw enforced throughout the isthmus strip: Eliminate standing water. Remove trash and rubbish. Keep buckets and tubs upside down. Fill all cisterns. Coat all undrainable surface water with oil. Keep roofs and gutters clean. Change water in flower vases at least every three days. Keep empty cans off the premises. Keep cellars dry. Treat malaria sufferers promptly.

Such was conclusive proof of insanity in 1914 when the lank, leather-brown engineer left the isthmus to become public-health engineer for New Orleans. After distinguished success in reducing malaria rates of New Orleans and its adjacent deltas, LePrince became senior sanitary engineer of the United States Public Health Service. During 1923 he directed yellow-fever control in the Mexican oil fields, and in 1927, following the great flood of that year, he directed all malarial control activities in the Mississippi Basin.

When the premier mosquito fighter returned from Panama

the United States was spending nothing for malaria prevention. But presently the Southern railroads, engineering colleges and boards of health began to show "malaria consciousness." Congress granted a first $17,000 for combating mosquitoes in the Southern states.

Yet when World War I began, some of our biggest Army camps were placed in notorious malaria centers. By direction of the great Gorgas, then surgeon general of the Army, LePrince changed to Army khaki and directed drainage and mosquito riddance for thirty-six Army and Navy posts throughout the United States, and noted with due pleasure that the malaria rates of our armed forces had reached an all-time low. Also, Major LePrince had the exceptional pleasure of launching air warfare against mosquitoes. That began early in 1918 at Quantico, the great Marine base on the Potomac. At tidewater the river is crowded with floating eelgrass—ideal for mosquito breeding, since the grass serves to protect the mosquito larvae from fish and other natural enemies. Destroying the larvae with oil was impractical because the grass prevented the oil from spreading over the water. So LePrince undertook "dusting" the waters with toxic powders such as Paris green, spread from hoppers placed in low-flying scouting planes. That stopped the mosquitoes, blasted malaria out of the Marine base and introduced airplane dusting of mosquito breeding places as an outstanding strategy in malaria control.

Retired from the Public Health Service in 1931, the frail crusader returned to the study of mosquitoes. In the vicinity of Memphis he has captured specimens of malaria-carrying mosquitoes which were originally discovered in Canada, Central America, the Caribbean islands, even Africa. He has completely disproved the erroneous belief that malarial mosquitoes live only in warm countries. He assembled a colony of *Anopheles walkeri* (a Canadian species of malaria carrier), let their eggs hatch in clear water, and froze the larvae or wrigglers in the freezing compartments of a refrigerator. Each day for a week he took out a cube of the frozen larvae, thawed them out, and noted that the mosquito wrigglers still lived. That demonstrated that some types of malarial mosquitoes can survive long hard winters; that cold weather cannot be trusted to safeguard people from malaria.

LePrince completed voluminous experiments to prove that some of the most effective mosquito killers are unpaid and generally unappreciated. Spiders, for example. Many species of spiders are superb mosquito destroyers. So is the humble, warty toad. But mouth for mouth and pound for pound fish are the most effective destroyers of mosquitoes. They feed upon the pests during the aquatic stages—while the larva or pupa must live in water and breathe air. Use of fish to destroy the water-bound embryos of mosquitoes is cheaper, more convenient and safer than coating standing water with oil or poisoning—so long, of course, as the quantity and quality of the water are sufficient to keep fish alive.

In Panama some thirty years ago LePrince began trapping mosquitoes, spraying them with gaudy-colored dyes and releasing them. Panama natives were flabbergasted or terrified to see bright-green or livid-red mosquitoes zooming through their open doors. Some reported to the priests that the devil had taken the form of mosquitoes. More recently in Memphis local doctors were confronted by startled patients who thought themselves going color-blind. "Doc—last night I saw a pea-green mosquito on my wrist. I swatted it, went to sleep, and this morning the darned thing was still green. Look at it, Doc, and tell me if I've gone crazy!"

The doctor examined the squashed mosquito and swabbed his forehead—"I think we're both crazy!"

The standard device for locating mosquito breeding places is the LePrince "direction trap." LePrince takes two strips of glass, coats both surfaces with a sweetened stickum mixture and places the glass in the open so that a coated surface faces in each principal direction. Next morning he checks the mosquito catch. If a dozen or so mosquitoes are on the north face of the glass, that suggests the dominant flight direction is from the north; if about the same number of mosquitoes are stuck to the north and east faces, it is probable that the mosquitoes are flying in from the northeast. Knowing the direction of origin, the species of mosquitoes caught and its flight range, one can usually proceed to the breeding place. Recently Colonel LePrince walked southwest 3,000 yards from his home, stopped at a suburban cottage, and asked permission to empty a water barrel that was cradling unnumbered thousands of malarial mosquitoes.

"How did you know the mosquitoes are coming from my rain barrel?" the cottager demanded.

The colonel winked solemnly and made circulatory gestures about his right ear. "The mosquitoes told me . . ."

Disease is the age-old enemy of Middle America and malaria is the foremost communicable disease. Combating malaria is an ever resolute and ever personal enterprise; a merging of enlightened medicine, sanitation, and diplomacy. LePrince is an illustrious example of malaria fighters. But today scores and hundreds more are carrying forward his great work in Middle America, Africa, southern Europe, China, the South Pacific and elsewhere; studious and diligent men sufficiently brave and sure to admit that much remains yet to be learned about malaria and mosquitoes. And much more waits to be done by way of education and legitimate persuasion; never by evasion; never by ramming real or alleged remedies down the throats of harassed publics.

Even congressmen are becoming aware of the deep seriousness of malaria. In the congressional records of 1943 one finds many references to the menace of the greatest and still mystifying disease. This one is typical: "Malaria in its many forms constitutes one of the great scourges of mankind today—if not the greatest. It poses problems of the utmost immediate and future importance." And: "It is estimated that malaria now afflicts one-third of the world population, or perhaps as many as 800,000,000 people." "Malaria is an arch enemy to prosperity and the hope for peace."

The story of quinine, which is the one decisive therapeutic defense against the disease, is also a continuing and vital story. Malariologists of many countries are urgently pointing out that the time has come when quinine can no longer remain in the pace of so-called pure commercialism, that today the production of quinine is in the realm of a major national and international responsibility. Various American governments are seeking nobly to place effective stepping-stones to a possible international accord with respect to quinine and malaria control; such worthy efforts as those incorporated in the joint malaria-control program of the Health and Sanitation Division of the Co-ordinator of Inter-American Affairs and the various Latin-American republics where malaria is a major health problem.

The latter program aims primarily toward correlation of efforts to destroy the aquatic and adult stages of anopheline mosquitoes and their breeding places; to establish medical and educational facilities; and perhaps most important of all, to ascertain the needs and to facilitate the distribution of quinine and other antimalarials to the various American nations. An equitable distribution of quinine according to national requirements can be made and perhaps, in time, extended to other nations. The procurement program of the Office of Economic Warfare involves the development of

methods for collecting and processing the barks of wild cinchona trees, the exploring of heretofore unused stands of cinchona, and the cultivation of cinchona as a valid field crop.
One can visualize an extension of all these projects to other
nations beyond the Americas in an international fighting front
to control of endemic malaria by means of equitable distribution of cinchona bark and quinine on a nonprofit or controlled
basis, which would enable hundreds of millions of people
to buy antimalarials and scores of governments to carry out
highly necessary health programs. Totaquina, a comparatively inexpensive quinine solution made from mix-grinding
all beneficial alkaloids in cinchona barks (totaquina is now
officially accepted in United States medicine), and the com-
plementary antimalarial synthetics, atabrine and plasmochin,
are all of distinguished importance in the antimalaria program. But quinine is a superior prophylactic which can be
administered safely by nonmedical persons; whereas many
accredited authorities believe that the synthetics require experienced medical supervision.

Nowadays, however, medical researchers are on the whole
well agreed as to the desirability of treating malaria with a series of doses of quinine or totaquina, atabrine and plasmochin.
Every one of these remedies shows a wholesomely destructive
action on the parasite in one of its phases of development in
the human organism. As yet, no drug can guarantee the prevention of relapses.

While fervently labeling the cinchona the tree of life for
the hundreds of millions who suffer from malaria, it is also
well to remember that there are also sustaining industrial
uses for cinchona alkaloids—quinine and others—in metal-
lurgy, paint and rubber manufactures, textile industries, and
in the manufacture of Polaroid—important in scientific instruments and eyesight-testing equipment and scores of
other uses. These uses are factors of protection against the

still vague possibility of overproduction of quinine which might conceivably result from eventual victories against malaria, or possible, though still improbable, discovery of a totally effective suppressive drug.

At this date the latter is merest wishful thinking. Malaria is still the great incapacitator.

Middle America suffers from other diseases which are frequently ruinous and more frequently perplexing. The entries are as varied as the foibles of man and are rather vitally related thereto. And in Middle America as in other tropical countries there are many serious diseases about which modern medicine knows nothing, little, or not enough—foremost American enemies which headlines usually fail to mention.

One supposedly indigenous morbid entry is *pinta*, a tropical skin disease; really a group of tropical dermatomycoses caused by spirochetes that produce variously colored patches, frequently of grotesque design and strongly contrasted with the surrounding healthy epidermis.

Dr. Eduardo Urueta of Colombia defines pinta as an ancient disease chronicled in the earliest history of the Aztecs.[1] But the range of pinta still reaches far into the American tropics, from Mexico intermittently through Central America and northern South America—though in each country the disease seems rigidly limited to sections, outside of which it rarely or never occurs. Pinta sufferers usually react positively to the Wassermann and Kahn tests (pinta is not syphilis, however).

Pinta makes black men white, and during the process it can temporarily paint human skins most of the colors of the rainbow. For generations it has continued as a curse of the Caribs—the somewhat fabulous "black Indians" for whom

[1] Eduardo Urueta, M.D., *Pinta or Carate*, p. 524. International Conference on Health Problems in Tropical America, Kingston, Jamaica, B.W.I.

the Caribbean is named. Lieutenant Colonel James Cran, of Britain's Royal Army Medical Corps, has estimated that approximately half of all adult Caribs in British Honduras are blotched with pinta, usually beginning with the black or dark-blue varieties and finishing up as the white. In a recent *Journal of the American Medical Association* Dr. Eugene P. Lieberthal reported three clearly developed cases of pinta in Chicago—the first identified within the United States. Dr. Cran contends that good hygiene and cleanliness are the best defenses against this weird malady of skin blotches, and obviously that conditions of hygiene and cleanliness improve only as earnings and living standards increase.

The same applies to several other more or less mysterious diseases of the southern countries. It is true of ainhum, sometimes called "barefoot leprosy," or better defined as "a condition of parasitic origin, the infection taking place probably through the small superficial lesions or wounds which may be found in people going barefoot."

Ainhum is a malady of vanishing toes. The arteries leading to the toes develop sclerosis. Festering bands appear about the toes, most commonly the little toe. The bone structure begins to vanish. The outer skin hardens and shrinks. Presently the little toe remains attached to the foot only by a few fibers of muscle. After a time the toe falls off. The victim feels little or no pain. The cure, according to the renowned Costa Rican physician, Dr. A. A. Facio, consists of cleanliness and the wearing of stockings and comfortable shoes; a prescription not easily filled by tropical people who are desperately poor.

Many graver diseases are wedded and welded into Middle American tragedies of preventable poverty. Typhus is a perennial example. Typhus still spreads sickness and death throughout the highlands of Mexico (where the malady is called *tabardillo*) and throughout widespread areas to the south. Occasional cases appear in the United States, proving that the challenge of typhus still confronts all of the Americas. In general the history of this murderous fever belongs to the dark ages of the world, to times when famine, war and misery generally are at hand.[2] During the seventeenth, eighteenth and early nineteenth centuries severe epidemics of typhus spread through Europe and the British Isles, and time and time again its murdering waves swept through the Americas.

In Middle America as in many other parts of the world the story of typhus remains sad. The disease strikes furiously, dealing violent headaches, giddiness and nausea which are followed by burning fever. Within a fortnight the sufferer is usually either dead or headed toward recovery. The disease harasses the heart. About the fifth day of the affliction red, rashlike eruptions appear on the abdomen, the flanks and chest. Frequently delirium occurs by the end of the first week. Sometimes terrifying hallucinations besiege the sufferer— hallucinations that apparently cause the great number of typhus suicides. Acute circulatory weakness sometimes establishes tendencies of gangrene, usually in the toes. Severe coughs, bronchitis and bronchopneumonia are common complications. As in black plague the clouding of consciousness is commonplace, and as in plague the sufferer frequently behaves as if he were exorbitantly drunk.

Among adults its death rates range from 15 or 20 to 60 percent. Benefiting treatment is costly in time and effort, for it requires painstaking nursing and careful attention to heart conditions, insomnia, delirium and diet. Typhus remains linked to cruel poverty and chronic squalor which is also one with abject, continuing poverty.

[2] E. R. Stitt, *Diagnostics and Treatment of Tropical Diseases* (5th ed., P. Blakiston and Co., Philadelphia, 1929), pp. 362–86.

South American trypanosomiasis is another grievous tropical malady carried to man by mites, ticks, bedbugs, triatoma (a flying bug that infests stables and pigsties) and perhaps other vermin from dogs and cats, armadillos and opossums and other animals. The infections are most commonly reported from the South American tropics, particularly Brazil, Venezuela, Peru and northern Argentina, but the disease is known to Central America and some of the Caribbean islands. Most of its victims are extremely poor people who live in deplorable hovels.[3] The mobile and highly destructive parasite invades many areas of the human body including lymph nodes, thyroid, heart muscles, ovary, testicles, bone marrow and so on. Acute forms of the malady frequently occur in young children, causing them to suffer high and continued fever. Their faces become puffy; thyroid areas swell; spleens become enlarged. The disease is highly fatal. Adults usually suffer the chronic types, frequently marked by swollen throat, heart irregularities, sometimes by cerebral afflictions and insanity.

In man as well as in lower animals the infection produces its own immunity—how or why nobody knows. Actual knowledge of the disease remains pitiably scant. According to Stitt, no curative agent has as yet been proved consistently effective.[4]

Medicine remains lamentably ignorant of many other rodent-carried diseases that harass the American tropics; even those with perfectly forthright names, such as relapsing fever (also carried by ticks and lice and still common to parts of Central America and north South America), infectious jaundice (thought to be transmitted through the infected urine of men or rats), ratbite fever (hellishly painful, marked

[3] *Ibid.*, p. 97.
[4] *Ibid.*, p. 99.

by successive waves of syphilislike eruptions and known principally to the West Indies). Still another malady of Middle America is the parasitic disease called blinding filaria (*Onchocerca caecutiens*). About a quarter of a century ago this disease was reported in the highland Pacific slope of Guatemala. Researchers discovered that thousands of highland Guatemalans (in limited areas as many as 97 percent of the entire population) suffered nodules upon their scalps —swellings about the size of a walnut and sometimes vivid green in color.

The nodules are commonly associated with chronic eye ailments. Surgeons discovered that highland peoples who had been almost blind are frequently all but miraculously cured after the filarial cysts are removed from their scalps. Inside the scalp node is a closely coiled and gigantic worm, sometimes as much as fifteen inches long.

Other tropical filariae are still farspread and insufficiently known: among them the nightmarish *Filaria bancrofti*, still widely prevalent in the West Indies and much of Central America and South America; as well as in Arabia, India, China, the South Pacific islands, Africa and to some extent in our own Southern states. This is another deceptive malady. Its embryos are frequently present in the blood streams of persons who show no symptoms of the disease. The symptoms are varied, and usually distressing. Knowledge of the disease is still groping and feeble.

Like malaria, yellow fever and dengue, this particular filaria is mosquito-borne. After entering the human host the uninvited guests make their way to the lympathic vessels or glands where the female worms, duly fertilized by the males, shed more larvae.[5] From the lymph stream the damaging embryos proceed into the blood circulation. Adult worms may be present in a body in great numbers and give off thousands of em-

[5] *Ibid.*, p. 554.

bryos into the blood before the victim shows any clear evidence of illness. The actual development of filarial infections is ironically puzzling. Sometimes they appear as virulent red swellings of the flesh, or as varicosed groin glands. Sometimes the adult filarial worms cause deep, sickening abscesses in the flesh, the bladder or other organs. Elephantiasis, a malady of grotesque swelling, is a not uncommon aftermath. Barbados leg is one of its more common appearances. The lower legs, calves and ankles swell to appalling dimensions. Sometimes the elephantiasis occurs in the areas of the breasts or the penis. There are many other torturous filarial maladies, all far too little known. Their cure or arrest frequently calls for costly medication and skilled surgery and skin grafting.

To some extent Middle American areas are cursed with ticks, mites, sandfleas and chigoes that burrow into human skin and flesh. There are many kinds of tropical tarantulas and scorpions, giant tropical centipedes, venomous snakes, "stinging" fish and other "natural enemies" to man. But none of the latter can be listed as principal causes of sickness or death. In general the damages dealt by snakes, scorpions, or spiders are exaggerated to the proportion of fable. The hidden killers are infinitely more ruinous.

The tragedy of dysentery is a good example. In the American tropics, as elsewhere, the term "dysentery" has become a convenient label for almost any disease of the bowels. One of the most justly dreaded is amoebic dysentery, which results from invasion of the intestines by a virulent animal parasite. Bacillary dysentery is a label that covers a huge group of intestinal maladies caused by bacteria. Another vast group of dysenteries results from mechanical irritants or poisonous materials in the digestive track. Still another group results from the more advanced stages of other chronic diseases, especially tuberculosis, cancer, nephritis, malaria, heart diseases, pellagra and typhoid.

In all, dysentery remains among the most damaging and invincible of inter-American afflictions. Amoebic dysentery exists in greater or less degree in most parts of the tropical world. At present it is a foremost health enemy in Brazil, Central America and the West Indies; and a major menace to Indo-China, North Africa, Egypt and the Philippines. It is known in our own Southern states. Some of the amoebae that live in man are harmless. The parasite amoeba called *Endamoeba histolytica* is insidious—tough enough to bore its way into the intestinal submucosa, where it causes infection by shedding offspring.

According to Stitt the earlier contention that water, fruit, or vegetables, from which one can isolate amoebae on culture, are sources of the infection must be abandoned.[6] The principal factor in its spread seems to be the long-lived amoebae encysted in human faeces. These can be carried by flies, or washed from dried stools into water supplies or carried in blowing dust to lodge upon unprotected foodstuffs.

Amoebic dysentery is rarely fatal in its first attack. Its greatest menace lies in its capacity to persist, to intersperse latent and active periods, to cause abscesses and otherwise bring about chronic invalidism. Its most widely accepted cures are emetine and prayer. Some medical authorities oppose the use of emetine. In all events the treatment is tedious and slow. Latin-American centers of amoebic infections are usually centers of liver abscess. According to various accredited researches, 60 to 90 percent of cases of liver abscess occur in company with dysentery.[7]

Amoebic dysentery is not an epidemic disease. Frequently bacillary dysentery is epidemic. Unlike the amoebic the bacillary forms frequently appear outside of the tropics and sub-

[6] *Ibid.*, p. 187.
[7] *Ibid.*, pp. 200–1.

tropics, defiant both of boundaries and casual diagnosis. They follow armies and tides of immigration. They attack babies and young children, invade asylums, prisons and barracks. They are enormously contagious since they can be spread by human carriers, flies, soiled clothing, blown dust or drinking water.

The disease's incubation period is brief, usually from one day to one week. Initial diarrhea is followed by characteristic dysentery stools and by intense pains that tend to center about the umbilicus. Fever flares. In acute cases the stools become almost pure blood and as numerous as a hundred a day. The pulse quickens and becomes weak as the heart is put under merciless strain. Sometimes arthritis appears as a complication. Sometimes the mucosa becomes gangrenous.[8] Frequently death invades before medication can be made effective. Mortality rates vary widely, from less than 2 percent to more than 20.[9]

Medical researchers still work to perfect successful vaccines. They are making progress. Meanwhile, successful treatment demands capable hospitalization, painstaking medication and sanitation—all well beyond the means of the great majority of sufferers from dysentery.

Yaws, another disease of skin lesions and flesh sores, is another little known and front-rank menace to the American tropics. Sometimes called "false syphilis," yaws produces many of the loathsome sores that one sees so frequently in Haiti and other Negro lands of the Caribbean.

Defending people against yaws is inevitably costly and complicated. It involves raising standards of sanitation, of income and living. It requires segregation and studied treatment of each sufferer. Yaws is another malady of abject pov-

[8] *Ibid.*, p. 220.
[9] *Ibid.*, p. 225.

erty. The needed medication is usually costly. The treatment is usually laborious and painful. Yaws remains a disease of many mysteries. Generations of medical men have termed it "syphilis under tropical conditions." At present this definition is largely discarded. Workers of the Rockefeller Institute, and others, have proved with considerable finality that the organism of yaws is substantially different from that of syphilis, despite the fact that the sufferer usually reacts positively to the Wassermann test.

Haiti is this hemisphere's hardest stricken victim of yaws. According to Dr. Paul W. Wilson of the United States Navy Medical Corps, the affliction was brought to Haiti more than four centuries ago with the first import of African slaves.[10] The havoc of the disease has continued. Haiti's economic losses from yaws have been enormous—and are still. In fact it has been estimated that between a fourth and a third of all Haitians were afflicted by this loathsome disease of festering flesh sores.[11] (Dr. Aldo Castellani has described districts of Ceylon where four-fifths of the inhabitants were cursed with the disease; where all industries and commerce have waited and rotted as a result of it.) [12]

Yaws continues as an inter-American menace that cannot be halted by prayer or wishful thinking, or economical handouts of salves and powders. It remains among many front-rank challenges to American medicine and commerce; another ruining tropical disease that has been wedded and welded to abject poverty.

[10] Dr. Paul W. Wilson, Medical Corps, U. S. Navy, Port-au-Prince, Haiti; an address before the International Conference on Health Problems in Tropical America, Kingston, Jamaica, B.W.I., 1924, pp. 586, 588.
[11] *Ibid.*
[12] Aldo Castellani, C.M.G., M.D., F.R.C.P., London, Lecturer, London School of Tropical Medicine, from a report to the International Conference on Health Problems in Tropical America, Kingston, Jamaica, B.W.I., 1924, p. 589.

Much the same may be said of hookworm, a lingering malady of our own cotton-growing South, and a grim rival of malaria as tormenter and weakener of the American tropics. Fortunately hookworm is one of the better known of parasitic maladies and, as the Rockefeller Foundation has so brilliantly proved, one of the more controllable. Hookworm is spread by means of human excreta, open privies, contaminated soils and bare feet. In the United States the disease halts growth, saps energy and weakens bodies, but rarely causes death. In the tropics hookworm infections are far more severe and if no treatment is given hookworm death rates have sometimes reached alarming heights—as many as forty deaths per thousand people each year.[13]

But hookworm can be cured. In Jamaica, a five-year campaign staged by the Jamaica Hookworm Commission, under joint auspices of the International Health Board of the Rockefeller Foundation and the government of Jamaica, succeeded in reducing hookworm infections enormously—in some areas from half the total population to less than one-tenth within four years. With progress in this heroic effort Jamaicans have become healthier; employment has improved; and sickness and deaths from typhoid, malaria, colds and dysentery have diminished. As the great antihookworm campaign in Jamaica so conclusively proved, co-operation and common effort of local health boards, independent physicians, farm owners, schoolteachers, businessmen, preachers and public officials are essential. The war against hookworm is not yet won. There is good reason to believe that between the Mason-Dixon line and the River Plata millions of Americans still suffer from the disease, which is tragically unnecessary.

[13] This statement by Dr. Friederick Fulleborn, professor, Institut für Schiff und Tropen Krankheiten, refers to hookworm casualties on Netherlands Indies plantations.

Pellagra is another dark road into the blackish realms of inter-American diseases; another dietary disease, widely associated with the eating of corn—the foremost crop of this hemisphere.[14]

It is distinctly possible that thousands or millions of Americans, from Missouri south to Cape Horn, have pellagra and don't know it. Some of its victims recover. Still more survive. But any inter-American wanderer is likely to become unhappily acquainted with the advanced type of pellagra; a distressing malady of fever, sore tongue and mouth; of eruptions on feet and hands, colitis, ulcers and diarrhea. Most advanced cases spell lingering, painful death, since the pellagra-ridden system frequently becomes unable to assimilate food, and leaves the victim to die of starvation.[15]

Americans still die of pellagra; and the cure calls not only to medicine, but to commerce and agriculture as well. For there is commanding evidence that only well-nourished people can stand against pellagra, or a score of other ruining diseases that continue to spread sickness, despair and death throughout the Americas.

In Middle America, as anywhere else, improvement of diet is vastly complicated by forces of tradition, commercial exploitation of incompetent foods; by human laziness, apathy and ignorance. Diet is welded into the practical and variable business of agriculture, which in turn is tethered to factors of climate, geography and economy.

Leprosy is another disease of poverty. The bacilli of leprosy, like those of tuberculosis, often wait dormant for years, then awake to intensely active life. In Middle American and

[14] Siler, Garrison and MacNeal, "Studies in Pellagra," *Archives of Internal Medicine*, 1914, Vol. XIV, p. 293.

[15] Goldberger, *The Cause and Prevention of Pellagra*, U.S.P.H.S. Reports Nos. 218 and 311, Washington, D. C.

other tropics there seem to be notable similarities between the problems of leprosy and those of tuberculosis; though the latter, not the former, are now of foremost concern. Both leprosy and tuberculosis are most frequently contracted in the course of prolonged contact, particularly in overcrowded, ill-ventilated, unsanitary quarters. In both, the greatest risk of contagion is during babyhood or childhood. Like tuberculosis leprosy is accentuated by malnutrition. The late Sir Arthur Newsholme pointed out: "No satisfying evidence has been advanced to prove that inadequate food has any influence on the origin of leprosy, though this may be so." [16] Like tuberculosis, leprosy is lingering and chronic, frequently with long latent intervals. Like tuberculosis leprosy usually occurs among poor people, badly housed and little learned in hygiene and sanitation. Like malaria and tuberculosis its links of infection can be gradually worn down, though perhaps not entirely obliterated.[17]

Among tropical Americans tuberculosis shows alarming increase. For the past thirty years or so, medical statisticians have pointed out that tuberculosis is on the increase throughout much of the tropical world, and that its occurrence within the tropics has more to do with the people, housing and everyday living ways than with the climate as such. In all events the common citizen's ability to resist tuberculosis is far less in most of Central and South America than in North America. Apparently the essential defense lies in better sanitation and hygiene, better housing and perhaps most important, better diet. Our southern neighbors are working heroically to employ these defenses. They have built and staffed dozens of public sanitariums, many of outstanding excellence. They have assembled staffs of renowned clinicians. The heroic de-

[16] *Ibid.*, p. 791.
[17] Dr. F. L. Hoffman, "Leprosy as a National and International Problem," *Journal of Sociologic Medicine*, Vol. XVII, No. 2, April 1916.

fense continues. But south of the border, problems and dangers of tuberculosis remain acute.

Clinically, the progress of the disease is usually more rapid and virulent in the tropics than in temperate climates. Death-bringing stages are frequently and quickly established after primary lesions of the lungs. In general, tuberculosis of the bone, joint and skin is less common in Middle America than in the United States. But pulmonary tuberculosis is superlatively murderous to the poor of all races. So, unfortunately, is pneumonia. Throughout the world pneumonia remains a persistent and insidious killer. In the tropics its ravages are more than averagely destructive to bodies previously weakened by other diseases.

The disease enemies of man in Middle America are formidable. Diseases of livestock are also numerous and serious. In addition are the many natural enemies of valuable crops, agricultural pests that are proportionately more destructive in the tropics than out of the tropics. Agricultures for the Americas range from arctic growths to deep tropic crops, from crops of the wet, steamy jungle to the cold, dry mountaintops. But all the crops are needed if our nearest American neighbors are to live well and prosper. Like the organisms of diseases, insect pests have no respect or regard for natural boundaries or for man-made boundaries. P. N. Annand, Chief of the Bureau of Entomology and Plant Quarantine of the United States Department of Agriculture, summarizes the situation: "The pests that annoy man and waste his crops and stores may be classified roughly as cosmopolitan, introduced and native. No one knows when the first mentioned began their depravations, but since the early days of sailing vessels they have come to all human habitations."

There is not room in this book to list all the insect pests that actively threaten the agricultural stability of Middle America.

Entomologists are inclined to estimate that more than 90 percent of all insect species of the world are still undescribed, and for practical purposes, unknown. So-called new species are being described at the rate of 10,000 to 12,000 per year. Mr. Annand has suggested that thus far in the science of entomology only about 625,000 kinds of insects have been described, and that one may, therefore, conclude that there are more than 6,000,000 kinds of insects in the world. The tallies of Middle American insect enemies are substantially greater than those of the United States. The sterile winters and other natural control factors, of great consequence in insect control within the United States, are substantially missing in the American tropics. Furthermore, the American tropics are in the most direct line of migration and infiltration by insect enemies of other continents and far-distant islands.

Among the more serious of introduced pests, for example, is the San Jose scale, which is native to China and now all too well established as a premier enemy of fruit crops throughout most of the Americas. Many other scales have invaded the American tropics by way of the importation of nursery trees and planting stocks, among which are the Florida red scale, the California red scale and the purple scale. The cabbage butterfly which menaces vegetable gardens throughout all the Americas is native to Europe. So is the coddling moth or apple worm, which throughout three-fourths of our hemisphere is now a foremost enemy to the apple crop.

Earlier in this book we noted something of the use of predator insects as weapons for controlling at least some part of the crop-destroying insects. This endeavor grows more important with passing time. Obviously, the more immediate and the more formidable problem is co-operative warfare against the long-ranging insect destroyers of crops. This involves co-operative effort among all American nations, the persistent, ever-continuing collection and classification of insect species from all American lands, and meeting one of the gravest agrarian problems now common to the Americas—plentiful and inexpensive supplies of insecticides. We noted, too, recent experiments in the introduction of cultivated rotenone crops to the American tropics. Because rotenone is among the more valuable of insecticidal materials these experiments are of particular importance. But there is not enough rotenone or any other highly effective insecticidal material to fulfill all existent needs. There may not be enough for a long time to come. The distribution of various strategic insecticides has been ably directed by our government and other American governments. Basic insecticidal minerals such as lead arsenite and calcium arsenite have actually been increased rather than decreased during the late war period. But the physical and financial problem of procuring and supplying insecticides remains one of the major and unsolved Pan-American problems.

In a general way the same is true of insect quarantine measures. In some degree every American nation has enacted laws to regulate the importation or movement of seed, food products and other commodities in which or on which the egg, larvae or other forms of insect pests are or can be carried. These Pan-American adventures in plant quarantine are proved enormously valuable to all of the Americas. They have benefited man's stand against the myriad insects that would destroy him, and they have resulted in invaluable research in the diagnosis and treatment of plant disease and in the fundamentals of agronomy and practical pathology. They have wakened not only the scientist but to some measure the lawmaker and the administrative official to the vital importance of the great unfinished task in insect control. Left to breed, multiply and migrate as they would, insect and fungus pests can substantially destroy Middle American agriculture. They can do much to destroy men and nations of men and to restore the unproductive jungle and desert. It is heartening to see that valuable protective enterprises, such as the United States Department of Agriculture's Bureau of Entomology and Plant Quarantine, work in controlling the notorious citrus black fly by the use of natural predators and with the active assistance of the Cuban Government; to see the able co-operation between the United States and Mexico, particularly as regards the spread of the Mexican fruit fly, clover beetle, and peach mosaic—a virus disease of the common peach tree. The same co-operation has been effected in the fight against black stem rust of wheat and oats, in which instance rust-immune strains of wheat from the United States have been introduced to Mexican fields. From the standpoint of persistence in co-operation, United States and Mexican combat of the pink bollworm of cotton is a superb instance of scientific Pan-Americanism dating back to 1917. It is one of the best examples of international co-operation in plant pest control, and it constitutes a valid symbol for future co-operation.

Sagely the Chief of the Bureau of Entomology and Plant Quarantine, United States Department of Agriculture, remarks: ". . . what we have achieved is only the beginning of Inter-American co-operation in pest control."

Middle America Information Bureau

elfry in Church Tower at Panama City

Middle America Information Bureau

Municipal Gate, Ruins of Antigua, Guatemala

La Merced Cathedral, Front View, Antigua, Guatemala

Middle America Information Bureau

Middle America Information Bureau

Hospital from Beach, at Puerto Limon, Costa Rica

Photo by Iris Woolcock

A Farm Home, Costa Rica

Hospital, Second-class Ward, at Puerto Limon, Costa Rica

Middle America Information Bureau

CHAPTER NINE

MIDDLE AMERICA AND THE FUTURE

MANY and serious problems are facing Middle America today and tomorrow. But there is no one of these problems that cannot be substantially solved or favorably alleviated by the creation or improvement of better average incomes and valid trade.

The need for protection against ruinous diseases of people and crops is outstandingly urgent. But the objective reporter must concede the historical reality that when and as Middle American income and living standards make possible the maintenance of health, comparatively good health standards are maintained; and that when competent agronomy is applied to suitable soils the resulting developments of crops compare favorably with results obtained anywhere else. It is equally well proved that tropical health cannot be lastingly maintained merely by broadside handouts of pills and powders, or the temporarily subsidized initiation of nonindigenous sanitation endeavors.

Three years have proved beyond any reasonable doubt that the demanding health or economic problems of Middle America and the other Americas will not be solved decisively or otherwise by fourteen easy lessons in Spanish; or by any quantity of chatty rationalization of the facts that the American tropics have suffered terribly from war-effected shipping shortages and war scleroses of essential goods and equipment; or by the inescapable fact that incessant "field parties" cannot stabilize war-strained agricultures and war-depleted credits and invoices merely by talking and deluging the local presses with nineteen-carat self-publicity.

The Co-ordinator of Inter-American Affairs' Health and Sanitation "program"—potentially the most valuable of C.I.A.A. efforts thus far attempted in several areas of Middle America—impresses this reporter as another re-enactment of the following rather ancient and sardonic metaphor.

A man sets out to push a heavy wagon up a steep hill. He pushes hard, sweating and swearing beneath a burning sun. Presently in exhaustion he sinks down to rest. Instantly the heavy wagon begins rolling backward down the hill, gaining momentum as it nullifies the hombre's hard toil, finally coming to a standstill hundreds of yards below the point where the long hard push began.

That is, in tropical sanitation efforts, as in tropical business generally, a noble enterprise if abruptly abandoned or insolvently begun frequently is far worse than no enterprise at all. Through the centuries the tragic consequences of abandoning good works prematurely are the first fear and dread of the realistic tropical planner. This has been true for many centuries longer than the Office of the Co-ordinator of Inter-American Affairs has been in existence, and neither Mr. Nelson A. Rockefeller nor his associates can be held responsible.

But it seems to this reporter that the Office of the Co-ordinator of Inter-American Affairs, despite all the broadsides of criticism and lambasting, and its frequent mistakes in the selection of personnel, has gone a great deal of excellent work in arousing and directing American interest in the other Americas. Its motion-picture division, with the superb contributions of Walt Disney, is easily the best in the United States Government. Its relations with schools, colleges, steering committees and study groups throughout the many American capitals are excellent enterprises.

In particular, the Co-ordinator's Health and Sanitation Department deserves credit for recognizing the existence of major and continuing health menaces of the American tropics and for setting out to help native medical talent make a stand against the many-sided onslaughts of the prime destroyers of health. So do certain efforts of the Co-ordinator's Food Supply Division, which has undertaken the ever formidable task of sponsoring more and better subsistence crops for the American tropics, and the Emergency Rehabilitation Department which has endeavored to strengthen the basic agrarian structure of the American tropics during a hard-straining war era. This reporter believes that the Americas are definitely better off because of the creation of the Office of the Co-ordinator of Inter-American Affairs.

But the insistent likelihood that no barrage, foxhole or fighting corner in the perennial battle of Washington can, per se, solve the demanding problems of Middle America is as evident as the realistic certainty that the greater part of the lasting solutions of Middle American problems must be developed in Middle America by way of Middle American enterprise applied to the rich soil and other durable resources of Middle America. But certainly the government of the United States is morally obliged to avoid hindering. There is no particular point in here repeating the involved, greedy and rather dismal saga of real or would-be dollar diplomacy. The era in question is now ended and even though it is unburied, it is dead, and nothing short of a complete collapse of moral character on the part of our national government can possibly cause its resurrection.

Now is the time to look to the future. Accordingly, as one American who watches beside and along with many other Americans, this reporter respectfully suggests that because of the basic, indisputable interdependence of the Americas, our hemisphere should produce in some measure all the strategic tropical deficit crops that can be grown effectively in Middle America and other of the American tropics—not to the exclusion of the importation of these crops from proved and existing sources but sufficiently so that with the occurrence of the next war the Americas will not again be completely or principally cut off from such indispensable tropical staples as natural rubber, strategic fibers, irreplaceable palm oils and palm waxes, and so forth.

The benefits derivable by all the Americas seem to me as evident and as secure as the advantages to military defense. For example, if even one-sixtieth of the minimum United States requirements of natural rubber could be purchased in Haiti, the export trade of Haiti would thereby be doubled, to the distinguished benefit of Haiti and ourselves. If even one-fourth of the United States pre-Pearl Harbor imports of natural rubber could be bought in Central America, the combined export trade of the six Central American republics would be approximately doubled. One-half of the United States peacetime requirements for abacá fiber would easily double the total value of Nicaraguan exports. These are pertinent "ifs," important alike to United States security and to the so long proved reality that valid continuing trade means life, health and survival for Middle America.

As previously noted, Middle America is not cartel country; we hope it may never be; and accordingly it cannot endure abject wage competition with the seventeen-cent-per-day pittance of the Sumatra rubber coolie, or the seven-cent-per-day wage of interior China, or the Javanese sugar wage of eleven cents per day for men and six to eight cents for women and children. The fact that in localized highland areas of Guatemala the daily wage is still as low as twenty-five cents, that in certain areas of Mexico it is thirty cents and in Haiti twenty to thirty cents is certainly not to be lauded or perpetuated.

For Middle America can never be solvent with or because of crushingly low wages. Wages far higher than existing averages need to be established and perpetuated. More and better labor unions are urgently needed, unions that are bona fide and adaptable to the needs and the laws of the particular countries concerned.

But progress toward desirable wage levels cannot be effected without real justification. Middle America's strategic nearness to United States markets which are far and away the world's strongest; Middle America's rich lands, some of them already productive through twelve months of the year, most of them comparatively cheap and lightly burdened with taxes —these are among the factors that provide or that can be made to provide economic justification for better wages for Middle American workers. So is the outstanding adaptability of Middle American farm workers. So are the bright opportunities for improving sea, air and land transportation to the end of better exploiting Middle America's mutually beneficial proximity to the United States. So, too, are the ever growing opportunities for mechanical improvements in Middle American farming practices and processing of crops (currently proved in the superb mechanization of the recently established Middle American abacá industry, the essential oil industries, and the newer techniques for processing of various valuable oil nuts).

Middle American wages and the entire agrarian and commercial structure of these Americas can and by all means should be further strengthened by research. In the past, and on the whole, research in American tropical agriculture has been chronically inadequate; frequently of almost kindergarten caliber in comparison with the well-co-ordinated government and privately subsidized research of the Dutch-directed experiment stations of the East Indies. The one consoling thought here is that while the greater part of the Dutch research, however excellent, was designed and executed for the benefit of limited groups or associations only, inter-American agricultural research has remained comparatively accessible to interested and literate people. Further, that since 1942 both the quantities and standards of research in American tropical agriculture are greatly increased, for which fact much gratitude and much glory are due the United States Department of Agriculture, which has drastically expanded and streamlined its long anemic stake in tropical research; the United Fruit Company, which now outdistances any other commercial operator in the scope, variety and practicality of its tropical crop researches; Britain's ever valuable Imperial College of Tropical Agriculture of Trinidad; the distinguished Experimental Farms of Guatemala; Costa Rica's College of Agriculture; Honduras' Lancetilla Experiment Station; Colombia's Coffee Experiment Stations; the increasing agricultural facilities of the Mexican Government, the Cuban Government, the Dominican and Haitian governments and other research institutions that are working ably and well for the good life of American tropical agriculture.

But a great deal more research is needed; capable laboratory work, experimental stations and practical field work, rural community establishments; public-school and public-health work, particularly for the great rural spaces of Middle America which support and otherwise shape the lives of about four-fifths of all Middle American peoples.

The practical and benefiting interpretation of research in tropical agriculture is also essential. The same is true of able and up-to-date agricultural education for the citizen youth of Middle America. At this time the need for such education simply cannot be exaggerated.

That Middle America is capable of growing practically all

the crops required by people, including approximately all the great tropical crops, is no longer open to question. Since Pearl Harbor the visible beginning for a new era of American tropical agriculture has been made. More than a score of experimental crops are succeeding, some of which can be grown successfully by independent citizen farmers.

But successful tropical agronomy is no longer a simple or easy enterprise. Today much up-to-date technical knowledge, supported by much theoretical study and practical work, is essential to the success of any new crops for the New World. Unless the talented youth of the American tropics can be capably taught how to cope with that exacting demand of the current and postwar era in tropical agriculture, neither the new fields of agriculture nor those already established are likely to succeed or endure.

In line with this decisive need at least one new development in agrarian education is being pioneered by and for Middle American youth. The name of the school is Escuela Agricola Panamericana; the location is inland Honduras about twenty-five miles from Tegucigalpa, the capital. This school was endowed initially late in 1941 by the United Fruit Company, with lands, buildings and other physical properties costing somewhat more than $800,000. The United Fruit Company additionally pledges the permanent maintenance of the school—which will endure as long as the company endures.

The school is being built in the Zamorano Valley at the intersection of the two highways that lead from Tegucigalpa to the towns of Danlí and Guinope. Its horticultural section, with nurseries, orchards and vegetable gardens, is situated on the road to Danlí. Along the other road is the livestock section, equipped with dairy barns, stables, poultry houses, refrigeration and creamery buildings, etc. The school's forest lands extend westward into the mountains. Down the valley are experimental fields and pastures, the former planted to corn, beans, rice, potatoes and other annual crops. The campus, farms and ranges cover about six square miles, with altitudes ranging from about 2,000 to 5,000 feet—and capable of growing practically any crop known to this hemisphere.

The school supplies its students with lodging, clothing, board, books, laboratory equipment, medical and dental services, transportation, and all other necessary supplies—entirely without cost. Each student works in fields, orchards, with livestock, or in gardens or orchards four hours each weekday and devotes four hours to study. The course covers three entire years with a fourth year of specialization. Student ages range from sixteen to twenty-one years. The curriculum is planned to develop practical agrarian leadership for Middle America in both independent agriculture and government extension services. The first year is devoted to preliminary courses in English, Spanish, general science and mathematics. This is followed by intensive study of agronomy, livestock husbandry, land survey, soil analysis and the planning and building of roads, irrigation and drainage systems; there is elementary instruction in physiology, hygiene and first aid, with particular emphasis on the treatment of common tropical diseases; in farm economy and farm marketing of tropical products; rural legislation and various other studies of urgent importance to contemporary agriculture of the American tropics.

The Department of Agronomy and Forestry provides basic laboratory experiments in chemistry and geology, which is followed by training in classification of soils and the use of fertilizers and crop-rotation techniques as adapted to the common needs of Middle America. The forestry course includes practical training in replanting native trees, establishing tree nurseries and transplanting small trees from nurseries to open woodlands. The course in agriculture begins with practical instruction in the propagation of common plants by means of seed, sprouts, bud-grafting or other planting stocks. Each student prepares and cares for a model nursery which includes 100 or more grafted fruit trees including oranges, mangoes and avocados. These fruit trees become the student's property at the time of his graduation, and he is urged to plant them on his own farm or in his own community. The courses in practical gardening include study of the nutritional value of the common vegetables.

The farm engineering department directs the study of irrigation and drainage—both particularly important throughout Middle America—and provides various courses in the use and care of farm machinery, including tractive machinery, staple hand tools and horse-drawn implements; also home carpentry and farm blacksmithing. A department of animal industries provides practical tutelage in breeding and keeping tended horses, mules, swine and poultry in the American tropics; provides study of principal contagious and infectious diseases and parasites of livestock in the tropics; and of animal vaccination and autopsy.

South of the Rio Grande agricultural, mechanical and engineering schools have always been in shortage. The shortage grows ever more acute, now that the defense of basic crops and livestock from fungi, microorganic diseases and virulent insect enemies becomes ever more commanding. Escuela Agricola Panamericana is a first deliberate answer to a challenge and need that simply cannot be evaded. It is not a preparatory school for banana farmers. It is entirely divorced from personnel requirements of any particular company or commercial employer. But I believe that it is a distinguished adventure in practical Pan-Americanism of the future.

The school's first admission of seventy-four students represents Mexico and all the six republics of Central America. Full-strength enrollment and its opening have been delayed by war conditions, but by Columbus Day, 1944, the school will be formally opened with the minimum authorized enrollment of 160 fellows—all own sons of Middle America; all rural youth; most of them poor boys who could not otherwise attend college; most of them from remote communities whose local school systems are limited to the first four or five elementary grades.

Even during its beginning year the school's farms are producing foodstuffs ample for its needs. Fields and gardens are already planted and in bearing. The livestock herds include more than 500 cattle, 80 horses, also poultry, swine and sheep. During 1943, the first year of experimental gardening, attractive vegetables were actually produced during ten and a half months of the year. Various garden and other staple food crops were quickly adapted to the Honduran study center from various nearby Americas: melons from Cuba, sweet corn from Puerto Rico, grafted avocados from California and Mexico, white potatoes from Florida, tomatoes and leafy vegetables from various areas of the United States South.

The beginning faculty personnel is distinctly inter-American. The head of the Department of Agronomy and Soil is Alfred F. Butler, cobuilder of the Lancetilla Experiment Station of Honduras, an English-trained agronomist who has done extensive work and research in agronomy, plant pathology and soil chemistry in Jamaica and other islands of the British West Indies. Dr. H. A. Von Wald, graduate of the University of Wisconsin, is head of the Department of Engineering. He has spent sixteen years in tropical America as supervising engineer for irrigation and drainage projects, rice plantations, livestock farms and other agricultural construction. The head of the Livestock Department is E. A. Rivera, a native Puerto Rican, a graduate of the College of Agriculture of Mayagüez, Puerto Rico, and for eleven years the director of the livestock and dairy department of the Venezuelan Government.

The professor of natural sciences is a Costa Rican, until recently the director of the National Museum of Costa Rica, Dr. Juvenal Valerio R. The professor of English is Augusto Aris, a Guatemalan. The professor of horticulture and director of the school is Dr. Wilson Popenoe, internationally renowned authority on tropical agriculture. The school's board of directors includes Luis Landa of Honduras, Carlos Miron of Guatemala, and Fernando Casto Cervantes of Costa Rica. The regents are responsible for the selection of scholars, each one of whom must be investigated and proved thoroughly accredited as to good character, industry and general intelligence. Thus far, all admissions have been of poor boys, and thus far not one accepted fellow has failed to prove a satisfactory record.

The school is not yet completely proved. Of necessity it may be variously revised and changed. But the school is there and at work; expertly planned and dedicated unequivocably to the premier agrarian need of the American tropics.

Escuela Agricola Panamericana is a reality as this book is written. More are needed; perhaps from two to six or more for every one of the Middle American nations. No better use of credit or money can be made. But the establishment of adequate vocational schools of agriculture, research institutes and experimental centers is inevitably costly; and here again, the provision of funds or enthusiasm for establishing such a school or research center, without the wherewithal to assure the competent operation of the school or center, is but another unhappy repetition of lethal anticlimax.

In the small, war-cramped Caribbean countries, the support of necessary schools is a hard-straining obligation. But this does not in any sense nullify the reality that timely and technical education, particularly in agriculture, is a pre-eminent need of Middle America today, an instant need that few or none of the Middle American nations can instantly fulfill.

In time they can probably provide and maintain these agricultural schools and other types of schools which are also certain to become increasingly necessary. But governmental burdens are heavy in Middle America; during the global-war period they have been staggering, and the burdens are sure to remain heavy during the several years immediately ahead. The more prosperous and better life for Middle America is certain to be predicated on increasing technological needs and on Middle American youth who are qualified to accommodate these needs.

The weight of evidence holds that Middle America will remain preponderantly agricultural, winning or losing by its climates, its producing lands and the people who till those lands—from which must be borne the staff of life, the indispensables of health, and the bases of living standards.

Now, as in the centuries gone by, the people of Middle America must stand together against the stubborn forces that would destroy them: the crowding jealous jungle; the violence of disease, flood and hurricane; the conspiracies of ruthless commercialism which play designingly in and with international politics.

In national tempers and in traditions the countries of Middle America stand clearly apart. But more than even before they are learning to stand and work together in commercial and social enterprises. They are proving the validity of co-operative efforts: of producer, consumer and labor co-operatives (for the most part still localized and in some cases still in experimental stages, but nevertheless promising). In this facility to work, produce and deliver in democratic groups, each member profiting in proportion to his contribution, we may even now see the talisman key that may open ever more precious doors to good lives for Middle America and all the American tropics.

But perhaps the most telling of all the keys to a brighter Middle American future is molded and sized from the indigenous character of tens of thousands of young men and young women of Middle America, with a genius born of uncounted generations of land-loving and land-tilling forebears, for the most part Indian but in some measure of other races; a genius that directs and inspires the contemporary generation; a genius that directs men and women to work the land gladly and to view it feelingly: actually to live and work on the *finca* or the *rancho;* to plan, supervise and personally effect the planning, tillage and harvesting of crops; to work as one with the habituated toilers of the field; to search and experiment with new crops and new ways of agronomy; to wear sweated working clothes; and, when the dudish tourist passes by and inquires for the *patrón,* to direct him to the farmhouse, hurry up the short trail home, enter the farmhouse by the back door, change hats and so welcome the naïve *turista* who believes that tropical agriculture is a whimsical color fantasia perpetuated by the gran señor who spends most of his time at the watering places of south France and other Mediterranean spas, since such has been the way of the glamorized caballeros of old.

But it is their way no longer. Middle American blood, talents, and devotions are again the priceless ingredients of Middle America. That is well for Middle America and for the United States. For the good of these Americas is inevitably our common good.

CHAPTER TEN

RESOURCE SUMMARY

THE following commercial and encyclopedic summary of the Middle American nations is included with the hope that it will prove useful to the readers who are exporters, importers or otherwise commercially or professionally associated with Middle American trade. Also it is hoped that the summaries will prove helpful to travelers, tourists and to those who seek condensed factual information regarding the ten American nations to the immediate south.

Conditions incident to the global war have considerably impeded, restricted or delayed the orderly collection and publication of factual material about Middle America. For this reason some of the statistical and record materials herein listed are marked as estimates or approximations; and certain statistics are considerably outdated.

However, I have tried to include the most authentic statistics available at the time of publishing this book, and here wish to express my gratitude for able assistance received from the Foreign Department, Chemical Bank and Trust Company of New York; the Foreign Department of the First National Bank of Boston; the United States Department of Commerce; the United States Consul at San Salvador, the United States Consul at Ciudad, Trujillo, and the United States Consul at Port-au-Prince.

MEXICO

General: Area 760,290 sq. mi., or about one-fourth as large as U. S. Climate is temperate in most regions, period of peak rainfall extending from June to October, with remaining months normally dry. Thermometric extremes (Fahrenheit) for Mexico City are 56° January and 66° June; in other leading cities the readings range some 10° higher. Government is republican in form, with three separate branches, and has its seat at Mexico City. Monetary unit is peso, valued at U. S. $0.2054. Population equals 19.4 million, giving density of 25 per sq. mi. *vs.* 44 in U. S.

Banking: System is headed by Banco de Mexico, which the government owns. It has sole authority to issue bank notes, without limitation, and no minimum metal reserve there against is legally prescribed. Statement of major items:

DATE	MET. RES.	NOTES	CAPITAL, ETC.	TOTAL RESOURCES	RES. VS. NOTES	DISC. RATE
		(in millions of pesos)				
12/31/41	188.7	559.6	41.5	885.2	33.7%	4%

Gold holdings of Banco de Mexico as of 2/28/42 were valued at U. S. $28 million. The banking organization has been expanding in recent years through the establishment of lending institutions supported by either public funds or private capital.

Budget:

YEAR	INCOME	OUTGO	BALANCE	COMPARATIVE PER CAPITA OUTGO
		(in millions of pesos)		
1942 (Est'd)	554.7	554.7	—	pesos 28 = $5.60 *vs.* $130.00 for U. S.

Main receipts 1941: Customs, export duties, industrial taxes, commercial taxes, income tax.

Main expenses 1941: Defense, public education, federal debt, communications, agriculture.

Collections: Dollar engagements resulting from merchandise imports are, with few exceptions, paid promptly.

Consulates: Consular representatives of Mexico and the United States are located in all the most important commercial centers of each country.

Debt: Not the subject of official disclosure in recent years. As of 12/31/39 it was estimated that Mexico owed pesos 3,506 million to foreigners and pesos 346 million to its own citizens.

Exchange: Free of governmental restrictions. In February 1940 Mexican bankers organized an unofficial Control Commission to supervise currency and credit, and this agency has achieved satisfactory results.

Exports: Certain articles require the prior approval of the Office of Control and Supply, established 2/6/42. This agency, which is under the jurisdiction of the Minister of National Economy, may expand or contract the list of affected items as immediate conditions dictate.

Foreign Trade:

YEAR	IMPORTS	EXPORTS	BALANCE	IMPORTS FROM U.S.	EXPORTS TO U.S.	BALANCE
	(in millions of pesos)			*(in millions of dollars)*		
1940	668.4	959.4	+291.0			
1941	887.4 *	688.6 *	−198.8 *	139.4 *	95.2 *	−44.2 *

* Provisional or approximate figures based on incomplete data.

Main imports: Vehicles, textiles, machinery, equipment, copra, metalware, cellulose, wool.

Main exports: Gold, silver, lead, zinc, copper, petroleum, mineral precipitates.

Gold: Production in 1941 valued at $29.0 million ($30.9 million 1940), with exports to U. S. amounting to approximately $16.5 million ($30.0 million 1940).

Imports: With respect to their Mexican deliveries, our exporters are, as a condition precedent, required to deposit 5% of their value with the consul who visas the relative invoices. Constituting prepayment of import duty, the sum in question may be charged to the buyer in Mexico. Certain shipments are, however, exempt from this provision. Essential covering documents on sea-borne cargoes are: commercial invoice, bill of lading and packing lists; on overland freight, a consular manifest is necessary, besides those papers just mentioned. Special certificates are prescribed where seed and cattle importations are involved. To co-ordinate its importing operations with our export restrictions more effectively, Mexico has established an Office of Control and Supply. This agency is empowered to issue certificates of necessity covering purchases from us of vital supplies, the exportation of which we have placed under governmental allocation, priority or license. It has drawn up a system whereby each Mexican importer who files a proper application therefor will be assigned a purchase quota of our controlled exports, based on related statistical totals computed by our economic authorities.

Industries: Agriculture—corn, wheat, cotton, sugar, chickpeas, henequen, vegetables, fruit, coffee, alfalfa, rice, tobacco. Communications—radios 310,000,* broadcasting stations 125,* telegraph lines 170,000 * kilos., telephones 180,000 * (with wire length 1.2 * million kms.). Forest—timber, rubber, chicle, naval stores. Manufacturing—textiles, shoes, metalware, cigars, cigarettes, drugs, beer, flour, paper, cement, pottery, foodstuffs, building materials, glass. Mining—gold, silver, copper, lead, zinc, antimony, tin, bismuth, cadmium, mercury, etc. Pastoral—cattle, pigs, goats, sheep, horses, hides, skins, dairy products. Power—150* generating plants, with water major source of energy. Transportation—airlines cover 15,000 * mi., linking all sections of nation; highways 63,000 * mi.; railways 24,000 * mi., passengers yearly 30.5 * million, freight 16.0 * million metric tons. Shipping—merchant fleet 60,* gross tons 39,000; * about 25,000 ships either enter or leave Mexican ports each year.

    * Provisional or approximate figures based on incomplete data.

Miscellaneous: Language is Spanish. Mail—regular 3–4 days, 3¢ per oz.; air 1–2 days, 10¢ per ½ oz. Weights, etc.—metric.

Prices: Official controls in effect for certain commodities and are likely to be further extended.

Trade Status: Our State Department announced 4/4/42 an intention to negotiate a reciprocal trade pact.

U. S. Credits:

Date Ext'd	Lender	Borrower	Amount	Purpose	Expires
3/27/37 *	Ex.-Imp. Bk.	Nat'l R'ways	$ 0.5 mil.	rolling stk.	
11/19/41	U. S. Treas.	Bco. de Mex.	40.0 mil.	cur'cy stab.	
11/19/41	U. S. Treas.	Bco. de Mex.	25.0 mil.	silver purch.	covers 1 yr.
11/19/41 †	Ex.-Imp. Bk.	Nac'l Fin. S. A.	30.0 mil.	highways	3 yrs.

    * Current status of this credit not disclosed.
    † Carries guarantee of Mexican Government.

Note: The Export-Import Bank has agreed to consider other suitable projects for financing offered by the Mexican authorities.

U. S. Investments: Direct investments end of 1936 placed at $480 million. Portfolio holding not estimated. Private sources

have appraised (1938) the value of total U. S. investments
in Mexico at $1 billion.

GUATEMALA

General: Climate varies with altitude; is tropical along coastal
lowlands where temperature averages 80°F. and moderate
at elevations approximating 5,000 feet, where mean annual
temperature is 58°F. Seasonal rains occur from May to October. Government is republican in form, with executive, legislative and judicial departments. The president is General
Jorge Ubico. Re-elected in 1937, the Constitutional Congress
of 1941 voted to continue him in office until 3/15/49. Language is Spanish. Mail—ordinary 8 days, 3¢ oz.; via air 1 day,
12¢ for ½ oz. Measures are metric. Monetary unit is quetzal,
same value as our U. S. dollar. Population equals 3.1 million,
giving density of 70 per sq. mi. *vs.* 44 in U. S.

Banking: System is headed by government-controlled Banco
Central de Guatemala S. A. (Central Bank), the state own-
ing 40% of the capital stock; remainder is held by banks, cor-
porations and citizens of the Republic. It retains the exclusive
right to issue currency and buy gold and silver, and also
conducts a general banking business. Major balance-sheet
items are:

DATE	GOLD, ETC.	FOREIGN EX.	CIRCULA- TION	SIGHT DEPS.	CAPITAL	GOLD VS. NOTES
		(in millions of quetzales)				
6/30/41	10.2	3.3	8.9	11.7	1.9	108%
5/31/42	9.5	9.3	13.4	12.4	1.9	71%

Note: Banks must maintain a reserve in gold and silver in
its vaults or in sight deposits abroad payable in gold of
not less than 40% of its circulation. At least one-third of the

40% reserve must be held in its own vaults, but this may include silver coins up to 10% of circulation. Executive decree 8/5/42 permitted issuance of paper currency up to 10 times paid-in capital.

Budget:

YEAR	INCOME	OUTGO	BALANCE	COMPARATIVE PER CAPITA OUTGO
(in millions of quetzales)				
6/30/42	10.2	10.2	—	
6/30/43	10.0	10.0	—	quetzales 3 *vs.* $250 for U. S.

Receipts: Taxes, public services, patrimonial revenues, national lottery, monopolies.

Expenses: Defense, personnel, education, finance, development, agriculture, debt.

Note: Budgetary trend in recent years has been downward from peak totals of quetzales 13.8 million for year ending 6/30/39.

Collections: Dollar engagements covering merchandise imports are usually paid on time.

Consulates: (main) Guatemala in U. S.: Washington, New York, San Francisco, Chicago, New Orleans. U. S. in Guatemala: Guatemala City, Puerto Barrios, San José de Guatemala.

Debt:

DATE	EXTERNAL	INTERNAL	TOTAL	COMPARATIVE PER CAPITA DEBT
(in millions of quetzales)				
12/31/41	9.2	0.5	9.7	quetzales *vs.* $600 for U. S., Aug. 1, 1942

Note: Debt has been reduced from peak of quetzales 22.7 million as of 12/31/33.

Exchange: No foreign-exchange restrictions are operative in Guatemala.

Foreign Trade:

Year	Imports	Exports	Balance	Imports from U.S.	Exports to U.S.	Balance
				(in millions of quetzales)		
1941 (12 mos.)	13.4	12.8	—0.6	10.0 *	10.2 *	+.2
1942 (4 mos.)	5.0	6.8	+1.8			

* Provisional or approximate figures based on incomplete data.

Imports: Machinery, textiles, drugs, chemicals, iron and steel products, fuel, flour.

Exports: Coffee, bananas, chicle, gold ($156,000), wood, honey, hides, rubber.

Suppliers: U. S., United Kingdom, Peru, Mexico, El Salvador.

Customers: U. S., United Kingdom, Canada, El Salvador, Mexico.

Note: We trade with Guatemala under a reciprocal agreement in force since 4/24/36. Official regulations apply to the importation and exportation of numerous commodities, these involving tariff, price and profit controls. Normal covering documents on freight shipments are commercial invoices, bill of lading and certificate of origin.

Industries: Agriculture—coffee, bananas, sugar, lemon grass, cereals, vegetables, cacao, tobacco. Communications—radio sets 14,000,* broadcasting stations 2, telephones 2,500 * (wire length 2,100 * mi.), telegraph lines 3,000 * mi. Forest —rubber, chicle, cinchona, mahogany, cedar. Manufacturing—sugar, cement, textiles, soap, candles, shoes, hats, ice, confectionery, cigars, cigarettes, furniture, lime, bricks, tiles. Mining—gold, silver, lead, ochre, mica, salt, iron, copper, marble, sulphur, coal. Pastoral—cattle, horses, asses, sheep, goats, pigs, mules, dairy products, poultry, meat. Shipping—lines 3, estimated arrivals and departures each 1,000 yearly, with approximate tonnage 2 million. Transportation—airlines 3, highways and roads 3,600 * mi., motor vehicles 3,000,* railroad 700 * mi.

* Provisional or approximate figures based on incomplete data.

Terms: On merchandise sales to Guatemalan importers our exporters specify settling methods that vary as follows: letter of credit; sight draft, documents *vs.* payment; sight draft up to 90 days maturity, documents *vs.* acceptance; open account, up to 90 days for liquidation.

U. S. Investments: Direct investments of the U. S. at the close of 1940 were placed at $68.2 million. Our investors held, as of 12/31/41, dollar bonds of Guatemala to a total of $1.6 million, and an additional $1.0 million in bonds guaranteed by the Republic.

HONDURAS

General: Climate along the coastal plains is tropical, that of interior highlands moderate. Rains prevail on the Atlantic side from September to January, on the Pacific from June to September. Government is republican form, with executive, legislative and judicial functions differentiated. Seat is at Tegucigalpa. Monetary unit is lempira, valued legally at U. S. 50¢, but free circulation of U. S. currency is allowed. Population equals 1 million, giving density of 22 per sq. mi. *vs.* 44 in U. S.

Banking: Honduras has no central bank but the establishment of one is currently under consideration. Two commercial banks, Banco Atlantida and Banco de Honduras, the former controlled by foreign capital, the latter by native interests, provide relative facilities and issue their own notes, which are secured by a statutory liquid reserve of 40%. Banco de Honduras may emit its notes up to twice its paid-up capital, while Banco Atlantida's bill circulation is limited to lempiras 1.7 million. Reserves may include U. S. dollars, gold coin, or lempira deposits in the two banks specified. Comparison of major items of both institutions as of 6/30/41:

	CASH	LOANS, ETC.	GOV'T BONDS	DEPS.	NOTES	CAP. FUNDS
(in millions of lempiras)						
Banco Atlantida	1.7	2.2	0.4	2.7	0.6	2.1
Banco de Honduras	2.6	1.6	—	1.9	0.5	1.4

Budget:

YEAR	INCOME	OUTGO	BALANCE	COMPARATIVE PER CAPITA OUTGO
(in millions of lempiras)				
6/30/41	10.8	10.8	—	
6/30/42	11.4	11.4	—	lempiras 11.4 = $5.70 *vs.* $250 for U. S.

Main receipts: Customs, monopolies, services, special stamps. Main expenses: Development, defense, treasury, government, education.

Note: Preliminary fiscal totals for budgetary year beginning 7/31/42 placed at lempiras 12.2 million.

Collections: Dollar engagements resulting from approved merchandise imports by well-rated merchants are, as a general rule, paid after short delays.

Consulates: Honduras in U. S.: Washington, New York, Boston, New Orleans, other large cities. U. S. in Honduras: Tegucigalpa, La Ceiba, Puerto Cortés, Tela.

Debt: As of 7/31/40 the national debt aggregated lempiras 17.4 million, of which lempiras 5.1 million were external and lempiras 12.3 million were internal. Per capita debt equaled lempiras 17 = $8.50 *vs.* $600.00 for U. S. as of August 1, 1942.

Exchange: Subject to control since 6/1/34. Transactions supervised by Committee for Control of International Exchange and Stabilization of Monetary System, which distributes foreign exchange monthly on the basis of quotas determined by the importer's purchases abroad over a period of years.

Value or volume of such quotas, as well as commodity ratings thereunder, are subject to revision depending usually on exchange balances and commodity supplies. In collecting foreign commercial obligations, the local bank is required to deliver shipping documents to the importer upon his payment to it of official lempiras, after which the bank then applies, on his behalf, to the committee for permission to allow it to effect the necessary conversion and remittance.

Exports: No official restrictions have been invoked at this writing.

Foreign Trade:

FISCAL YEAR	IMPORTS	EXPORTS	BALANCE	IMPORTS FROM U.S.*	EXPORTS TO U.S.*	BALANCE
(in millions of lempiras)						
6/30/40	20.2	19.3	0.9			
	20.5	20.2	0.3	16.0	19.3	+3.3

* We trade with Honduras under a reciprocal agreement executed 3/2/36.

Main imports: Ironware, petroleum, textiles, machinery, sugar, fertilizers, wheat.

Main exports: Bananas, silver, gold, mineral waste, cattle, coffee, timber, tobacco.

Suppliers: U. S., El Salvador, Netherlands W. I., United Kingdom.

Customers: U. S., El Salvador, United Kingdom.

Gold: Production during calendar year 1941 was valued at approximately $1.0 million, which equaled amount shipped abroad in fiscal year ending 6/30/41. Silver worth $1.3 million was mined in Honduras during calendar year 1941.

Imports: No governmental permits are required but quantitative quotas are in operation. Covering documents on freight shipments: consular invoice, certificate of origin, commercial invoice, bill of lading.

Industries: Agriculture—bananas, coffee, sarsaparilla, plantains, fruits, coconuts, sugar, vegetables, cereals. Communications—radio sets 16,000,* telephones 3,500,* lines 6,500 * mi., telegraph lines 5,000.* Forests—mahogany, rosewood, cedar, balsam, rubber. Manufacturing—flour, tile, soap, candles, shoes, beverages, matches, clothing, lard, tobacco products, straw hats. Mining—gold, silver, antimony, cinnabar, copper. Pastoral—skins, cattle, hides, dairy products. Power —potential water-power resources estimated at 1 million hp. Transportation—airlines 2, auto vehicles 2,000, highways 500 mi., railways 900 mi., shiplines 3, with merchant marine tonnage 84,000.*

* Provisional or approximate figures based on incomplete data.

Miscellaneous: Language is Spanish. Mail—ordinary 7 days, 3¢ per oz.; air 2–3 days, 12¢ per ½ oz. Weights, etc.—metric.

U. S. Credits: On 2/11/42 the president of Honduras was authorized to negotiate with our Export-Import Bank for a loan of $15 million, for the purpose of (1) construction on the Pan-American Highway; (2) construction on the Interoceanic Highway; (3) construction on the Interoceanic Railway; (4) establishing a central bank; (5) establishing a farm-loan bank; (6) retiring the external debt.

U. S. Investments: U. S. direct investments in Honduras at the close of 1936 were placed at $36.4 million, mostly in banana plantations and mines. In recent years there has been a gradual increase in U. S. capital outlays here.

EL SALVADOR

Commercial travelers, when proceeding to El Salvador on sales or survey trips or for similar purposes, should be in possession of a letter from their firms accrediting them as such. This should be authenticated by an official of a chamber of commerce, merchant's association, or similar body, and should be visaed (gratis) by a Salvadoran consul. A fine of colons 25 will be imposed for failure to present this document.

General: El Salvador, which is the smallest of the 6 Central American republics, has an area of about 10,000 sq. mi. (approximately the size of Vermont) and is the only country of Central America without an Atlantic seaboard. It is mountainous and is subject to frequent slight earthquakes. Along the seacoast and in the lower regions it is hot, tropical and during the rainy season (May to October), damp and unhealthy. In the foothills and in the higher interior regions the climate is semitropical and healthy the year round. The total rainfall of the country averages about 75 in. and the average annual temperature about 74°F. Extreme temperatures are about 51° and 98°.

Population, Race and Standard of Living: The Republic is the most densely settled of the Central American countries, having an estimated population of 1,829,816 or 183 persons per sq. mi. The capital, San Salvador, which is the commercial and financial center of the Republic, has an estimated population of 140,000.

Language, Weights, Measures and Currency: The language of the people is Spanish and some of the old Spanish weights and measures still are employed, although the metric system generally is used. The nation's currency unit is the colon, the value of which in American dollars has not varied more than 1¢ from 40¢ since November 1934.

Leading Occupations and Industries: El Salvador is essentially an agricultural country, almost entirely dominated by primary industries, principally the cultivation of coffee, which normally represents 75 to 85% of its exports by value. Corn, beans, rice, sugar, fruit, cotton, henequen (sisal) and tobacco are grown, and gold, balsam, henequen, sugar and uncured hides are exported. Stock raising is sufficient to supply the local demand. There is some manufacturing for local consumption, but the country has developed few industrial raw materials. Power resources are limited. Manufactures consist principally of shoes and leather goods, cotton yarn, piece goods, some clothing and furnishings, sugar, rum and alcohol, beer and soft drinks, wheat flour, cigarettes, henequen bags, soap, candles, matches, vegetable oils, furniture, ironware, tiles and bricks, salt, lard, and printed articles. Labor is largely unskilled and receives wages that little more than cover the cost of living. There is no national shipping.

Leading Imports and Exports: Total imports in 1941 were valued at $8,330,991, of which the U. S. supplied 77.75%. Manufactured goods comprised the bulk of importations. Principal imports were cotton piece goods, cotton yarn, rayon piece goods, machinery and automobile vehicles, medicines, toilet goods and other chemicals, petroleum products, foodstuffs, and wines and liquors. Total exports in 1941 were valued at $11,304,375, of which coffee amounted to $8,464,570. The U. S. received 79% of all exports.

General Customs Policy and Regulations: The Salvadoran import customs tariff is high and is levied under a dual schedule, of which the second is three times the first. The preferential Import Tariff Law of 1934 (revised) operates to give nations that import substantial amounts of Salvadoran products the benefit of the lower tariff. Countries that import little or nothing from El Salvador are required to pay the higher duties on merchandise they send to this country. Salvadoran imports from the U. S. are assessed at the minimum rate. The rates of import duty are fixed in American currency, although collected in colons (at the rate of $1.00 equals $2.50), and are assessed per kilo (2.2 lbs.) of total gross weight (i. e., including packing).

The following special duties are also applicable to imports: a Salvadoran consular fee amounting to 6% of the value of the import, and a tax of 2% of the value of the customs duties paid.

The customary set of documents received by the local banks for freight shipments from the U. S. consists of a Salvadoran consular invoice and two copies of the commercial invoice, appropriately visaed by the consulate of El Salvador in the U. S. nearest the port of shipment, bill of lading, certificate of origin, insurance papers, and a statement of contents, weights, and measures.

United States–El Salvador Trade Agreement: A trade agreement between the U. S. and El Salvador, which went into effect on May 31, 1937, provides for substantial reductions in former import duties into El Salvador on certain meat, fish, fruit, vegetable and cereal products, lumber, rubber products (including tires and tubes), leather products and phonograph records. Trade statistics, since the effective date of the agreement, show considerable gains in importations into El Salvador from the U. S. of most of the products mentioned.

Postal Regulations and Rates: Postage on ordinary letters is 3¢ per oz., from the U. S. to El Salvador; on air-mail letters, 12¢ per oz.; on parcel-post packages 14¢ per lb., with a very small surcharge on parcels sent via Puerto Barrios. The air-express rates to San Salvador from Brownsville, Texas, and Mexicali, California, both on the U. S.–Mexican border, are $0.61 and $1.07 per lb., respectively.

Merchandise by freight reaches any of the Salvadoran ports (Acajutla, La Libertad, La Union-Cutuco) by sea direct, and also by sea to Puerto Barrios, Guatemala, and thence to San Salvador by rail. Rates from any port in the U. S. to San Salvador are the same, irrespective of the route by which the goods are shipped.

Only two American shipping lines at present serve El Salvador: the Grace Line, 2 Pine Street, San Francisco, California, and the United Fruit Company, Pier 3, North River, New York.

Character of Packing Desired: Owing to the tropical climate and to rough handling, which is unavoidable in landing imported goods at final destination, particular care should be taken in preparing merchandise for shipping. Packing, however, should be as light as practicable, as the import duty is levied on the gross weight. To avoid claims, packing instructions furnished by individual importers should be strictly adhered to. The packing of different classes of goods together is inadvisable.

Credit Conditions and Price Quotations: There are no definite financing rules applicable to this Republic. The bulk of foreign business is done on a sight-draft basis. Credit reports can be had from American banks doing foreign business, from commercial reporting agencies such as Dun and Bradstreet, from banks in San Salvador, or from the Bureau of Foreign and Domestic Commerce and its district offices. Quotations should be made C.I.F. Salvadoran ports or Puerto Barrios, Guatemala (for rail transit to El Salvador), whenever possible, and a note added that such quotations include, or do not include, Salvadoran customs and consular charges.

Banks in El Salvador: The bank of issue in El Salvador is the Salvadoran Central Reserve Bank (Banco Central de Reserva de El Salvador), established in 1934. The private banks are the Banco Occidental, Banco Salvadoreno and Bank of London & South America, Ltd., all located in San Salvador. The important, semiofficial Mortgage Bank was established in 1935. It is advisable that shipments in most cases, whether freight or parcel post, be consigned to one of the local banks, irrespective of whether the draft has been made payable at sight or on time, but to avoid delays in delivery, cases should be marked with the name of the house for which the goods are ultimately intended. Merchandise remaining in the control of the Salvadoran Customs Administration for a period exceeding 6 months is liable to confiscation.

Sales Methods in El Salvador: From the standpoint of an exporter entering this market, El Salvador should be considered as a single sales area to be covered from San Salvador, as about 85% of the nation's business is handled through this city. There are three principal methods: (1) appointment of a local importer as exclusive agent, (2) appointment of several importers as agents, and (3) appointment of a manufacturer's agent as sole representative for the entire country.

NICARAGUA

General: Largest Central American country. Climate on eastern side of mountains generally tropical with rainfall spread liberally through the year. In the western districts, where the major population centers are, wet and dry seasons rotate, with former lasting from May to December. Government is republican in form, having three distinct branches, with seat at Managua. Monetary unit is cordoba, with official value of U. S. $0.2000. Population equals 1.3 million, giving density of 22 per sq. mi. *vs.* 44 in U. S.

Banking: System headed by Banco Nacional de Nicaragua, which is fully owned by the government and holds exclusive note-issuing privilege. Statement of major accounts in Issue Department (in millions of cordobas):

Date	Stab. Fd.	Fiduc'y Circ.	Total Circ.	Res. *vs.* Total Circ.
6/30/41	15.2 *	4.1	14.6	104%
12/31/41	9.7 *	4.1	17.7	55%

* Gold reserve equal to 60% of notes outstanding in excess of fiduciary issue must be held in New York City.

Budget:

Year	Income	Outgo	Balance	Comparative Per Capita Outgo
		(in millions of cordobas)		
1941	25.5	25.5	—	
1942	34.0	34.0	—	cordobas 26 = $5.20 *vs.* $130.00 for U. S.

Receipts: Internal taxes, customs, railways and ship revenues, national bank fees, etc.

Expenses: Governmental agencies, railways, ships, public debt, national bank costs, etc.

Note: Surpluses have actually resulted in each fiscal year from 1936 to 1941.

Collections: Dollar engagements arising from approved merchandise imports by well-established merchants are, as a rule, currently settled without undue delay.

Consulates: Nicaragua in U. S.: New York, San Francisco, honorary consulates in other important cities. U. S. in Nicaragua: Managua, Matagalpa, Puerto Cabezas.

Currency: Cordoba worth U. S. 20¢. General circulation composed of notes of the Banco Nacional de Nicaragua and metallic units, and various subsidiary coins. The U. S. dollar, as well as fractional denominations thereof, also circulates rather freely.

Debt: As of 1/31/41 national debt aggregated cordobas 22 million, composed of following obligations:

Ext'l Bonds	Int'l Bonds, etc.	Nat'l Bk.	Frozen Com'l	Ex.-Imp. Bk.	Other
7.9 mil.	0.4 mil.	2.2 mil.	5.2 mil.	5.7 mil.	5.0 mil.

Comparative per capita debt: Cordobas 22 = $4.40 for Nicaragua *vs.* $600.00 for U. S. as of August 1, 1942.

Note: Substantial reductions were effected in some of the above figures during 1941.

Exports: Certain limitations imposed thereon in the interest of hemispheric defense, unless items in question are moving to markets in the two Americas.

Exchange: Restrictions have been in force since 1931. Law of November 4, 1940 requires that foreign exchange accruing from exports be delivered to Exchange Control Commission. Its use by the credited exporter in payment of licensed imports is, however, allowed, providing liquidation of the relative engagement results within 60 days. Exchange acquired through other transactions, except those involving tourist expenditures or freely marketable obligations, may not constitute the subject matter of a private contract. In rationing exchange, commodity imports receive preference, with issuance of the relative authorizations (exchange-import certificates) determined by the status of Nicaragua's cash balances abroad. Exchange-import certificates are available to Nicaraguans who maintain their own accounts with foreign banks, for remittance purposes. While official selling rate of the Banco Nacional is 5 cordobas per U. S. $1.00, the actual quotation, including the 10% sales tax and ½% commission, equals 5.52½. The Banco Nacional buys dollars at 4.97½ cordobas per U. S. $1.00, arrived at by deduction of ½% commission from its fixed price. On the curb market the present cordoba-dollar rate ranges around 5.32 plus 10% tax.

Foreign Trade:

YEAR	IMPORTS	EXPORTS	BALANCE	IMPORTS FROM U.S.	EXPORTS TO U.S.	BALANCE
	(in millions of dollars)					
1940	7.5	9.5	+2.5	—	—	—
1941	10.5	12.0	+1.5	9.0	11.5	+2.5

Main imports: Machinery, equipment, cotton, textiles, metalware, chemicals, foodstuffs, oils, vehicles, fuel.
Main exports: Gold, coffee, bananas, lumber, cotton, silver, cattle, hides, skins, ipecac.
Suppliers: U. S., United Kingdom, Peru.
Customers: U. S., Peru.
   Note: Imports are valued f.o.b. port of origin. Exports include gold, which is largely foreign owned, only an estimated 60% of its value reverting to Banco Nacional in foreign exchange. Certain types of overland and transit trade excluded from above figures.

Gold: Virtually entire production, valued at $7.5 million in 1941, up from $5.8 million in 1940, was exported. Foreign-owned mines accounted for 77% of output. Shipments abroad prohibited unless routed through Banco Nacional.

Imports: An emergency law empowering president to control imports, originally enacted in September 1939, was extended for an additional year on September 12, 1941. Before placing merchandise orders abroad, the importer must have applied for an exchange-import certificate. Since clearance of an incoming cargo will not be allowed without presentation of this certificate, our exporters should insist on proper assurances to that effect, before proceeding with their shipping preparations. In addition, the normal covering documents, where freight shipments exceed $50 in value, viz., consular invoice, bill of lading, commercial invoice and certificate of origin, are required.

Industries: Agriculture—coffee, cereals, vegetables, sugar, cotton, fruit, bananas, cacao, tobacco. Communications—radios 4,000, broadcasting stations 4, telephones 1,390 * (wire length 4,000 mi.), telegraph lines 5,000 * mi. Forest—mahogany, cedar, cocobolo, lignum vitae, dyewoods, gum, medicinal plants. Manufacturing—sugar, alcohol, cigars, cigarettes, textiles, leather goods, rubber articles, cement, dairy products. Mining—gold, silver, copper. Pastoral—cattle, horses, pigs, goats and sheep. Power—10 stations, capacity 3,261 kilowatts. Transportation—airlines 3, local 1, international 2; auto vehicles 1,000,* highways 500 mi.; railways 400 mi.; shipping—approximately 800 ships, tonnage 840,000, enter and leave Nicaraguan ports each year.

* Provisional or approximate figures based on incomplete data.

Miscellaneous: Language is Spanish. Mail—regular 6–9 days, 3¢ per oz.; air 2 days, 12¢ per ½ oz. Weights, etc.—metric.

Prices: Controls and ceilings have been applied to an increasing number of commodities.

U. S. Credits:

DATE EXT'D	LENDER	BORROWER	AMOUNT	PURPOSE	EXPIRES
5/17/39	Ex.-Imp. Bk.	Banco Nac.	$ 0.5 mil.	buy U.S. goods	12/31/41
5/17/39	Ex.-Imp. Bk.	Repub. of Nic.	2.0 mil.	buy U.S. goods	12/31/41
3/ 3/41	Ex.-Imp. Bk.	Repub. of Nic.	2.0 mil	buy U.S. goods	—
1/16/41	P.W.A.	Repub. of Nic.	12.0 mil.	Pan-Am. H'wy.	—

U. S. Investments: Latest official estimate of U. S. direct investments is $4.5 million at end of 1936. No figures available on portfolio holdings. Our capital stake has increased substantially during recent years, chiefly in metal-mining and oil-drilling explorations.

COSTA RICA

General: Capital is San José. Monetary unit is the colon, officially valued at $0.1781. Population equals 625,000, giving density of 27 per sq. mi. *vs.* 44 in U. S.

Banking: The system is headed by the government-owned Banco Nacional de Costa Rica (National Bank), which operates three departments: Issue, Commercial and Mortgage. It has the sole right to issue bank notes. Statement of the Issue Department showed the following accounts:

DATE	CIRCULATION	GOLD	FOREIGN ASSETS	TOTAL ASSETS	GOLD *vs.* CIRC.
		(in millions of colons)			
12/31/40	29.2	4.5	2.8		14%
12/31/41	37.5	4.4	9.1	49.4	12%
5/30/42	39.0	4.4	12.4	48.3	11%

Note: No legal minimum gold reserve is specified. Ratio of gold and foreign assets to circulation 5/30/42 equaled 38%. Per capita circulation 12/31/41 equals colons 62 = $10 *vs.*

$100 for U. S. today. Resources: 12/31/41 Mortgage Department colons 29.9 million; Commercial Department colons 38.4 million. Total bank deposits 6/30/42 estimated at colons 66.0 million, equaling per capita sum of colons 105 = $17 *vs.* $615 for U. S. today.

Budget:

YEAR	INCOME	OUTGO	BALANCE	COMPARATIVE PER CAPITA OUTGO
(in millions of colons)				
12/31/41	42.6	53.0	−10.4	colons 85 = $14 *vs.* $250 for U. S.

Receipts: Customs, liquor monopoly, railway earnings, export tax, direct taxes, conversion tax.

Expenses: Public works, education, public safety, debt, financial, interior.

Note: Deficits for 1940 and 1941 attributed to added outlays on Pan-American Highway; budget usually balances or shows a moderate-sized surplus. Above figures apparently include certain special accounts, operation of which is not disclosed, inasmuch as ordinary budgetary totals stood at colons 35.6 million each. Monthly returns suggest another deficit for the fiscal year ending 12/31/42.

Consulates: Costa Rica in U. S.: New York, Chicago, New Orleans, San Francisco and other large cities. U. S. in Costa Rica: Puerto Limon and San José.

Debt:

DATE	EXTERNAL	INTERNAL	TOTAL	COMPARATIVE PER CAPITA DEBT
(in millions of colons)				
12/31/40	100.9	35.4	136.3	colons 220 = $37 *vs.* $600 for U. S.

Exchange: Decree of 8/15/42 authorized Exchange Control Board to apply equal treatment to all transactions in controlled exchange, regardless of the type of goods involved, thereby repealing decree of 2/6/40, under which approval of such applications had been based on different merchandise categories. The rates for dollars in controlled and uncontrolled colons are 5.62 and 5.64 respectively. The former is obtained from commodity exports, the latter from other sources.

Foreign Trade:

YEAR	IMPORTS	EXPORTS	BALANCE	IMPORTS FROM U.S.	EXPORTS TO U.S.	BALANCE
	(*in millions of colons*)			(*in millions of dollars*)		
1941	99.7	56.7	—43.0	13.0 *	9.5 *	—3.5 *

* Provisional or approximate figures based on incomplete data.

Imports: Flour, gasoline, cement, textiles, chemicals, automotive products, petroleum.

Exports: Coffee, bananas, cacao, gold, rubber, timber, fruit, hides, skins, fish.

Suppliers: U. S., United Kingdom, Peru, Canada, Mexico.

Customers: U. S., Canada, Argentina, Panama.

We trade with Costa Rica under a reciprocal agreement effective 8/2/37.

Gold: Production of gold bullion and concentrates has declined in recent years from an annual average of approximately $500,000 to an estimated $300,000 for 1942.

Industries: Agriculture—coffee, bananas, cacao, citrus fruit, coconuts, sugar, vegetables, cereals, tobacco, cotton. Communications—radios 11,000, stations 20, telegraph offices 235, telephones 4,000. Forest—rubber, hemp, timber, dyewoods. Manufacturing—shoes, soap, candles, beverages, alcohol, cigars, cigarettes, furniture, textiles. Marine—shark, tuna, pearls. Mining—gold, salt. Pastoral—cattle, swine, horses, mules, hides, skins, dairy products, honey, meat, milk. Shipping—vessels numbering 731 (aggregate tonnage 1.5 million) entered and cleared during 1939. Transportation—airlines 2, automotive vehicles 5,000, highways 300 mi., railways 413 mi.

Miscellaneous: Language—Spanish. Mail—ordinary 9–15 days, 3¢ oz.; air, 2–3 days, 15¢ ½ oz. Measures—metric.

U. S. Credits:

DATE EXT'D	LENDER	BORROWER	AMOUNT	PURPOSE
10/12/39	Ex.-Imp. Bk.	Banco Nacional	$1.0 mil.	U. S. purchases
9/23/40	Ex.-Imp. Bk.	government	4.6 mil.	U. S. purchases
7/ 1/41	Ex.-Imp. Bk.	Banco Nacional	.5 mil.	dollar ex.
1/16/42	P.W.A.	government	8.0 mil.	Pan-Am. H'way
7/ 1/42	Ex.-Imp. Bk.	government	2.0 mil.	pay bills, etc.

Note: U. S. agreed 1/16/42 to grant lend-lease credits of $550,000.

U. S. Investments: Our direct holdings in coffee plantations, mining lands, cattle ranches and public utilities were appraised at $24.7 million at the end of 1940, while at the close of 1941 our investors owned an estimated $6.4 million worth of Costa Rica's dollar bonds. Under stipulations of the Coupon Purchase Offer of 3/20/39, expiring 12/31/41, interest on coupons of these bonds was paid at the rate of 30% of face value. Arrangements for continuation of coupon-purchasing program is now pending.

PANAMA

Panama, with a population estimated in 1941 as 635,836 and an area of 33,667 square miles (comparable to that of Indiana), remains one of the most strategic land surfaces of the world. Commercially the country tends to be divisible

into the Canal Zone and Panama Republic. The ports of
Panama City and Colón are commercial strongholds for both
the Zone and the Republic, and with the war in progress the
military and civilian personnel of the renowned "Zone" are
heavily increased, with proportionate increased demand for
construction materials, general supplies and war material of
almost every type. Outside the "Zone" and the principal
cities, Panama is a rich and thus far little developed jungle
and mountain country, with some extremely rich soils and
extensive mineral resources.

Trade volume is rapidly increasing. In 1939, Panama's foreign trade totaled $27,290,000—on a per capita basis one of
the highest tallies in the Western Hemisphere. The $20,464,-
000 worth of imports featured in this order: textiles, cigarettes, automobiles, butter, wheat flour, cotton textiles, gasoline, construction lumber, cotton and silk cloths, perfumes,
dresses and suits, processed meats and cement. The principal
exports ($6,826,000 in 1939) are bananas, cacao, cattle, gold
dust, coconuts, hides, antiques, wild rubber and tortoise
shells. In the area of Gatun, the Goodyear Rubber Plantations Company has established one of the most important
hevea rubber nurseries of the hemisphere. In the Caribbean
plains area the United Fruit Company established 10 years
ago this hemisphere's first seed plantation of abacá. The company is now planting the crop extensively in the Almirante
area. To Panama goes the honor of having produced and exported for the benefit of our fighting Navy the first tonnage
of Manila hemp produced in the Western Hemisphere.

CUBA

General: Climate is semitropical, temperatures ranging from
60° to 98° F., with two seasons: May to November warm and
moist, December to April dry. Government is republican in
form, with three distinct branches, and has its seat at Havana.

Monetary unit is peso, officially valued at U. S. $1.00. Population equals 4.2 million, giving density of 95 per sq. mi. *vs.* 44 in U. S.

Banking: Each bank must maintain at least 25% of its total deposits with the Insular Treasury in the form of a legal reserve. The government alone is privileged to issue currency. Money in circulation as of 4/30/42 consisted of pesos 90.7 million and U. S. $89.4 million. The former, which were increased by pesos 10.0 million in early June, are backed 98% by U. S. dollars on deposit with the Treasury. An agreement signed by Cuba and the U. S. on 7/6/42 will enable Cuba to buy gold from us for the purpose of eventually using it to supplant the dollars it now holds in its currency reserve.

Budget:

YEAR	INCOME	OUTGO	BALANCE	COMPARATIVE PER CAPITA OUTGO
		(in millions of pesos)		
1942 (Est'd)	89.4	89.4	—	pesos 21 = $21 *vs.* $250 for U. S.

Main receipts: Taxes, direct and indirect, customs, communications, consular.

Main expenses: Defense, education, debt, finance, health.

Note: The Budget Law of 1938, since modified from time to time, has governed fiscal procedure in each succeeding year. Subsequent budgets represent extensions by legislative decrees of the policies then inaugurated.

Collections: Dollar engagements resulting from approved merchandise imports are usually paid on time.

Consulates: Consular representatives of Cuba are located in all our most important business centers. In Cuba we have full consular offices at Havana, Matanzas, Antilla, Cienfuegos, Nuevitas, Santiago.

Debt: As of 10/31/41 the insular debt aggregated $213.8 million, composed of the following obligations:

External	Internal	Floating	Total	Comparative Per Capita Debt
		(in millions of U. S. dollars)		
$116.4	$7.4	$90.0 *	$213.8 *	$50.0 as of Aug. 1, 1942

* Provisional or approximate figures based on incomplete data.

Exchange: Transactions have been supervised in varying measure since 6/15/39, at which time an Exchange Stabilization Fund was established. Exporters must deliver to the Exchange Stabilization Fund a certain percentage—it is raised or lowered according to market conditions—of their dollars, receiving therefor pesos at par. After setting aside debt-service requirements, the balance of such receipts is allocated proportionately to importers of essential goods. Regulations pertaining to money movements to and from Cuba were tightened 6/19/42. Dollar imports from sources outside the Americas are forbidden, and exports of this currency require governmental approval.

Exports: Many items are subject to prior authorization of the minister of commerce, who acts in conformity with advices rendered by the Exportation and Importation Agency, another official bureau.

Foreign Trade:

Year	Imports	Exports	Balance	Imports	Exports	Balance
		From U.S.*			To U.S.*	
		(in millions of pesos)				
1941	133.6	211.5	+77.9	117.1	181.2	+64.1

* We trade with Cuba under a reciprocal agreement signed 8/24/34, supplemented or amended 12/18/39 and 12/23/41.

Main imports: Foodstuffs, textiles, automotive machinery and vehicles, chemicals, fuel, paper, etc.
Main exports: Sugar, derivatives, tobacco, vegetables, fruits, minerals, animal products, lumber, fish, canned goods.
Suppliers: U. S., United Kingdom, Mexico, India, Canada.
Customers: U. S., United Kingdom, Canada, Spain, Mexico.

Gold: Not listed as an important producer. No special restrictions apply to its export or import.

Imports: The allocation of imported materials is carefully regulated by the official Importation and Exportation Agency on the basis of quarterly quotas. Certificates of necessity are likewise prescribed for purchases made in U. S. markets. Normal covering documents on ship cargo are the consular invoice, bill of lading and commercial invoice, but certain shipments require a certificate of origin as well.

Industries: Agriculture—sugar, tobacco, fruits, vegetables, coffee, cereals, peanuts. Communications—radios 170,000,* telephones 62,000 * (wire length 272,000 mi),* telegraph lines 9,000 mi. Forest—mahogany, ebony, cedar. Manufacturing —sugar, molasses, cigars, cigarettes, rum, glycerin, twine, beeswax, sponges, alcohol, honey, machinery, foodstuffs, furniture, cement, tile, toiletries, beer, textiles. Mining—iron, manganese, chrome, copper, asphalt, nickel, petroleum, salt. Pastoral—cattle, hides, meat, milk, dairy products, horses, mules, hogs, sheep. Shipping—in 1940 ships entering and leaving Cuban ports numbered respectively about 3,700, with tonnage under each heading amounting to about 14.7 million. Merchant fleet numbers 39 * steamers, with gross tonnage 30,000.* Tourist—in 1940 arrivals equaled 127,400 but substantial declines noted in seasons of 1941 and 1942. Transportation—automotive vehicles 50,000; * airplanes in service 3,600; * highways 2,500 mi.; * railways 6,800 mi.

* Provisional or approximate figures based on incomplete data.

Miscellaneous: Language is Spanish. Mail—ordinary 4 days, 3¢ per oz.; air 1 day, 10¢ per ½ oz. Weights, etc.—metric.

Prices: Controlled by Office of Price and Supply Regulation since 5/13/42. Frozen as of 3/2/42.

U. S. Credits:

DATE EXT'D	LENDER	BORROWER	AMOUNT	PURPOSE	EXPIRES
6/13/41	Ex.-Imp. Bk.	Gov't.	$ 11.0 mil.	m'kt sugar	?
3/28/42	Def's Sup. Corp.	Gov't.	150.0 ° mil.	sugar purch.	12/16/42
4/ 8/42	Ex.-Imp. Bk.	Gov't.	25.0 mil.	general	?

* Provisional or approximate figure based on incomplete data.

Note: U. S. signed lend-lease agreement with Cuba 11/7/41 under which latter will receive war materials and we will buy its sugar, tobacco, manganese, etc.

U. S. Investments: As of 12/31/40 U. S. investments in Cuba's dollar bonds were placed at $60 million. In August 1940 our capital investments were estimated at $1,140 million, including $600 million in sugar, $235 million in railways and public utilities, $80 million in factories, hotels, buildings and real estate, $50 million in mines, $30 million in miscellaneous businesses, $45 million in agriculture. Cuba's dollar bonds consist of 6 separate issues:

HIGHEST PRICED	QT.	LOWEST PRICED	QT.	AV. OVER-ALL QT.	TOTAL OUTSTANDING
Public Works 5½s '45	112	Ext'l 4½s '77	80	99	$98.3 million

DOMINICAN REPUBLIC

General: The Ciudad Trujillo Consular District embraces the entire Dominican Republic, with an area of 19,332 sq. mi., which occupies the eastern two-thirds of the island in the West Indies known as Hispaniola. Haiti is situated in the western portion of the same island. Except for certain regions in the highlands, the climate of the Dominican Republic is tropical and enervating throughout the greater part of the year. November to March are usually the coolest months. Four mountain ranges cross the country from east to west. The Pico del Yaque and Pico Trujillo in the southwest rise to heights of approximately 10,000 feet.

Population, Races, Language, Standard of Living: On December 31, 1941 the population of the country was officially 1,768,163. On the basis of these figures it has been calculated that about 12% are whites, 20% Negroes and 68% of mixed blood. Ciudad Trujillo (pop. 79,000) is the capital, largest city and chief port and principal commercial center of the Republic. Other cities of importance are Santiago de los Caballeros (pop. 34,655), San Pedro de Macoris (pop. 19,-147), Puerto Plata (pop. 11,891), La Romana (pop. 11,000), and San Francisco de Macoris (pop. 10,397). While Spanish is the language of the country, the majority of the more important commercial organizations are able to correspond in English.

Leading Occupations and Industries: The economy of the Dominican Republic is largely agricultural, with sugar, cacao, coffee, starch, molasses, tobacco and corn as the principal export crops. Other important agricultural products are beans, rice, oranges, bananas, coconuts, pineapples and mangoes. Leading manufactures are shoes, cigarettes, beer, rum, cigars, furniture, shirts, straw hats, tiles, soap, starch, matches and sole leather.

Imports and Exports: Imports for 1940 amounted to $10,511,-403, while exports amounted to $18,330,135. Of the total imports, 67% come from the U. S., as against 25% of Dominican exports sent to the U. S. Leading imports into the Dominican Republic were: cotton and manufactures of cotton $910,603; rubber and manufactures of rubber $861,432; machinery and apparatus $826,583; jute bags $692,222; chemical and pharmaceutical products $632,815; paper and manufacturers of paper $442,170; construction materials (iron) $438,801; gasoline $351,201; automobiles $299,196; cement $188,279. Cotton and manufactures came chiefly from the U. S. (46%), Japan (39%) and England (9%); machinery and apparatus from the U. S. (96%); chemical and pharmaceutical products from the U. S. (65%) and France (9%); jute bags from British India (68%) and the U. S. (22%); paper and manufactures from the U. S. (82%); gasoline from the Dutch West Indies (60%) and the U. S. (40%); structural material (iron) from the U. S. (94%); cement from the U. S. (90%); automobiles from the U. S. (93%) and from Germany (7%); rubber and manufactures of rubber from the U. S. (58%) and Canada (28%). Principal exports in 1940 were raw sugar $12,882,807; cacao $1,617,104; coffee $769,975; molasses $546,996; gold $280,180; corn $175,020; bananas $151,983; cattle $128,909; tobacco leaf $96,215. Raw sugar went mainly to the United Kingdom (59%), Canada (22%), France (9%), U. S. (4%); cacao to the U. S. (93%); coffee to the U. S. (59%), Cuba (23%), Netherlands (12%); starch to the U. S. (99%); tobacco leaf to the U. S. (54%); gold to the U. S. (100%); corn to Puerto Rico (65%) and Dutch West Indies (27%); molasses to the U. S. (98%); cattle to the Dutch West Indies (78%) and French West Indies (20%); bananas to the U. S. (100%).

General Customs Policy and Regulations: Customs duties are levied on most of the products imported into the country. In addition, special taxes, designated as internal revenue under Law No. 854 of March 13, 1935, are collected. Since these taxes are assessed on imported articles, that law is in effect a supplementary customs tariff.

Communications: Postage on letters to be carried by ordinary mail from the U. S. to the Dominican Republic is the same as between cities in the U. S. Although the air-mail rate from the U. S. is 10¢ per ½ oz. or fractions thereof, the return postage from the Dominican Republic to the U. S. is 13¢. Dutiable articles should not be sent in letters or in letter packages. Packages weighing not more than 44 lbs. may be sent by parcel post. The Dominican Republic is served by RCA Radio, All American Cables, and by radiotelephone service to the U. S.

Transportation: The New York and Porto Rico Steamship Company maintains a weekly schedule of combined passenger and freight ships between New York and Ciudad Trujillo via San Juan, Puerto Rico. Combined freight and passenger ships of the Lykes Brothers Steamship Company sail occasionally from gulf ports of the U. S. to this Republic. Two steamship lines operating from American ports using ships of foreign registry include the Bull Insular Line, with a fortnightly service between New York and Dominican ports, and the Aluminum Line, also with a fortnightly service between New Orleans and Caribbean ports via Ciudad Trujillo. Ships of Cuban and Dominican registry make frequent calls at various ports of the country in connection with their general Caribbean trade. Airplanes of the Pan American Airways System from Miami arrive in San Pedro de Macorís, 50 miles from the capital, both northbound and southbound, at least 3 times a week.

Packing: Ordinary export packing is generally sufficient for merchandise intended for the Dominican Republic.

Credit Terms: Importers and dealers usually request terms ranging from 30 to 90 days. While there are many firms to which such credit should be safely granted, American concerns will do well to obtain reliable credit reports before business relations are entered into. The Banco de Reservas de la Republica Dominicana, the Royal Bank of Canada, and the Bank of Nova Scotia have branches in Ciudad Trujillo which will furnish reports upon requests from other banking institutions.

Currency, Weights and Measures: The United States dollar is the monetary standard of the country, although subsidiary coins are of Dominican issue. While the metric system of weights and measures is used officially and must be stated in consular invoices, units such as the pound, gallon, yard, etc., are widely employed and may be used on imported articles without penalty.

HAITI

General: The Republic of Haiti occupies the western third of Hispaniola, the second largest of the Caribbean islands. It is about the size of the State of Vermont with an estimated area of approximately 10,200 sq. mi. The eastern two-thirds of the island is the Dominican Republic. Haiti is 1,543 miles due south of New York City.

Climate: Haiti lies wholly within the tropics and tropical clothing is worn throughout the year. At Port-au-Prince the annual mean temperature is 81° F. and the daily temperature range averages 19° F. There is a spring and an autumn rainy season. Certain sections of the country are arid whereas in others the precipitation is heavy.

Topography: The country is rugged. The mountain ranges traversing it from the Dominican border to the sea rise in the north to 4,600 feet and in the south to almost 10,000 feet. There are extensive, though often arid, coastal plains, fertile mountain valleys, and many water courses; rivers are few. The forests have been almost entirely cut down.

Population: The estimated population is 3,000,000. Port-au-Prince, the capital, with an estimated population of 100,000, is the only large city. More than 90% of the population are Negroes. There is a small, influential minority of mulattoes, concentrated in the towns. There are possibly 1,500 foreigners.

Language: French is the official language. While Creole, a French-African patois, is the language of the countryside, a knowledge of it is not necessary for business purposes. Spanish is not used and communications and catalogues in that language should not be sent to Haiti.

Standard of Living: Low generally. Agricultural methods are comparatively primitive and holdings small. Food, clothing, and shelter are the peasant's chief needs, and he is usually able without much effort to satisfy most of his simple wants from the produce of his own land.

Occupations and Industries: There is little manufacturing. Agriculture is the principal industry, and coffee is by far the most valuable crop. Other exports in the order of their importance are sugar, sisal, bananas, cotton, cacao, goatskins, cottonseed cake and logwood. There are no large-scale agricultural enterprises except the U. S.-operated sugar-cane, banana and sisal plantations. There is no mineral production except marine salt.

Imports and Exports: The following table gives the total value in U. S. currency of imports and exports for a 5-year period, and in addition, the value of the trade with the U. S.:

Fiscal Year	Imports		Exports	
Oct. 1 to Sept. 30	Total	From U. S.	Total	To U. S.
1936–37	9,215,132	4,698,380	8,970,890	2,500,350
1937–38	7,594,778	4,105,525	6,946,390	2,972,123
1938–39	8,180,737	5,092,082	7,267,635	2,502,207
1939–40	7,940,115	5,767,295	5,399,040	2,787,437
1940–41	7,431,109	6,177,222	6,657,307	5,842,873

Cotton textiles usually account for one-fourth of total imports. Other leading imports are wheat flour, fish and other foodstuffs, iron and steel manufactures, gasoline and kerosene, lumber, cement, household utensils, soap and agricultural implements.

Customs Policy and Regulations: While revenue from internal taxes is gradually increasing, the government still looks to the customs for its principal revenues. Customs receipts were 96% of total revenues in 1917 and 80% in 1941.* Import duties are collected on most articles either at a specific or an ad valorem rate. Import duties collected in 1921 amounted to 49% of the value of the imports of that year, while export duties were nearly 10% of the value of all exports.

* Provisional or approximate figure based on incomplete data.

Postal Regulations and Rates: The postal rate on letters from the U. S. to Haiti is 3¢ per oz. or fraction thereof; the air-mail rate is 10¢ for each ½ oz. or fraction thereof.

Communications between the U. S. and Haiti: Pan American Airways System operates passenger, mail and express service between Miami and Port-au-Prince on its Miami–Antilles–Port-au-Prince–San Pedro de Macorís–San Juan route. The schedule provides for a plane daily, except Sunday, from Miami to Port-au-Prince, and a plane daily, except Friday, from Port-au-Prince to Miami. The company operates a service of a plane each Tuesday and Saturday from Port-au-Prince to Maracaibo, and a plane each Wednesday and Sunday from Maracaibo to Port-au-Prince. In addition, Port-au-Prince is a stop on the San Juan–Pedro de Macorís–Port-au-Prince–Santiago–Kingston service of the company every Friday westbound and every Saturday eastbound. Shipping service between the U. S. and Haiti is normally maintained by 4 companies, including the Standard Fruit and Steamship Company, the Aluminum Line, the Lykes Brothers Steamship Company, and the Royal Netherlands Steamship Company.

Banking: There are two commercial banks in Haiti: the Banque Nationale de la République d'Haiti, which is the bank of issue, and a branch of the Royal Bank of Canada. The Banque Nationale has its principal office in Port-au-Prince and branches in all important towns. The New York office of the Royal Bank of Canada is at 68 William Street.

Currency: The unit of currency is the gourde, which is exchangeable on demand and without expense, at the fixed rate of 5 gourdes for one American dollar. The gourde is divided into 100 centimes. U. S. currency circulates freely.

Weights and Measures: The metric system has been adopted officially but American weights and measures are employed commercially to a large extent.

Credit Terms: Prevailing terms for imports are sight draft, documents against payment, and to a lesser degree 30 to 60 days sight, documents against acceptance. Practically no business is done on open account. Credit reports on firms in Haiti may be had from the two banks mentioned in the paragraph under Banking above.

Commercial travelers are subject to a license tax of $50 and a communal tax of $40 per annum, payable quarterly. However, only $22.50 is collected on arrival, and no further payment is necessary unless the stay of the traveler exceeds 3 months. Travelers' samples must be declared as intended for re-exportation and separately from personal effects, which are duty free. Samples of no commercial value are admitted duty free if verified as such by the appraising officer. Samples having commercial value are dutiable at the prescribed rates, but duty paid is refundable if the samples are re-exported within 6 months. The application for refund, however, must be made within 30 days after payment of duty.

Packing: Goods intended for Haiti should be securely packed and crated to withstand rough handling and as a precaution against pilferage. Merchandise sensitive to climatic conditions should be well protected against tropical heat and moisture.

General Trade Information Service: The United States Consulate is prepared at all times to furnish to American manufacturers and exporters information concerning trade conditions in Haiti.

INDEX

A

Abacá, *see* Fibers

Acajutla, 52

Agriculture: Aztec, 40; Dominican Republic, 69-70; El Salvador, 52; Guatemala, 51; Honduras, 48-9; Maya, 25; Mexico, 59; Middle America, 18; United States, 84

Agronomical Institute (Campinas), 100

Aguilar-Meza, Dr. Ricardo, 218-28

Ahuitzol, 52

Airways: Aerovias de Guatemala, 203; Braniff, 214; British West Indian, 203; Compania Mexicana de Aviacion, 204; Inter-American, 203; Pan American, 74, 75, 203, 204, 214; Transportes Aereos Centro-Americanos, 75, 156, 202, 203, 204, 214; Transportes Aereos Hondureños, 201

Alajuela, 54

Albemarle, Lord, 65

Almirante, 58, 105, 295

Alta Verapaz, 51, 92

American Export Company, 214

American Jersey Cattle Club, 76

Annand, P. N., 253, 254

Arica, 98

Aris, Augusto, 267

Aromatics: citronellol esters, 137; geraniol, 137; synthetic menthol, 137

Arsenic, 62

Art, Mayan, 24, 37-8

Artibonite, 67-8

Aviation, 206, 208; *see also* Transportation

B

Badu, 161

Bagasse, 138, 141

Balboa, 57

Banana, *see* Fruit

"Banana republic," 186

Banking: Costa Rica, 291; Cuba, 296; El Salvador, 286; Guatemala, 275; Haiti, 306; Honduras, 278-9; Mexico, 271; Nicaragua, 287

Baptism, 31, 36

Barranquilla, 98

Barrios, General Justo Rufino, 90

"Basket fields," 39-40

Bats, 233-4

Beals, Carleton, 41, 43, 44, 45

Belize, 154

Benitez, Alberto Terones, 61

Benitez, Jorge M., 93, 94

Berlanga, Tomas de, 180

Bismuth, 62

Bolivar, Simon, 57, 58

Bolivia, 98, 99, 100

Boquete, 58

Brazil, 127, 138

"Brazilette," 175

British Honduras, 22, 44, 134, 149, 202, 242

Budget: Costa Rica, 292; Cuba, 296; Guatemala, 276; Honduras, 279; Nicaragua, 287

Buna S., 168, 169

Burden, William A. M., 204

Bureau of Entomology and Plant Quarantine, 81, 256

Butler, Alfred F., 266

C